TURNING POINTS
IN
Rock and Roll

TURNING POINTS

IN

Rock and Roll

The Key Events That Affected Popular Music in the Latter Half of the 20th Century

Hank Bordowitz

CITADEL PRESS
Kensington Publishing Corp.
www.kensingtonbooks.com

CITADEL PRESS BOOKS are published by

Kensington Publishing Corp.
850 Third Avenue
New York, NY 10022

All Kensington titles, imprints, and distributed lines are available at special quantity discounts for bulk purchases for sales promotions, premiums, fund-raising, educational, or institutional use. Special book excerpts or customized printings can also be created to fit specific needs. For details, write or phone the office of the Kensington special sales manager: Kensington Publishing Corp., 850 Third Avenue, New York, NY 10022, attn: Special Sales Department; phone 1-800-221-2647.

CITADEL PRESS and the Citadel logo are Reg. U.S. Pat. & TM Off.

Image of Edison gramophone: Photo by Hank Bordowitz; phonograph and cylinder courtesy the New York Public Library. *Robert Johnson:* Columbia Records publicity photo. Photo courtesy Columbia Records. *Les Paul:* Photo by Hank Bordowitz/Starfile. *American Bandstand:* Dick Clark photo courtesy Dick Clark Productions, Inc. *Elvis Presley:* "Million Dollar Quartet," including Elvis, RCA publicity photo; photo from CD booklet. Photo by Marion Keisker MacInnes, used with permission of Colin Escott. *Alan Freed:* Photo courtesy www.alanfreed.com. *Blackboard Jungle:* From the author's collection. *CD and 8 track:* Photo by Hank Bordowitz. *Chuck Berry:* LP cover, *London Chuck Berry Sessions* used with permission of the Universal Music Group. Art by Tim Lewis. *Buddy Holly:* LP cover, *Buddy Holly: Legend* used with permission of the Universal Music Group. Art by Phil Carlig. *The Beatles:* McCartney photo from BMI. Photo used with the permission of Broadcast Music, Inc. *Bob Dylan:* Columbia Records publicity photo. Photo courtesy Columbia Records. *Crawdaddy! magazine:* Crawdaddy! #4 cover, courtesy Paul Williams/Crawdaddy! magazine. *Eric Clapton:* RSO Records publicity photo, courtesy the Universal Music Group. *Monterey, Woodstock, Altamont:* Photo of Michael Lang courtesy Michael Lang. *Sex Pistols:* John Lydon, publicity photo from Elektra Records courtesy Elektra Records. *MTV:* MTV logo. Photo courtesy MTV. *Live Aid:* Boomtown Rats publicity photo from Columbia Records courtesy Columbia Records. *Nirvana:* Photos from CD booklet. Nirvana, *Nevermind* cover art courtesy the Universal Music Group. *MP3 and Napster:* Rio portable player. Photo by Hank Bordowitz.

First printing: August 2004

10 9 8 7 6 5 4 3 2 1

Printed in the United States of America

Library of Congress Control Number: 2004106000

ISBN 0-8065-2631-9

This book is dedicated to the people who helped oversee the turning points in my life (whether they knew it or not):

Mom & Dad
Beth & Richard
Harold, Jeff, Hy & Sydell
Steve Julty
Joe Zitt & Joel Spector
Bob Shannon, Arthur Levy, Jim Green & Jane Freidman
Chris Watson & Pat Vitucci
John Swenson, Roy Trakin & Brian Jackson Griffith
Bobby Colomby, Dave Marsh & Ken Richardson
Jeff Jacobson & Bruce Colfin, my longtime legal guardians
Mark Zuckerman, my minister of finance (such as it is)
Barry Hirschberg, Juggy Gales, Ed Cramer & Mickey Gensler
Dr. Ron Sadoff, Pierre Lamoureux, Rich Stumpf, Barry Ehrman, Steve Zuckerman & Andy Skibins
Fran Leibowitz
Richard Carlin, Ben Schafer, Margaret Wolf, John Cerullo & Michael Messina
Mr. Shags (You know who you are)
Jim Fitzgerald

and of course
Caren, Michael, Larry & Billy

"To everything there is a season."
—Pete Seeger, after *Ecclesiastes*

Contents

Foreword
by Dave Marsh

If I had to choose just one thing to teach denizens of our culture, it would be this: All things change. I'd choose that lesson because as long as we believe in the immutability of our current circumstances, we're trapped by them. In our society, virtually all of us fear change, because stability seems our key to survival, often—maybe, especially—when the opposite is true. Not that change isn't dangerous, but the danger certainly can't be lessened by merely standing by, pretending that what's happening is a temporary aberration, illusion, correctable mistake.

Many say that rock'n'roll's history encompasses nothing but change, but in reality, much of the alteration comes from no instinct stronger than a desire to maintain the status quo. Just as rock'n'roll itself came into the world against the kicking and screaming of the Tin Pan Alley songwriters, so too arrived Beatlemania, "rock" (in Hank Bordowitz's use of the term), punk, and certainly hip-hop, which transformed the entire face of American popular music in a way for which there are very few precedents, rock'n'roll chief among them. Each of these met resistance from those already rocking on the day of the new thing's arrival: Four Seasons and Beach Boys and doo-wop fans tried to stand their ground against the Beatles and the British Invasion just as staunchly as a later generation, wed to post-psychedelic "rock," opposed disco to the point of leaving themselves vulnerable to the far deeper incursions of punk, which was "compromised" in its turn (despite the best efforts of its stalwarts) by incorporating aspects of disco to become "new wave." Hip-hop, like the earliest rock'n'roll, seemed prepared to loot everything that had come before it in search of change. This, of course, meant that those with a stake in what had already happened declared it an aesthetic void.

Such are the perils of knowing history in a culture that seems determined to forget yesterday the instant it's over. In the world that invented rock'n'roll—the "world turned upside down" of quite another Anglo-American revolution—the idea that turning points exist may seem controversial or even chimerical.

So the value of what Hank Bordowitz does here can't be measured simply by whether we think he defined all the turning points correctly. I'm not sure there is a correctly, because history rarely turns on such tiny points as whether it was Chuck Berry making "Maybellene" or Little Richard squalling "Tutti Frutti" that hurled the stone that felled Goliath. It's down to the minutiae of individual observation, and the two of us, having observed and recounted more than our share, are entitled to disagree, as is the person who thinks that the launching of *Sixteen* was more important than the founding of *Crawdaddy!* Far more important, Hank not only describes what happens as each of these rocks is hurled onto the surface of the placid stream that we believe is our lives but traces each of their ripples as they spread and collide with those that preceded them and those that follow. What we get to see is not only cause and effect but how difficult it is to keep the individual events separate: the way that they combine to create the meaning of one another; the way one could not have happened without the other and a third happened despite the other two; and how curious it is that MTV launched the most elaborately and determinedly superficial musical phenomenon of our time at almost the same moment that Bob Geldof—to some extent a made-for-MTV pop star—launched a movement that brought to the forefront the music's deepest political instincts and its most important sociological contradictions.

Those fully attuned to our ahistorical society (as no one who reads and writes history can be) seem to presume that the main purpose of studying and describing events in the past must be to divine the future. By ending where he does—by ending where he has to, given the circumstances, and not flinching from it—Hank Bordowitz shows that the real purpose of all this going on about the past is to create the tools with which to understand the present. (Undeniably, this provides a key to shaping the future, but the ahistorical don't believe the future *is* shaped; like the past, it simply occurs as a kind of prospective inevitability.)

Turning Points in Rock and Roll is yeoman's work, appropriately enough, since rock'n'roll and the music that arrived with it and alongside it and succeeded it has been the yeoman's voice. It's a map through a forest not quite so dense as it first appears, and properly used, it will help lead at least some to the clearing in that forest where they find their own voices. May they do it soon, and may they have a chronicler as reliable and loving as Hank Bordowitz to tell their tales.

Acknowledgments

Margaret Wolf at Citadel Press for dropping this project in my lap. The conversation went something like this:

> "How would you like to do a book called *Turning Points in Rock and Roll?*"
>
> "I've been training for that book for the last twenty-five years!"
>
> "Well, then, I think you should do it, don't you?"

Jim Fitzgerald, of the James Fitzgerald Agency, agent extraordinaire. I could never say enough nice things about Jim, but it makes him blush.

The staff at the Lincoln Center Library for the Performing Arts, The Suffern Free Public Library, The Mid-Manhattan Library, The CUNY Graduate Center Library, The Newman Library at Baruch College, and the Fifth Avenue Central Branch of the New York Public Library. So much information!

The keepers of Lexis-Nexis, Findarticles.com, Google, EBSCO Masterfile Premier, Yahoo!, All Music Guide, and so many more references placed at our fingertips in the digital age.

David E. Weekly, Stan Soocher, Vic Steffens, Paula Amato, Dave Marsh, and John Swenson for timely information.

Michael Messina, John Cerullo, Paul Williams, Wanda McSwann, Colin Escott, Sujata Murthy, Rhonda Malmlund, Joann Duran, Phuong K. Baum, Tom Cording, Kevin Kennedy, Judith Fischer Freed, Greg Pollard, Paulette Lee, Jeff James, Dr. David Sanjek, Shannon Tourney, Bruce Pollock, and Vickie Sarro for help getting together the artwork for this book.

Introduction:
Rock and the Voice
of Post-1950 Youth

The late, great promotion guru Juggy Gayles hated the phrase *rock and roll*, although he is one of the unacknowledged champions of the sound. He was at the lunch with Alan Freed and others where Freed had to rename his radio program *Moondog Matinee* to avoid legal entanglements. He was the only one who objected to calling it *The Rock and Roll Show*. "Anyone who spent time in the colored neighborhoods knew that 'rock and roll' meant fucking," he said.

Rock and roll both reflected and triggered revolutionary times in the history of the United States and the history of the world. Very few eras were quite as fomentive as the last half of the twentieth century, and rock and roll was the soundtrack to this change. Humanity began to question the values that they had lived by for centuries. Science and technology brought us bigger, better, more, and different. Change was around every corner and no one could predict "the future" without a crystal ball.

Inventions like "the pill" and mind-altering chemicals led to scenes like Woodstock's "three days of peace," mud, drugs, sex, and music. Similarly and simultaneously, the armed conflict in Vietnam coupled with rock and roll spurred the first mass, long-term opposition to armed conflict by the people who would be sent to fight it.

From the ability to capture music in a replayable form (i.e., records) to the digitizing of music, from the relative innocence of "Rock Around the Clock" to the outright seductiveness of "Soft and Wet," from white artists like Pat Boone sanitizing black hits for the suburbs to Run-D.M.C. urbanizing rock for the 'hood, popular music in the twentieth century had more turning points than your average highway, and like the highway, not all roads led to the same place.

Of course, this all begs the question of what is rock and roll. There are nearly as many opinions on this as there are listeners. The basic answer, the one given by so many jukebox jury members and dancers on *American Bandstand*, might be the best: "It has a beat, you can dance to it."

"If it doesn't swing," added concert promoter extraordinaire George Wein, "there's nothing happening. It's one of the things the rock kids took from jazz musicians and it's why rock is so popular."

The Rolling Stones' early impresario Andrew Loog Oldham agreed with Juggy Gayles, but rather than be offended by the connection of rock and roll and sex, he understood that one was the essence of the other. He celebrated it and took it further: "Pop music is sex and you have to hit them in the face with it."

Dancing was as important an element of early rock and roll as anything else. Gayles, who promoted everything from Irving Berlin while a song plugger in the '30s to EPMD as the co-owner of Sleeping Bag Records in the '80s, once told me he got his start in the music business because he was a great lindy-hopper. "Dance music," he said, "never changes. Disco, hip-hop, it's all just a different way of lindy hopping!"

Similarly, legendary boogie-woogie pianist Sammy Price, whose *Rib Joint* record is one of the seminal prerock albums, said he got started in music by dancing. "I was a Charleston dancer with Alphonso Trent," he said. "I used to sit behind the piano and listen."

Even though no less an authority than protorocker Brownie McGhee once wrote, "The blues had a baby and they called it rock and roll," this oversimplifies the issue. For one thing, rock and roll really isn't just one music. What do songs that fall under the rubric of rock like "Reeling and Rocking," "A Whiter Shade of Pale," "Paranoid," and "Reeling in the Years" have in common, besides a very broad, very wide genre? Do they all really fit under this same umbrella? "The real story," Colin Escott asserts, "is numbingly complex. How can you say where rock and roll came from when you can't really say what it is?"

"Rock and roll is one of those catch-all phrases," legendary song-writer Mike Stoller concurs, "and in some cases it means something to specific people, and it could be different things. It could be something that differentiates music that became more broadly popular, even if it's based more on blues than rhythm and blues. . . . Some people consider anything they hear on the radio that isn't classical to be rock and roll."

Rock and roll has always been about pushing the envelope. It takes the youth culture born of the postwar baby boom to its extreme, just one of the boundaries the music and the lifestyle that surrounds it push. "Rock and roll," noted journalist Dave Marsh says, "imposes this whole thing on you where you're not supposed to grow up, you're not supposed to *want* to grow up."

Really simple, elemental, the beat is the core of music from nearly any culture. As John Martyn once observed, "My ancestors painted themselves blue. You just get up off your arse and wail."

The primal beat got a little lost along the way until swing and jive, the great precursors of rock, came around. Even Benny Goodman said of rock and roll, "I guess it's okay, man. At least it's got a beat."

Therefore, it's kinda tough to be *definitive* where rock is concerned. Ask me what my favorite rock album is on any given day, for example, and you're likely to get a different answer, depending on my mood. I probably wouldn't even come up with the same top ten. And some of my favorite rock music, groups like Parliament-Funkadelic for example, and nearly all of the "purer faith" of soul and other "black music" tend not to fall into modern definitions of rock at all.

So many different roots and routes to rock and roll present as many options for defining turning points. Goodman himself might have merited a chapter for having the first integrated popular American band, but like so many other turning points, that story gives way to what I considered more overriding touchstones. Some of my choices are bound to be controversial, and I'm as likely to agree with any other turning point someone else might suggest as not. It's all pretty subjective. Given the time and space constraints of this book, though, I think I've put together a pretty interesting bunch, but there is just so much you can deal with in a hundred thousand words. Let the flames commence.

This is all well-trod ground, yet no one has really come up with any really satisfying answer. To do a project like this with any pretense of being comprehensive would involve twenty volumes rather than twenty chapters. It could be someone's life work. It won't be mine. That's why this book doesn't even try to offer answers, really, just a couple of the better-beaten paths in that well-trod ground. I've tried to select twenty turning points I thought crucial, but in addition to Goodman, there are so many other possibilities:

- Ry Cooder's *Bop 'til You Drop*, the first all-digitally recorded rock album

- Bruce Springsteen's *Born to Run* getting him onto the cover of *Time* and *Newsweek* simultaneously

- David Sarnoff starting the Radio Corporation of America (radio in general gets short shrift)

- The Jimi Hendrix Experience's *Are You Experienced*

- John Hammond's Spirituals to Swing concert, a veritable coming-out party, introducing African-American musical debutantes to white society on the white man's turf, Carnegie Hall

- The Who's *Tommy* and the whole idea of rock opera and concept albums

- The rise of rap; how it coopted rock, and then became coopted by rock

- Tom Donahue and his hand-picked retinue of deejays starting the album-rock, FM station KPMX in San Francisco, the dawn of progressive FM

- Hair Metal vs. Thrash

- The entire British blues revival from John Mayall and his "kids," like Eric Clapton and Fleetwood Mac, to the Rolling Stones, who probably should have had their own chapter, but don't

- Timothy Leary, acid, the rise of reefer, and the dangerous proliferation of heroin

- The rock resurgence featuring the Strokes and the White Stripes

I could have started the book in Congo Square or even Nigeria and dealt with slavery, or with the spread of popular culture on a worldwide basis due to the revolution in communications, in which rock played a major role—rock and roll within McLuhan's global village—but that would have gotten too scowlerly and highfalutin'.

I've tried to include some of these alternatives in the context of one essay or another. Many of the issues I deal with in a chapter or even a paragraph have entire shelves devoted to them in libraries. Again, my brief is to be . . . brief, to keep things informative and entertaining. It is, after all, only rock and roll (but I like it).

So, I've tried to capture the phenomena that are Elvis and the Beatles in five thousand words, a neat trick and one I hope I've pulled off satisfactorily. There were a lot of ways I could have taken this on. Think of the book as a rock and roll version of Cliff Notes.

Beyond all that, this book deals with rock from a predominantly American viewpoint, so we'll be traveling the Interstates, spending way more time on Route 66 than the Reeperbahn. So, buckle in and get comfortable as I attempt, without the aid of a GPS, to follow these roads to some kind of conclusion. In many cases, as with many roads, the trip proves more important than the destination. Hopefully, the only airbag we'll encounter is me.

TURNING POINTS
IN
Rock and Roll

Edison Invents the Phonograph: Recorded Music Goes from Science Fiction to Big Business

Thomas Edison may have come up with a dozen different ideas for inventions on any given day, but he only pursued those that would make him money. A capitalist first and foremost, he didn't invent the light bulb to pull humanity out of the darkness. He did it because he saw the potential for profit.

Edison would seem an odd person to invent a medium for the transmission of sound. For one thing, he was exceedingly hard of hearing. While folklore would have it that a conductor pulling him onto a train by his ears had been the contributing factor to this, a family proclivity toward mastoiditis was more likely the culprit. This disability, coupled with the revolutionary changes of the time, however, proved instrumental in both Edison's career path and the invention and growth of the "talking machine."

So how is this important to rock and roll? Edison started it all. While many would maintain that rock and roll is primarily a live medium, for as long as the genre has been around the gauge of popularity has been how many records an artist sells. Before Edison, the only way to hear music was to either play it or go where it was being played. The phonograph (and subsequent incarnations like the gramophone and all its "grandchildren," from the tape deck to the MP3 player) made it possible for someone in Wyoming to hear a musician who never left New York. We take that for granted now, but at the turn of the twentieth century, it was revolutionary.

Most of Edison's early inventions had to do with the transmission of ideas. An adept sender and reader of Morse code when the prevailing medium for reading it was ticker tape, Edison found himself at a disadvantage as that medium began to switch to audio reading of the code. After inventing several improvements for telegraphy, he found himself floored by the improvement made by Alexander Graham Bell—telegraphy that actually sent the human voice.

Edison began experimenting with Bell's new telephone, coming up with the carbon transmitter still in use today. He felt that he could use it as a stenographic tool by capturing sound on some medium with a stylus, not unlike what the ticker tape did for the telegraph. He ran a floating stylus over a piece of paper coated with paraffin. Legend has it he pricked himself with another stylus. He noticed that the paper captured an image, and rubbing this back over the stylus, he heard a sound that approximated his voice.

He and his associate Charles Batchelor quickly drew up plans for a device that would capitalize on this discovery. They had his machinist, John Kruesi, create the actual machine. Within a year, Edison was astounding the staff at *Scientific American* with a machine that recorded speech:

> Mr. Thomas A. Edison recently came into the office, placed a little machine on our desk, turned a crank and the machine inquired as to our health, asked how we liked the phonograph, informed us that it was very well, and bid us a cordial good night . . . No matter how familiar a person may be with modern machinery . . . it is impossible to listen to the mechanical speech without his experiencing the idea that his senses are deceiving him.

Suddenly, audio could be preserved like a bug in amber. By 1878, the Edison Talking Machine hit the market.

The thrust of Edison's marketing of the machine wasn't geared toward entertainment, at least not musical entertainment. The machine itself went on tour, and continued to astonish and confound audiences across America as it would play back trumpet passages, various obscenities, and whatever else volunteers from the audience chose to transmit into the machine's hearing trumpet for transcription onto the machine's tinfoil cylinder.

However, Edison never conceived of the machine as an entertainment, but rather as a business tool. It simply cost too much to manufacture for the average family to afford. Businesses were a different matter, and Edison started selling it as a stenographic tool. However, the tinfoil was only good for one or two playings before it wore out. After the novelty value wore off, the price and the difficulty in actually using the phonograph—especially when you had to change the tinfoil—made it one of Edison's poor sellers. By the end of the 1870s, he had moved on to his work with the light bulb. The phonograph, with all its technical imperfections, languished.

This left the field open to archrival Alexander Graham Bell. As Edison had evinced interest in the telephone from the moment he heard about it, Bell became fascinated with the phonograph. By 1887, Bell and several associates, including his cousin Chichester, had made enough improvements on Edison's machine—including changing the tinfoil cylinder to wax—that they began marketing their own graphophone, also conceived as a dictating machine. Edison, in the meantime, had devoted enough time to his phonograph to equip it with a battery-operated motor (the graphophone worked on a treadle). Neither Edison's improved machine nor Bell's really caught on.

What really saved the phonograph from the relic heap of failed inventions (and both Bell and Edison had their share) was the innovation and invention of Louis Glass, who worked for Edison's Pacific Phonograph Company. He created a coin box for the phonograph. In the fall of 1889, he slipped on a cylinder with a song on it and put the machine into San Francisco's Palais Royal Saloon. This protojukebox created a sensation. Within a year and a half, the company had placed twelve hundred coin-operated phonographs, generating in excess of $20,000 a month.

Suddenly, there was a demand—a huge demand—for entertainment on wax cylinder. The Columbia Phonograph Company signed John Philip Sousa and the U.S. Marine Band to record marches on cylinders. By the mid-1890s, the business applications of the phonograph were all but forgotten, and it became an entertainment machine. With the change in application came a change in the basic commercial thrust of the device. Edison started making simpler machines at a price point that the rising middle class in America could afford, the cheapest selling for about three dollars.

At the same time, competition started to grow. Columbia offered its own machine at a price far less than Edison's. In 1901, The Victor Talking Machine Company started offering its own machine. These machines were not compatible with each other. The Victor machine, in fact, was the first to use Emile Berliner's new glass and lacquer disc-based system. Within a few years, this had begun to replace the more difficult, more delicate (but sonically superior) wax cylinders. What really jump-started the disc business was Victor signing Italian tenor Enrico Caruso to record discs for them. His recordings sold so well that Caruso became the first artist to demand—and receive—royalties on recordings, getting forty cents for each seventy-five-cent disc sold.

The speed was adjustable on nearly all early sound-reproduction devices. While Berliner ascertained that a speed of roughly 70 rpm offered the best compromise between sound quality and amount of material you could fit onto a disc, speeds ranged from 50 to 120 rpm, depending on the needs of the recording.

Early in the twentieth century, Victor joined forces with the British Gramophone Company. The British company got access to Victor's technology and catalog. Among other things, Victor adopted British Gramophone's logo, a little dog listening at the horn to "his master's voice." Their disc offered major advantages over the cylinder. One of the reasons Caruso signed on with Victor was that he only had to sing once and the record could be reproduced, something that wasn't the case with the the wax cylinder—pretty much each wax cylinder was a unique recording or a poor reproduction of a master cylinder. Eventually Edison came up with a method for creating electroplated master recordings so the cylinders (and ultimately discs) could be reproduced with even better quality and less expense.

Victor also advertised heavily. One particular ad caught the beauty of their product perfectly. It pictured a very robust Dame Nellie Melba singing with a shadowy, ghostly figure of Jenny Lind—the soprano who had taken America by storm some fifty years earlier when P.T. Barnum proved the efficacy of touring—looking on. The copy read, "Jenny Lind is only a memory, but the voice of Melba can never die. . . . There were no Victrolas to capture the fleeting beauties of Jenny Lind, but Melba's voice will be heard in centuries to come." And, indeed, as recorded all those years ago, you can still hear how Melba sounded in her prime on CDs currently in print.

By 1909, discs outsold cylinders by two to one. Within five years, the ratio was closer to nine to one. Columbia changed over to disc. By the 1920s, even Edison tried to introduce his own disc-based system with one-inch-thick, "artificial resin" and wood monstrosities played with a diamond stylus (the metal stylus of the Victor machine wore out after a couple of plays, and using a dull stylus destroyed the fragile records). These new discs played at thirty-three rotations per minute rather than the seventy-eight of most disc-based recordings. While the system didn't catch on in Edison's lifetime, it would prove to be about thirty years ahead of its time in both concept and the use of plastic in its construction. These discs were arguably the first industrial product to make use of the new scientific marvel (so new, it wasn't really rolled out for public consumption until the World's Fair nearly a decade later).

Over the course of two generations, the idea of hearing music without actually going to see the musicians went from unheard of and revolutionary to almost commonplace. During the 1920s, you could not only get the classical music represented by Caruso, but also blues, country, jazz, nearly any kind of music that had an audience. Spoken-word recordings were also popular: famous actors performing favorite soliloquies or presidents and other politicians reading speeches—both their own or classics like the Gettysburg Address.

By the late '20s, however, the emerging record business had several problems to contend with:

- A new medium of home entertainment was beginning to catch on: radio. Started by hobbyist David Sarnoff—who had earned notoriety when he "heard" the *Titanic* go down on his wireless set and got the news to the *New York Times* so that they had it published the morning after rather than several days later—the Radio Corporation of America and the National Broadcasting Company became media powerhouses, selling $80 million worth of their Broadcast Music Boxes over the course of three years. The record companies totally underestimated the impact this would have. Why, they reasoned, would anyone want to listen to what someone else played when they could select the music for themselves from their own collection?

- Movies began to talk and—more important—sing. Yet another challenge for the public's entertainment dollar, movies also had technological and business ramifications. Where the record business had made their recordings essentially the same way for thirty-five years, the advent of sound in motion pictures demanded an entirely new discipline that ultimately would carry over to the record side. For one thing, it hastened the move of the record business from an acoustic, horn-based system of recording and playback to an electronic, amplifier-based system. Where families could record on the old, horn-and-cylinder apparatus, the electronic phonographs and gramophones were strictly playback instruments.

- When the movie business left the broadcast capital of New York City for the dryer, sunnier climes of the Southern California desert, they also polarized the music publishing business. This end of the music industry, which controlled the copyrights of the actual songs, was no longer centered in New York. Most of the film companies opened their own publishing companies to better control and profit from the music in their films.

- By the end of the 1920s, there were fewer "entertainment dollars" available. The bottom fell out of the American economy, the nadir coming with the stock market crash of 1929. Suddenly, no one had seventy-five cents to spend on the latest disc when even buying food was a challenge, and besides, people could be entertained for free via the radio.

By 1929, Edison was out of the business entirely. Sarnoff's RCA had bought the oh-so-successful Victor Talking Machine company, changing its name to RCA Victor. Most of the other record companies were hanging on for their lives. Columbia Records, in an effort to consolidate its market position and compete with Sarnoff, purchased the struggling United Independent Broadcasters network, changing its name to the Columbia Phonograph Broadcasting Systems, which was eventually shortened to CBS.

One company that tried to beat the business at its own game, English Decca records, started selling their discs for thirty-five rather than the prevailing seventy-five cents. American Records, which owned Vocalion and Brunswick, followed this innovation. These labels predominantly released "race records," records by blues performers, other African-American performers, and anything that wasn't deemed mainstream. These fifty-cent and three-for-a-dollar records helped keep these companies afloat during the Depression, and some of their country recordings, like "The Last Roundup," even became bona fide hits. They also managed to sign and develop such mainstream talent as Guy Lombardo and his Royal Canadians, Al Jolson, and the Dorsey Brothers.

The U.S. entered into World War II in 1941 and the Depression started to ebb as the country's economy assumed a wartime footing. This should have been a good time for the record business, especially for Columbia Records, RCA Victor, and Decca, the companies that shook out of the Depression as the major players.

But the war, while generating the need for entertainment to divert people's minds from the grim realities in the Pacific and Europe, created a severe problem for the disc manufacturers—a lack of lacquer. The same medium that they used to capture sound for distribution since the 1910s was a major component of aircraft, and the companies that made shellac could barely produce enough of it for the aircraft manufacturers. It became a hot commodity on the black market.

"America was at war and there was a shortage of shellac, the material that records were made of then," recalled Atlantic Records Chairman Ahmet Ertegun who, along with his brother Nesuhi and funding from their dentist, founded the company shortly after the war. "As a result, the major labels only pressed records by their biggest stars."

Amid this fray, songwriter Johnny Mercer, movie mogul Buddy DeSylva, and a group of associates launched Capitol Records—despite a stranglehold on distribution by the majors and shortage of a major component of their physical product. What helped was that two of their first three records—Freddy Slack's "Cow Cow Boogie" and Mercer's own "Strip Polka"—hit the top ten. One of the things that Capitol did to aid in their production process was use early proto- types of plastic records for their demonstration and promotional records. They became the first record company to service radio with free records.

As the war drew to a close, the record business started revving up again. Rather than license soundtracks to other labels, many of the film and media giants started their own record divisions. Warner Brothers had had one for some time, a companion to the largest music-publishing holdings in the world through most of the twentieth century. The record label's level of activity vacillated wildly, however. MGM Studios started its own, to go with its already huge music- publishing holdings. During the late '40s and early '50s, it became a major force in country music, especially after signing Hank Williams.

The scarcity of shellac and various unsuccessful forays into other plastic products to replace the glass-and-lacquer disc had Columbia and RCA experimenting with other means of getting records made and improving the sound in the process. Columbia went back to the idea of Edison's Diamond Disc. In 1946 they introduced the long- playing vinyl disc. Similarly, RCA, loath to give up on singles, released a player with a larger center hole than the 33.3-rpm long player, which had adapted the 78-rpm player's spindle and, as in the case of many popular ten-inch EPs, their size. RCA's 45-rpm records, intro- duced in 1948, were similar to the 78s in that they contained one song per side. And a battle of the speeds began among the record companies.

The speed that fell by the wayside was the 78, especially after RCA and Phillips announced that they would only service radio with 45s. The 45 also had better sound than the early microgroove 33s. How- ever, it still made listening to cohesive pieces, which came in albums of four or five singles, an annoying experience. Sure, there were only seven seconds between the time one 45 ended and another started, but as one RCA executive put it, "You're in bed with your best friend's wife, and every five minutes the door opens. It isn't open long, only seven seconds . . ."

Ultimately, both won—at least for a while. The 33 became the standard for albums and the 45 for singles. Plastic became the standard material for the dissemination of music on records. This led two plastic manufacturers into the fray, turning them from producers of plastic novelties to successful music businesses. Circle Plastics in San Francisco was asked to press up an album by Dave Brubeck. Within a year, they had a record division called Fantasy. Irving Green Plastics in Chicago was approached by booking agent Berle Adams, and they formed the even more successful Mercury Records.

All this activity couldn't have come at a better time. Saying the postwar economy was robust would be an understatement. Returning veterans had jobs, money in their pockets, and actual leisure time. They snatched up sound recordings along with all the other consumables they could get. A new brand of salesman called a rack jobber made sure music was available in all kinds of stores. As the chain and department stores grew, these wholesalers became more important, making recordings a commodity like magazines and glassware.

By the late '40s, a novelty merchant named Sam Goody decided to expand the trade he did in used-jukebox records to selling new merchandise, using sophisticated marketing techniques that included advertising and steep discounts. What he lost in margin, he made back in a large way in volume. Thus began record discounting. In 1950, record sales totaled just under $200 million.

So, in a little over fifty years, the recordings went from a novelty to something nearly everyone owned. People could be identified by the kind of music they consumed as early as the '20s. Flappers bobbed their hair and danced to the latest jazz, while their more sedate sisters listened to Rudy Vallee or Caruso. The revenues had grown a thousandfold from the early days of the nickel record player to the postwar boom.

By the '50s there were six major record companies—that is, record companies that manufactured and distributed their own product: Columbia, RCA Victor, MGM, Decca, Capitol, and Mercury. Independents like Fantasy and Chess, another Chicago-based company that had formed to take advantage (in every possible way) of the burgeoning blues scene in the Windy City, were independent and had to rely on a network of distributors around the country.

Around this time, rock and roll started to kick in. While the rest of this book deals with the cultural impact of rock and roll, right here we want to deal with business ramifications. In the most basic, dollars-

and-cents measurements, by 1959 RCA Records alone had half a billion dollars in sales. The advent of rock and roll had sent the music business shooting into the economic stratosphere.

"The late '50s were a time of great opportunity," said former Elektra president Bob Krasnow. "So many people were not doing things, and it left these big, gaping holes. . . . There was no industry then. I remember, my parents used to say, 'What are you talking about, the music business? What is the music business?' . . . Then, it wasn't really a business. You found the music, you found the money to make the records, and then the other people tried to get paid for selling these records. As the major labels grew and the corporate structures began to grow, it fell to the independent labels to cultivate new ideas and untested genres. These independent labels were responsible for fostering all these new ideas, especially in the post swing and jazz era, and in the beginning of the rhythm and blues era. As things moved on, these labels became the guardians of, you might say, the sounds of uncouth Caucasian kids."

The profits generated by rock and roll led most of the major film and media conglomerates that hadn't already done so to begin their own record divisions. American Broadcasting teamed with Paramount to form ABC Records. Companies merged and consolidated, the "majors" acquired independent companies. English EMI bought out contrarian Capitol Records.

By the late '60s, rock was an institution. The music business had essentially become a rock-and-roll business. This suited the cast of characters who ran it, the likes of Morris Levy, who spent much of his professional life under a legal cloud, Allen Klein, and innumerable other street-smart hustlers.

By the mid '70s, a broad-spectrum definition of rock accounted for 80 percent of all records sold, in a business that grossed over $2 billion, nearly three times that of professional sports and 20 percent more than movies. Naturally, this attracted the attention of big corporations, which basically decided they could do a better job running things with their LDs and MBAs than could the people who had built the business. Thus:

- Kinney, a company noted mostly for parking lots, rental cars, and funeral parlors bought Warner Brothers. Over the years it mutated into Warner Communications and took in Elektra Records and Atlantic Records, as well as all their recording subsidiaries (not to mention Time Publishing, Turner Broadcasting, and eventually merging with AOL).

- Phillips, a major German manufacturer of both music and hardware, purchased Mercury Records, morphing by the '70s into PolyGram.

- MCA, which owned Decca Records and all its subsidiaries, merged with Universal. By the '90s, liquor giant Seagram's acquired the whole kit and caboodle before itself merging, first with the Phillips-owned PolyGram and then with French communications giant, Vivendi.

- Sony, also looking for a software company to fuel and complete its hardware interests, purchased Columbia Records and all the sub-labels it had spun off and acquired over the years.

- Paramount was bought out by Gulf and Western.

- Mighty RCA sold its recording interests to German publishing giant Bertelsmann.

While these companies knew the notes in terms of business, most of the models of doing business as a major corporation impeded the model that made the rock-and-roll business run. Public corporations—all the major labels, except Bertelsmann, are publicly held, and Bertelsmann has been itching to go public for years—need to show profit on a quarterly basis, or explain to their stockholders why they don't. Creative business can't run on that type of schedule. It takes years to develop artists to the point that they become profitable. Thus the emphasis shifted to:

- Entities proven on smaller independent labels. The prevailing wisdom being if an act can sell twenty thousand units as an indie with a limited budget, there's a good chance it could sell a hundred times that amount if "properly" promoted.

- Quick hits and novelty records. A dance hit like the "Macarena" could sell 4 million copies in the U.S. alone, enough to seriously jumpstart slumping revenues.

- Formulas. It's a time-honored tradition in the music business, but much more evident now. The folks who sign artists to record labels find what works, i.e., what the other companies had hits with, and go get their own version of it.

Part of Edison's vision for his talking machine was to bring grand opera into the home of every workingman. That facet of his vision has come to fruition in a very big way. In the 125 years since Edison placed his invention on a table in the offices of *Scientific American* and proceeded to astound everyone in the office, sound reproduction has grown from a novelty to an $8 billion-a-year business. Beyond that, entertainment of nearly any stripe is available to most everybody on disc, and the technology only continues to improve. At some juncture, holographic projection will allow three-dimensional home entertainment, bringing the live music experience that much closer to being captured on disc. Because as the entertainment experience has become corporatized, the need for new revenue continues to grow.

As much as the growth and consolidation of music into a business has catalyzed change, in its way this has led to the current downfall of rock and roll. However, the music has been down before, and it would be foolish to count it out just yet.

Robert Johnson Makes Forty-one Recordings in Texas Hotel Rooms, Offices, and Warehouses

Having landed in the relatively modern times of corporate cooption of popular music, we set the way-back machine for the 1910s to observe . . . the corporate cooption of popular music.

Robert Johnson signifies this and so much more. He might be the model for any rock star who wanted to play hard, live fast, die young, and leave a pretty corpse. This may be one of the reasons this blues-man who recorded but forty-one songs was among the first "early influences" inducted into the Rock and Roll Hall of Fame the year it was founded.

Perhaps the greatest of the Delta bluesmen—proclaimed their king by his initial release on LP—and certainly among the most influential, Robert Johnson's legacy affected everything that came after. You can hear his influence in the music of such protégés as Johnny Shines, Howlin' Wolf, Sonny Boy Williamson, and Elmore James. Yet his prime influence on rock and roll came with his stunning impact on the English white blues rockers of the '60s who revered him, such as the Rolling Stones and Eric Clapton. His twenty-nine-song canon remains one of the most covered in history.

Johnson's posthumous career is, in a way, a creation of the record business, and is largely based on about a week's work out of his twenty-seven-year-old life. The recordings themselves came out of the business's insatiable need for "race records."

Run, as it was, by white businessmen at the turn of the twentieth century, the music business—like so many other businesses in America—regarded the African-American population as largely unimportant. Initially, it was assumed that because the hardware was so costly, only white, middle-class, working people or those more affluent could afford it.

As the prices for the various record players came down, however, recorded music made its way into the hands of the masses, and that included the ten-to-fifteen-percent African-American minority. So when, in 1920, Mamie Smith recorded "Crazy Blues" for Okeh Records, and sold 75,000 copies in a month, mostly to black buyers, this caught the business up short, but it reacted with uncharacteristic speed. Soon many of the dominant labels had "race divisions," and independent labels started concentrating on the "race market" as well.

The prevailing music under this rubric was blues. Ironically, jazz was the popular music at the time, as at the time it was also dance music. Jazz made the '20s roar, which is why the decade is also called the Jazz Age.

However, in the 1920s, gospel music and the blues were styles nearly every African-American could identify and identify with—the promise of heaven on the one hand, the world as it is on the other. Yet these forms of music were largely unheard in the white community, except perhaps "vaudeville" blues, a very watered-down version of what was recorded by artists like Charlie Patton, Son House, and so many others. All most of these artists saw for their troubles was a small payment for making the recording and, if they had a hit, a bit more recognition when they went from jook joint to jook joint up and down the Mississippi, and beyond.

One of the interesting aspects of Johnson's career is that he was a second-generation bluesman. This is not to say that the blues were only around since the 1920s—evidence links it to the African Griot tradition that may well predate the Bible—but that Johnson was part of the second generation of bluesmen that started playing after radio and the record player had come into vogue. He was among the first generation of blues musicians that could learn to play from listening to players they might never actually see in their lifetime. By all reports, Johnson was especially adept at learning this way. He is alleged to have been able to hear a song once live, on record, or over the radio— even while having a conversation—and play it back perfectly.

In his early teens, Johnson became infatuated with music. The youngest of eleven children, with a fairly tangled family situation (for more on that, see Samuel Charters or Peter Guaralnick's excellent books on Johnson), Johnson was slightly built. As an adolescent he realized his physical stature would be a problem if he grew up to work on the Leatherman farm as his stepfather did. He took up the harmonica, and as Son House, who lived in the same area of rural Mississippi, recalled, he was pretty good at it. But he wanted to learn the guitar, so against the wishes of his stepfather, who wanted him to work the field, and his mother, who wanted to protect him, Johnson would sneak out at night and head to whatever jook joint House and his partner at the time, Willie Brown, were playing. When they took a break, he would pick up one of their guitars and start trying to figure it out. At the time he had a lot to learn.

But learn he did. By the time he was eighteen he had lost a wife and child in childbirth. As a young, married man, he had tried to make it as a farmer, working on his music after hours. With his wife and child dead, he hit the road. He played the jook joints for the WPA work gangs, lumber camp workers, and he learned his craft well. When he happened back to the town he left, he found House and

Brown again and asked to sit in with them. As House recalled, "So he sat down there and finally got started. And man! He was so good! When he finished, all our mouths were standing open. I said, 'Well, ain't that fast! He's gone now!'"

His sudden prowess on the guitar had people who-knew-him-when muttering about how he must have done a deal with the devil to get those chops. This was not an uncommon theory about blues-men, or anyone who played music outside the church in the rural South in the '30s. Not many bluesmen (with the possible exception of House, who was also an itinerant preacher) denied this. It added to their mystique. Peetie Wheatstraw called himself "the devil's right-hand man." So when Johnson would sing "Crossroads Blues," this resonated loudly and anciently for many African-Americans who remembered, even dimly, their heritage. Their view of the devil was colored by the Santerian deity Legba, the trickster, who often waylaid the unsuspecting at a crossroad, invariably sending the weak-minded or weak of spirit down the wrong path.

Whether by talent, practice, or demonic intervention, by the time Johnson hit his early twenties, nobody cut him on the guitar, hardly anyone could even touch him. "He went over some guitar," blues-man Henry Townsend recollected of his encounter with Johnson, "and I thought, *Well, this guy's got it*. I mean, he was amazing. I was a little bit older than him, but I didn't think anybody had seniority over me on the guitar, but this guy made me look little."

Johnson had become a seasoned pro at twenty-one. While he is best known for playing the blues, many of those who actually remember him say he could play *anything*. "He played ragtime, Dixieland, as well as the blues," his stepson Robert Junior Lockwood recalled.

His playing incorporated slide techniques (he used a jack-knife, which added an element of danger), boogie-woogie bass lines played on the lower strings while doing other amazing work on the higher strings—a technique that led Keith Richards, on initially hearing John-son, to wonder who the second guitarist was.

His playing had taken him to Canada and New York City and nearly every barrelhouse and jook joint up and down the Mississippi. The one thing he hadn't done that his mentors like Charlie Patton and Son House had was issue a record. He contacted H. C. Speir, who ran a Jackson, Mississippi, music store. Speir was known to be a scout for several record companies. By the mid-'30s, the companies that put out "race records" were ever vigilant for new talent. As the owner of a shop frequented by African Americans, Speir was in a unique position to tell them what African Americans would buy. He passed Johnson's name on to Ernie Oertle, a salesman and scout for the American Record Company's Vocalion label. The people at ARC were so impressed, they brought Johnson to San Antonio, Texas, to record.

In late November of 1936, Johnson was one of a variety of acts set to play for the microphone of record producer Don Law. In addition to recording Johnson, Law recorded a Mexican band, Andres Berlanga y Francisco Montalvo con guitarras, and a country band called the Chuck Wagon Gang in the same day. Over the course of three sessions, Johnson set down some songs that have become ingrained in the world's musical psyche: "Kindhearted Woman Blues," "I Believe I'll Dust My Broom," "Sweet Home Chicago," "Come on in My Kitchen," "Ramblin' on My Mind," "Crossroads Blues," and "Terraplane Blues," to name but a few.

A story from those sessions reveals an important aspect of Johnson. He got into trouble in San Antonio. Apparently, when they whisked him off to Texas no one checked to see if he had any money. He didn't. As Law sat down to dinner in the hotel, he got a call from the San Antonio police. They had Johnson in custody. Law got Johnson released, gave him forty-five cents for breakfast, and told him to stay put in the hotel for the rest of the night. A bit later on, Law got a call from Johnson himself, telling him he was lonely. "What do you mean?" Law asked. "I'm lonesome and there's a lady here. She wants fifty cents and I lacks a nickel."

As famous as he was in some circles as a bluesman, Johnson was notorious with the ladies. Although slight, he was good looking, had long, sensitive fingers, and a way with words. He also was not very discriminating about his women. Married three times, he sired any number of children from his various liaisons as well.

Vocalion released "Terraplane Blues" backed with "Kindhearted Woman Blues." "We heard a couple of his pieces come out on records," House remembered. "Believe the first one I heard was 'Terraplane Blues.' Jesus, it was good! We all admired it."

"Terraplane Blues" became Johnson's best-selling record during his lifetime, a minor hit for Vocalion. Although the subsequent records from the session didn't fare as well, Vocalion brought Johnson back to Texas the following June to record some more. The situation was similar, although in this case, ARC's engineers set up in a warehouse and office in Dallas. During one day, he shared recording time with the Light Crust Doughboys, a group notable for (a) their longevity (a band by that name still plays Texas swing all over) and (b) being the spawning ground for Bob Wills and his Texas Playboys (though Bob was long gone by then).

Though Vocalion and ARC would release eleven recordings during his lifetime (and one after his passing), he never had a bona fide hit 78 again. Because of that, ARC decided not to invite him to their next set of sessions. However, having had the hit with "Terraplane Blues" assured him good houses wherever he played. He continued rambling through life, still playing the jook joints, barrelhouses, picnics, and house parties up and down the Mississippi, using "Terraplane Blues" as his calling card and signature song.

While there are several stories about how Johnson died, the prevailing one points to his indiscriminate love of the ladies. Beyond his reputation as a fine player who could liven up any evening, he also earned nearly as much notoriety as a Don Juan. Between the liquor, the music, the party atmosphere, and his good looks, Johnson apparently had his choice of women and almost invariably chose badly. House was convinced it would be his undoing, at least in retrospect, when he remembered warning him, "You gotta be careful about that 'cause a lot of times they do that and they got a husband or a boyfriend standing right over in the corner. You getting all excited over 'em and you don't know what you doing. You get hurt."

That he did. In the summer of 1938, he played a house party and the hostess started fawning over the handsome young bluesman. Her husband saw this and sent Johnson a bottle of whiskey laced with strychnine. The poison didn't kill him, but it weakened him enough that he caught pneumonia, and that did. He was dead at the age of twenty-seven.

His early death, in addition to adding some romance to his story, brings up another element of Johnson's career that makes him so compelling, the "what-might-have-been" factor. In 1938, John Hammond began putting together a coming-out party for African-American music, perhaps the most important concert event of the twentieth century. Called Spirituals to Swing, it would bring the African-American music Hammond loved so much to his peers—Hammond was, after all, a Vanderbilt heir. "Upper-class white folks went up to Harlem in the '20s, slumming," Hammond once said. "I went out of passion. Anyone who did that had his life changed."

He had heard of Johnson, even as far north as New York, and asked his contacts at ARC to bring him up. Everyone involved knew this would be a problem: Johnson was an itinerant bluesman, and with more wanderlust than the norm at that. He might be anywhere along a 500-mile stretch of the Mississippi. Ernie Oertle became a hellhound on his trail, and soon learned that Johnson had died several months earlier.

Hammond had already had posters made for the show with Johnson's name on it. He had those withdrawn and brought in Big Bill Broonzy, a Delta bluesman of similar stature to Johnson in terms of having had a few records out and having spent his time touring up and down the Delta. But Broonzy had settled in Chicago, where he was building a new sound that would dominate the blues for years to come: the Chicago urban blues. In many ways, it would have been appropriate to have both Johnson and Broonzy on the bill: Johnson and his peers marked the high-water point on the levy, the crest of the Delta country blues; Broonzy represented the change coming on.

Because of that change, few cared to keep Johnson's legend and legacy alive. In 1940, folklore archivist Alan Lomax went searching for Johnson, only to find out that he was several years dead (he must have missed the news when Hammond went looking). Instead, he turned up one of Johnson's disciples, McKinley Morganfield, a.k.a. Muddy Waters, who also took his country blues to the city.

Part of the strength of Johnson's music was that it worked in the urban blues concept as well as it did in the Delta. In 1952, Elmore James paid tribute to Johnson, recording his "Dust My Broom," which became a sizable electric-blues hit.

So, for twenty or so years after his death, Robert's legacy lived on in the players he had influenced, but his name remained known only among rarified blues aficionados. In the late '50s, a major renaissance in folk and blues found record companies scouring their vaults for old blues records that might sound new again. Johnson's sides fit that bill nicely. When Columbia reissued Johnson's music in 1961 on the *King of the Delta Blues* album, no one knew very much about the man who made the music. "Robert Johnson came to me out of a distant time and place," wrote Tony Scherman of the experience of hearing *King of the Delta Blues* for the first time. "He came unadorned by facts or known photographs."

Johnson became a figure of almost mythical proportions, his story growing to fit the prodigious technique and emotion of his recordings. Word spread about this new album almost virally.

- John Hammond worked in the Columbia Records A&R department by then and had gotten a very early version of the record to his son John, Jr. John, in addition to his other studies at Antioch College, was majoring in guitar with fellow students like Jorma Kaukonen, who would later help launch the Jefferson Airplane (their name a conflation of Blind Lemon Jefferson and "Terraplane Blues"), with whom he shared this remarkable musical artifact.

- Ry Cooder was fourteen when he discovered the album, bought himself a bottleneck slide, and tried to make some musical sense out of it for himself.

- In 1962 Jaime Robbie Robertson was already a working musician in Memphis when he bought his copy.

- On the cover of *Bringing It All Back Home*, Bob Dylan poses with the album.

- Another blues fan, Eric Clapton, had his interest solidified by *King of the Delta Blues*. "It came as something of a shock to me that there could be anything that powerful," he recalled. "It was as if I had been prepared to receive Robert Johnson, almost like a religious experience that started out with hearing Chuck Berry then at each stage went further and deeper until I was ready for him."

- "There has not been a better album in the history of the recording industry," wrote critic Greil Marcus in his seminal book on popular music, *Mystery Train*.

- Brian Jones bought a copy and played it for his new buddy Keith Richards: "I've never heard anybody before or since use the form and bend it quite so much to make it work for himself," Richards remembered. "The quality of the songs themselves—I mean, he came out with such compelling themes . . ." (It seems ironic that Jones would be found dead at the age of twenty-seven, just a month older than Johnson was when he died.)

Johnson's life became a pursuit for writers and scholars. As they followed his trail, speaking to surviving blues musicians who remembered (or claimed to remember) Johnson, finding his relatives, uncovering legal documents like marriage and death certificates, a picture of his history started to emerge.

But all that was fueled by Johnson's music. Clapton followed him down to the "Crossroads," and it became one of his early theme songs and even a Top 30 pop hit, although "Ramblin' on My Mind" proved as good or better a vehicle for Clapton as a solo artist. The Rolling Stones recorded "Love In Vain." These artists sent interest in Johnson mushrooming. "I singled out the ones that seemed most accessible and then I tried to make them more so for today's market," noted Clapton, "so that people would like them, in a sense, on a somewhat shallow level, and ask questions afterward."

"'Love In Vain' was such a beautiful song," added Richards. "In a way, it was like, 'We've got to do this song one way or another.' Because it was so beautiful: the title, the lyrics, the ideas, the rhymes, just everything about it."

That two of the most influential British blues bands should evince such interest in Johnson's music triggered even more fans to follow. In 1990, Columbia collected together everything they had of Johnson in their vaults, which essentially represents everything he is known to have recorded. They put it through the best sonic cleansing they could without killing the music's essence, and released it as a two-CD, boxed set called *The Complete Robert Johnson*. The set outsold new recordings by contemporary pop performers like Madonna, Run-D.M.C., Iggy Pop, and Carly Simon, won a Grammy for Best Historical Recording, and sold more than a million copies. It was one of the musical events of the year.

Robert Johnson's influence continues into the new millennium: Alternative folk-rockers the Cowboy Junkies recorded "Me and the Devil Blues." Tracy Chapman paid homage with her own song called "Crossroads." Prince commissioned a film script based on the peripatetic bluesman's life.

Scherman suggested that, "Although it's hip, especially since his rise to pop iconhood, to call him 'the original rock and roller,' the notion is unilluminating at best."

While this is true, it would still be safe to say that way back in the 1930s, Robert Johnson started writing many of the rules that rock and rollers—for good or ill—live by today.

Les Paul Invents the Solid-Body Electric Guitar, Close Miking, the Multitrack Studio, and a Bunch of Other Stuff

Edison lived until Les Paul was a teenager. Otherwise, if you believe in such things, you might regard Paul as Edison's musical reincarnation. His inventions, which came fast and furious in the '40s and '50s, changed the way people made and recorded music. Yet, Paul claims to hold no patents, even though the list of his inventions and innovations is staggering: the humbucking guitar pickup, the solid-body electric guitar, sound-on-sound recording, electronic echo, and multitrack recording just for starters. There's even a book, Jim Dawson and Steve Propes' *What Was the First Rock 'n Roll Record?*, that maintains he (along with Nat "King" Cole and Illinois Jacquet and several others) invented rock and roll with the *Jazz at the Philharmonic* single "Blues Part 2" in 1942.

The song bears all the earmarks of what would follow a decade later—it works off a straight blues progression and a shuffle beat that you can dance to, Jacquet honks his sax viciously, and Paul solos and comps aggressively on that prototype solid-body electric guitar of his. If the song had vocals, people other than Dawson and Propes might have come to this conclusion. However, even in retrospect, the distinction caught Paul up short. "That probably was one of the forerunners of that kind of a thing," he decided. "In no time at all, that was what made Norman Granz and *Jazz at the Philharmonic*. I had to be Paul Leslie and Nat was Shorty Nadine. We used pseudonyms because we were under contract from other record companies.

"Norman Granz came over to my backyard and asked me if I would do this thing, and I said 'sure.' What had happened was that Nat Cole had called up Norman Granz and said, 'Hey, Oscar [Moore, Cole's guitarist] has some broad up in his house and he hasn't been out in a week. The sonuvabitch is giving us a helluva time. Could you possibly get Les Paul to fill in for Oscar?' Otherwise, this never would have happened.

"When I got down there, to the Philharmonic, I was in uniform. I was with Meredith Willson and the Armed Forces Radio Service. So I went to Meredith and said, 'Hey, can I do this?' And he says, 'I'll give you permission to do it, but you've got to stay in uniform and take all the identification off of you.' So I went down there and I had to play it for nothing, because in the Armed Forces, you can't play as a civilian. So, I did exactly that.

"When we got out on the stage and started [to] play, it didn't take long before Nat and I got into cat and mouse. As soon as we started to do the chase, they went crazy, and the more they went crazy, the more we were turned on. First thing you know, they're standing on their chairs, they're throwing their hats in the air. That just made it more fun for us."

"I saw that rock scene coming in," he added. "But I didn't particularly like to switch over, and neither did Sinatra and neither did Peggy Lee, and neither did Ella Fitzgerald or Bing Crosby or Benny Goodman. None of us wanted to go that particular route. To this day, I don't really go out of my way to dial in rock music, though I don't avoid it and I like it and I can listen to it. It's not something that I crave to play."

What Les fails to add is that when he saw that rock scene coming in, much of it came in on Les Paul guitars. One of his first major innovations, the commercial version of the Les Paul solid-body electric guitar, came out via Gibson in 1952. It came about for the same reason nearly everything Les Paul invented came about: It made making music either easier or better.

That solid-body electric guitar was the product of a quarter century of experimentation on Paul's part. The precedent was set early that the music always came before the innovation. Paul started playing out very young, when he was still called Lester Polfus in and around his original hometown of Waukesha, Wisconsin, on a five-dollar Sears and Roebuck Gene Autry guitar.

"Friday and Saturday nights they had roadhouses in those days where I could play," Paul says. "And I would play a drive-in hamburger place. Everybody in their cars couldn't hear me, so the first thing I did was build a PA system. They could hear my voice then, but not my guitar, so I made an electric guitar."

Paul's first electric guitar didn't look very much like the instrument he continues to play well into his eighties at his weekly Monday-night shows at New York's Iridium Jazz Club. Initially, he took a needle and cartridge and attached it to his guitar. Over the years, he tortured that guitar to try and get the sound he wanted.

"It just bothered me, somehow, I got an electric guitar and it feeds back," he says. "I filled it full of rags, filled it with plaster of Paris. I did everything in the world to it. Yeah, it's ridiculous, but I wanted to kill that sound, and I could care less. I just wanted to prove the point. That's more important."

A consummate pack rat, as well as inventor and guitarist, Paul has kept nearly everything—from the Atwater Kent radio that became his first amplifier and PA system to his early experiments with allowing for only the vibrating string to generate sound, without the vagaries of the acoustics that caused the feedback. One such experiment looks like a plank with a door-hinge tailpiece and a pickup that turns out to be the inner coils of an old electric clock attached under a piece of wire, drawn taut with a machine head. It looks a little like a jerry-rigged lap steel guitar.

"I was just trying to get the concept of the steel string and a pickup underneath it," Paul explained. "I was just trying to get my act together, find out what kind of wood to use. All I wanted to do was get a string to ring.

"Along with this one, I made a piece of railroad track, the same length and did the same thing. I wanted to try a piece of steel versus this piece of wood, to find out which sounded the best, soft wood or a very heavy mass, very strong dense material. I came up with the idea that the railroad track was the way to go, but I couldn't imagine Gene Autry on a horse with a railroad track. So, that went out the window and I went back to the wood. This was the concept."

In the meantime, Paul had gotten a somewhat more professional electric guitar. He became a Gibson guitar artist in 1928 when he got his first L5. Before that, to get enough volume, he had played one of the "guitarists' solutions" from the '20s, an instrument called a tympanic guitar, made by Dobro.

"They penetrated," Paul said of the instrument. "They had a characteristic sound of their own, very much like an electric guitar. I used them with the Mills Brothers, many records in the old days. The Delta Rhythm Boys, things like that. I used the Dobro a lot. It was right after I got the '28 L-5 that I tossed the Dobro in the corner and forgot about it, because the Dobro is anything but musical compared to an L-5. You couldn't play rhythm on a Dobro. I had a team, Sonny Joe and Rubarb Red. If you can imagine, when he played rhythm for me, I could cut him to pieces because of that Dobro. It jumps out. But when I had to play rhythm for him, this tin can playing rhythm was terrible. So, he says, 'You've got to get rid of that Dobro.'"

A Gibson Guitars engineer named Lloyd Loar had designed a very primitive pickup and put it onto the L5, Gibson's top-of-the-line jazz guitar. By 1931, the pickup technology improved. Rickenbacker introduced their first commercial electric guitars with a Spanish-style guitar called the Electro-Spanish in 1935 and a Hawaiian steel guitar they called the Frying Pan in 1937.

As the technology revolutionized the instrument, it started to change the way players—especially younger players—approached the instrument. With the guitar amplified, it changed the need for large bands to generate the volume required for groups to entertain dancers (and compete with the drummer). Beyond that, the guitar, which had primarily been a rhythm instrument, now could develop an expressive voice as a solo instrument. Paul saw this, as did a young African-American guitarist from Texas named Charlie Christian. As Frederic Grunfeld wrote in *The Art and Times of the Guitar*, "There is the guitar before Christian and the guitar after Christian, and they sound virtually like two different instruments."

"Sometime in the late thirties," Paul recalled, "in walked a kid named Charlie Christian and we became very good friends. . . . He got a guitar like mine and a pickup like mine but he played his own thing, he had his style of playing. And he went with Benny Goodman . . .

"Charlie and I would really battle each other—and we'd battle for blood. We go up on stage and chop each other to pieces and then go out to eat together."

Meanwhile, Paul was still fighting his feedback problems, with the help of Gibson. With his acoustic-electric guitars, he would stuff towels into the f-holes and take off the back and put in blankets. "I asked Gibson to make a guitar with no holes in it so that no sound came out of it at all. Charlie Christian ordered one like it. Whatever I ordered, Charlie ordered."

Another member of the live-fast-die-young-and-leave-a-pretty-corpse school, Christian was dead of tuberculosis by the time he was twenty-three, but like Robert Johnson, his effect on popular music is immeasurable. For all intents and purposes, Christian is the father of the guitar solo.

Paul continued to play one of Gibson's acoustic-guitars-with-a-pickup models. Feedback and distortion were constant foes. Now living in New York and playing with Fred Waring as well as his own trio, Paul continued to experiment. What he finally came up with was a 4 X 4 with two pickups and an Epiphone neck. To make it look less strange and more like a guitar, he sawed an Epiphone acoustic guitar body in half and attached it with hooks (so that they were detachable as well). He affectionately dubbed this instrument "The Log" and he played it pretty much through the '40s.

"This is the one I took to the Gibson people, this is the one that Leo Fender saw, this is the one that everybody laughed at," Paul said, then amended himself. "Some laughed at it. Gibson laughed at it. They called me that character with the broomstick with pickups on it. That's the way they visualized the whole thing. Others took it quite seriously and said 'Hey, there's some merit to this.'"

Paul continued to come back to Gibson with ideas. "I built the first pickup, Alvino Ray probably still has it in his collection. The first pickup I had them build was from the fingerboard down to the bridge. I called that 'The Mine Sweeper.' That was the damnedest thing you ever heard, the worst thing you ever heard. I sent it back to Gibson and said, 'Forget about it.'"

It took close to a decade for Gibson to take "The Log" seriously, and that was only because someone beat them to the punch. Leo Fender owned and operated a radio and electronics repair shop in Fullerton, California. One of the pieces of electronics he stocked were public-address amplifiers that he rented to local musicians. In talking with them, he learned of many of the problems, including the feedback and distortion problem Paul had dealt with by using his Log. By 1943, he and his partner Doc Kaufman had applied for a patent for a pickup, which they mounted onto a lap steel guitar.

Like Paul, although Fender didn't actually play the guitar, he designed his instruments to suit his customers. By 1948, he was developing prototypes of a solid-body electric guitar that would be simple to mass-produce and maintain. It had a pickup built onto the plate that held the bridge, and the musician had to put the strings through the body of the instrument. Fender called this utilitarian instrument the Broadcaster, but after some legal problems over the name changed it to the Telecaster. By 1950, the instrument went into production.

Even more important, the next year Fender introduced the Precision Bass. Now the bassist would no longer have to carry around an instrument taller than the average man and twice as cumbersome. The P-Bass (as it is affectionately called by musicians) was only a little longer than the Telecaster with a fretted neck demystifying the note positions for guitarists who had to also play bass. It was small, as loud as the amplifier and speaker allowed, and much easier to transport, even with the amp.

With this competition, and the demonstration that musicians

would embrace a solid-body electric guitar, suddenly Les Paul's "broom-stick with pickups" looked mighty good to Gibson.

"If Leo Fender hadn't decided to come out with it, Gibson proba-bly wouldn't have come out with a Les Paul model yet," Paul mused. "It just happened to be that he rattled their cage. The latter part of 1949, 1950, Gibson was making me prototypes with flat tops. No arch top. Then the president of CMI, Chicago Musical Instruments, got me. Not the president of Gibson. He didn't really know what was hap-pening. The guy that was really running that thing was M. H. Berlin. He was the chairman of the board and the guy who put this whole thing together. A beautiful man. He was the guy who said to me, 'Would you consider an arch top instead of a flat top?'

"The first one that came out on the market with the arched-top body was incorrectly made. The tailpiece, the neck joins the body and it's not on a bias, not on an angle. Consequently, they thought, 'Well, I guess what Les meant was the strings are supposed to go under the bridge.' So, you can't muffle the strings at the bridge. They made this wrong. When I got this guitar I said, 'Stop it! You're making the gui-tars all wrong.' There may be a thousand of these out. We had to stop them from making them."

With the economics of running a big band, along with the sea change going on in popular music in the wake of World War II, the dance orchestra was going the way of the dodo bird by the early '50s, and small combos—à la the Les Paul Trio—were becoming the pre-dominant kind of band. With a P-Bass and a couple of electric guitars, now three musicians could do the job of dozens. They could even play louder than the drummer.

Needless to say, these instruments caught on in a big way. Even if *Blues, Pt. 2* wasn't "the first rock and roll record," the artists who took up the flag of urban blues, the post–Hank Williams country, even bebop that evolved into rock, took to the electric guitar. It became synonymous with the new genre and the players. Elvis might have worn an acoustic guitar, but Scotty Moore, the power behind that musical throne, was a pioneering electric guitarist. Chuck Berry's elec-tric guitar allowed him to slice through the band with his unique double-stop technique. Buddy Holly created a standard for the rock band with his two-guitar, bass and drums line-up with the Crickets. The '50s were the breeding place of the guitar slinger.

In the meantime, Paul had developed quite a solo career of his own. Between 1946 and 1961 he rang up forty-two Top 40 hits, both solo and with his wife, singer Mary Ford. Ever the improviser, he had been cutting his own records for years with a transcription turntable he made from the flywheel of a Cadillac, rescued from a junker, in his father's garage in Waukesha. "The cutting lathe was a paring knife from my mother's kitchen drawer, just a plain paring knife," he said. "The two switches are from the barn. And these are 50-cycle motors, but I run them at 60. The belts are dental belts a drummer in my band got me. There were two of these, so I could go from one lathe to the other lathe, back and forth. This made 'How High The Moon.' All mastering was done on this lathe."

He had so impressed Bing Crosby with his recording prowess that Crosby funded a recording studio in Paul's Hollywood garage. If the electric guitar is the overt symbol of rock and roll, what Paul accomplished in that garage, and subsequently, is truly the heart, soul, and sound of rock and roll.

In the early '40s, recording techniques had actually changed very little since the days when Edison would set up a recording horn and have the musicians start playing. This had to be the way, because you only got one take. If one of the musicians messed up badly, they had to make another recording. If one of the musicians got too close to the mike, that instrument would be too loud. Paul, however, had another idea. He had been using his cutting lathes to make records for practicing for years. Why not, he reasoned, take this idea and expand on it? With two lathes, he could record one instrument on one, then play the recording along with another instrument and record the two together, and so on, until he had the recording he wanted. This allowed him to mike each individual instrument separately.

"Now this was the beginning," Paul said, "of what we call close mic [sic] technique—this had never been used. It had been pounded into [audio engineers'] heads that you should be three feet away from a microphone, no closer than two feet. . . ."

Using these techniques, Paul recorded music for Crosby, the Andrews Sisters (he had been a sideman for them for years), W. C. Fields, and many others. In 1946, he recorded the song "Brazil," laying down six separate guitar parts, bouncing from one lathe to the other.

That same year, he got something that rocked his world and then the music world in general. One of the spoils of World War II was the Nazis' improvement on an old, but inefficient, recording technique. Magnetic recording on wire had been around for some time, as Paul recalled, "I had a wire recorder years ago, with Fred Waring. Fred had them bring it over from RCA, from their display in the cases in the hallways at Rockefeller Center. They gave it to me for six months to play with. I said, 'Just as long as that wire is turning around and you have to tie knots in it, this is not the round wheel. Something better has got to come along than this thing. This is a dog.' So, it went back into the showcase and we forgot all about it, but the Germans didn't. It was just a question of getting the oxide on a flat tape so it wouldn't turn around like the wire did. The Germans took this thing and flattened it out."

The tape machine came to America with a Colonel Richard Ranger, who dismantled it, figured out how it worked, put it back together, and arranged for people to see it. "He. . . . showed it to me and Bing Crosby and Glen Glenn. . . . He showed me the advantage of tape over disc and it immediately turned my head. . . . When I got my first tape recorder, I immediately asked for a fourth head and they asked why and I said I just wanted one. I wasn't about to tell anybody what it was for—but it was to make sound on sound."

Similar to the technique he used with the cutting lathes, using sound on sound with tape was easier, but more dangerous—unless you made safety backups after each good take, one mistake and the whole project was ruined. It didn't take long for Paul to figure out a solution for this problem, however. "If you can do it with *one* machine, why not stack several of them up, stack eight up and do it that way?"

Paul took the idea to several companies before Ampex agreed to build it for him. By this time, he had moved to the exurbs of New York City, at the foot of the Ramapo Mountains, where he still lived when this book went to print. "We're about forty-five minutes from Broadway. I've timed it. I said, 'I can be at the Paramount Theater on Broadway in forty-five minutes. That's cool.' All the live shows were out of New York. We were in the perfect place to be.

"I just came to them with an idea and asked them if they'd make me one. I paid for it. In the meantime at home here I was building this console to match up with (the amplifier and tape machine). So, eleven guys are here designing the whole studio. Now, we're talking about the studio, the console, the patch bay going from one room to the other to do video, to do audio, to do everything."

By the time Paul and the engineers were through, he had the prototype for the modern recording studio just off the living room of his house. Ironically, as with so many of his inventions, he didn't file for a patent. He assumed that Ampex "had a line open to Washington and patented it right then and there when they saw what I was doing." Only in 2000 did Paul discover that they thought that he did, so *nobody* patented the original multitrack recorder. "I was busy doing other things, mostly," Paul explained about all of the patent applications he never filed. "I just go make them and there they are. You have to have priorities. Are you going to play the Paramount, be on the *Ed Sullivan Show* and record for Capitol Records, or are you going to sit around and screw with a piece of piezo? I decided I only had so much time."

The studio that he designed in 1951 does essentially everything that any modern studio can do. And, as of the turn of the millennium, the equipment still worked. Ironically, while he used it extensively for his television work on the shows he did at home with Ford through the '50s and early '60s, Paul made most of his hit records the old-fashioned way, using the sound-on-sound recorder. "This did everything," he said of the recording rig. "Everything done with Mary and I was done this way, with this mixer, this monitor and power supply, and that [points to the log] guitar. Here is the head of the sound on sound, the microphone, the earphones. This is how we recorded 'How High the Moon,' everything. Always, in a room, a basement. Las Vegas. Filling stations, under the grandstands, outdoors, indoors."

While the original studio is, of course, analog, Paul does understand the current digital technology—he predicted it in the early 1950s. Since then, the technology has improved some, has been tweaked. But the electric guitar hasn't changed all that much since the 1950s, and players value vintage instruments for their purity of tone and electronics. Any audio engineer checking out Paul's original eight-track studio would understand it immediately, as it isn't too different—just smaller—than a modern studio.

"This is the way I feel—I'm credited with a lot of things," Paul said. "When I did it, I was in it. Now, I'm out of it, and I look back and it's like another person did it. I just don't feel as though it's anything to rave about, or that it is important. I know it is, because there isn't anything you hear today that doesn't have delay on it, that doesn't have phasing, flanging, multitracks. I know that every studio has what I invented. But I never thought of it as being anything important, and I don't now. I'm not humble. I just can't get it in my head—not that I should—but when someone comes up to me like the Smithsonian Institute and says we want to put your museum in with Edison's, I look at it like it's ice cream and fat meat. It doesn't make sense to me. Edison was phenomenal. I'm just a guitar player that stumbled on this stuff. You couldn't buy it at Sam Ash, so I built it."

"American Bandstand"

Another famous first for Les Paul had to do with broadcasting. "The first TV show ever to come out of New York, we were on it, the Les Paul Trio," he claimed. "That was the broadcast from the 1939 World's Fair. So, in 1939, we were the first ones to go on the air and do it."

Ever since music and TV have had a strange and (occasionally) wonderful relationship. Most of the variety shows from the "Golden Age" of television relied as much on musical talent as the legendary comedy to make the age golden. The multitalented hosts and cast had to sing, dance, and do comedy, and since the shows were live, they had to do it all in one take. Most came from the Broadway stage or vaudeville, so the shows had a Broadway sensibility. A great many more made the transition from radio, especially the comedies and serials.

That was mostly in prime time, however. Until the '50s, TV channels tended to be on the air pretty sporadically. Even as recently as the early '80s, many stations signed off the air in the small hours of the morning.

With many channels, especially in the early days of TV, the daytime hours were not regarded as prime moneymakers, so the programming had to be done cheaply. Cooking shows, fashion shows, and the like filled the hours before 7:00 P.M. when the networks started to broadcast their prime offerings—the likes of Milton Berle and Sid Caesar.

In 1945, just after World War II and six years after Paul's appearance at the World's Fair, there were only 7,000 TVs in use, 6 television stations nationwide, and perhaps 15 hours of programming a week. By 1950, there were 8 million televisions in use in 5 million homes; sales of TVs were in the area of $1 billion and there were closer to 100 stations broadcasting.

So, with this influx of viewership and all this time to fill, many stations, especially newer and smaller ones, had to dig around for programming.

In addition to this, the radio variety and comedy shows began moving to television. As the talent pool made this shift, radio stations began to become the domain of men playing recordings—disc jockeys.

This had enormous impact on popular culture as well as popular music. For one thing, the postwar youth began to decide that the prevailing popular music was, in a word, boring. Performers like Dean Martin and Teresa Brewer personified white pop at the time. This is the sound that the people purveying the music, the record companies, thought the record-buying public wanted to hear. The deejays on the white-oriented middle-of-the-road (MOR) stations were playing this music and people were listening to it. It was pat, sweet, and nice, but it did not really speak for the younger people who were now demographically becoming the record buying public. Len Brown, coeditor of *The Rock and Roll Encyclopedia*, explained it this way:

> To me at the time, music wasn't ever going to change. It was going to keep going along on its same course, presenting novelties like "Sailor Boys Have Talked to Me in English," great show tunes like "(You've Gotta Have) Heart," and catchy instrumentals like "Poor People of Paris." What else was there? Who would want music to sound any other way? Me! . . .

People like Brown started to play with their radio dials and discovered what was still called "race music." This new sound (to them) had a beat. The lyrics made sexual allusions, and to a certain extent the songs far better addressed the frustrations and curiosity of this new audience than did most of the contemporary "white" popular music.

"The white pop music at the time," said songwriter Jerry Leiber, "was devitalized, by and large. Whenever there's a vacuum like that, someone comes along and fills it."

In those pre–civil rights days, the races did not mix socially, economically, or musically, especially on the airwaves. Television was outright a white medium and would pretty much remain so for another thirty years. Black performers on TV were few and far between. Amos and Andy and Eddie "Rochester" Anderson were exceptions that proved the rule, cartoonlike stereotypes created by white writers.

"They segregated everything in those days," noted Atlantic Records founder Ahmet Ertegun. "Certainly the South was fully segregated. But they couldn't segregate the radio dial. So, as we got our records played on radio stations that played black music, the white audience could turn the dial and get that station. So, a lot of the white kids started to listen to our music, which was really made for a black audience. That was really the beginning of rock and roll, because among those young white kids were people like Elvis Presley, who listened to Ray Charles and Chuck Berry and Little Richard. That was the beginning."

By the early '50s, many disc jockeys had begun to capitalize on this, and to the astonishment of all in the seats of power, these on-air personalities spinning this "race music" generated huge audiences—Alan Freed in Cleveland, Joe Smith in Boston, Buddy Dean in Baltimore, and a slew of others. In Philadelphia, the deejay *du jour* was WFIL's Bob Horn, and in 1952, to fill that void in the daytime programming, they asked him if he would do a television show that would appeal to his teenaged audience. They would put it on at 3:30, just after school let out. Initially he sat behind two turntables, kind of a cross between what he might do at the radio station, and one of the record shops prevalent in the '50s where you could have someone play the music before you bought it. Horn would pretend to spin a record and a promotional film of any of the hit-makers of the day would come on. They called the show *Bob Horn's Bandstand*.

"It all happened more or less by accident," recalled another WFIL deejay at the time, Dick Clark, "because they went on on a Monday. They opened the doors to the studio [for an audience] and the only people who would come to the damn thing were the girls from West Catholic High in their school uniforms, bored to death, sitting on those folding chairs in the studio, watching this atrocity that was going on the air. Out of sheer boredom . . . they got up and danced. Somebody took a picture of them dancing, two girls dancing together. We got a lot of telephone calls, not objecting to the girls dancing together but saying that was interesting, those young people dancing."

After a couple of weeks, some boys started showing up, and from 1952 until 1956, Horn ran a televised dance party that entertained Philly teens in the afternoon. Then Horn got arrested for driving drunk. The uproar was huge and negative, so WFIL-TV brought in WFIL radio personality Dick Clark, then perhaps a decade older than most of the dancers, but decidedly younger than Horn, to spin the platters.

Richard Wagstaff Clark was born and bred in the suburbs of New York. While at school at Syracuse University, he worked at his college station, WRUN in Utica, which his father managed, and at WOLF, a station close to school. Upon graduating, he became a newscaster at the local Utica television station. After a year there, he moved on to WFIL, first as a newscaster. However, as a major market newscaster, his youthful appearance worked to his detriment. The management at WFIL moved him over to their radio station, where he became a successful disc jockey. Thus, he was primed to fill Horn's post on *Bandstand*, where his still-youthful mien made him a natural.

Perhaps it was lack of choice on the other channels or all the publicity from the Horn incident or, maybe, it was just Clark's appearance (even into his 70s he looked decades younger), but not too long after he took over the show, it became the highest-rated local daytime TV show in the nation. This caused the networks to prick up their ears. On August 5, 1958, ABC broadcast the first ninety-minute weekday episode of *American Bandstand*. Within six months, it had been picked up by 101 stations on the network and reached an audience of 20 million viewers.

Clark did more than just spin records. The most popular artists of the day came on *Bandstand*, where Clark began to master the art of the three-minute interview. He had them lip-synch their hits, and had the audience play rate-a-record, where they would give their opinion of the songs to which they were dancing.

One of the things that made *Bandstand* so compelling was its subtext as the original reality show, bringing the latest hits into people's homes as a form of daytime drama with a rock-and-roll soundtrack. As the audience was generally made of kids just home from school, so generally were the dancers on *Bandstand*. People got to know Carmen and Carol and Denny. They learned dances like the Jerk, followed romances like that of Bob and Justine. They even took fashion tips from the show.

"The girls who came to our show," Clark recalled, "went to Catholic high school. They wore those little uniforms. Anyway, the priests objected so we made them wear sweaters over the uniforms. As a result, the little dickey collar stuck up over the top and it became know as the Philadelphia Collar. Every dime store in the country had a run on dickey collars. Kids would go in and say, 'Gimme a Philadelphia Collar,' not realizing that it was a Catholic school uniform they were buying."

From a cultural standpoint, this all pointed to something that

Bandstand alone offered the country in 1957—a single, nationwide point of view on popular music. Radio was local, but *Bandstand* was seen every day, all across America.

"It took all of twenty minutes after we went off the air that first day [on the network] for us to know we had a monster on our hands," said Clark. "The phones started ringing off the walls and suddenly we had this extraordinary concentration of power. Radio program directors and the disc jockeys who were on in the afternoon against us were getting slaughtered. Every kid in the country was watching the show."

The format was so simple, over fifty local stations ran their own version of it. The only one that survived, however, was *Bandstand*. Clark has a theory about that. Clark has always dressed in a suit and tie, kept neat, well-groomed, and like . . . well, an adult. He might've had a baby face even at seventy, but he always behaved like an adult. (When he told promoter Juggy Gayles about going network, Gayles smiled at him and told him "You can't lose. You've got the all-American face.") He was the older, wiser big brother, but never a peer. "I think it's sad that adults feel that they have to emulate their children," he said. "There's nothing more ludicrous than seeing a middle-aged, balding, cigar-smoking man trying to be one of the gang."

Clark was familiar with the cigar smoke and back rooms, however. By the time *Bandstand* went national, he was in bed with most of the coterie of music-business entities in Philadelphia. These record companies had a slew of local artists that had one thing in common: they were very videogenic. Of the stars of the "Philly Sound," brought national by *Bandstand*, Frankie Avalon was probably the most musical of the bunch. He played the trumpet, and by the time he was in his early teens was working on Atlantic City's Steel Pier (about an hour out of Philly) with a band called Rocco and the Saints. Bobby Rydell also belonged to Rocco and the Saints and got involved with the same producers, starting a career that would net him one gold record— "Wild One"—and nineteen Top 40 hits.

With Avalon's help, the producers discovered the third part of this Philadelphia triumvirate of banality. "We were talking to Frankie one day," said one of his producers of the time, Peter DeAngelis, "and he said he knew this fifteen-year-old kid at Southern High who looked like a cross between Elvis and Ricky Nelson. . . . He was so pretty, we just knew he had to be a commercial proposition." That singer was named Fabiano Forte, which his producer shortened to Fabian. All three used their record stardom and *Bandstand* as a springboard into the movies.

That *Bandstand* chose to run with the safe-as-milk artists that made up the Philadelphia sound, like Avalon, Rydell, and Fabian, was understandable. They were programming all across the country. ABC's previous attempt at a rock-and-roll TV show, *Alan Freed's Rock and Roll Dance Party*, ran briefly the previous year until it was unceremoniously pulled. African-American vocalist Frankie Lymon of the Teenagers ("Why Do Fools Fall in Love?") had the *audacity* to dance with a white girl on national TV. The Southern ABC affiliates were scandalized and appalled.

So Clark took care about such things. To his—and the producer's—credit, it didn't stop him from putting on African-American performers, from Dee Dee "Mashed Potato Time" Sharp and Chubby Checker—who was given his stage name by Clark's wife, Barbara, after Clark suggested he was like a young Fats Domino—to the Jacksons, Isaac Hayes, and Billy Preston. *Bandstand* was largely responsible for popularizing the dance craze "The Twist." "That made it all right to like rock 'n' roll music if you were an adult," Clark said. "That was a big change that happened right before the Beatles came along."

The show offered the first national media exposure to artists including Chuck Berry, Jerry Lee Lewis, and Buddy Holly. Many early acts on the show, however, were creatures of *Bandstand*, the "Philly Sound" that some would claim diluted the purer strain of rock and roll. Clark bought into a slew of publishing companies and local Philly record labels including Cameo-Parkway, Swan, and Chancellor, the labels releasing Sharp, Checker, Fabian, Rydell, and other artists frequently featured on the show.

"I was making a killing, racing around trying to get all the money I could," Clark said. "My tentacles went in every direction. I didn't want to let an opportunity go by. . . . You found a record breaking in Cleveland or Columbus and you'd charge in there and find some guy who didn't have the wherewithal and you'd lay a few dollars on him, take the master, give him a piece of the record, put it on the air and the next day it would explode all over the country."

While he doesn't deny that it was a flat-out conflict of interest, he really doesn't see the problem with it. "We would book two acts a day, fifteen a week total," said Clark. "One of the reasons why we used so many Philadelphia acts was because if somebody fell out, say there was a snowstorm or a last-minute cancellation, we'd just pick up the phone and call somebody in South Philadelphia. . . . I was a fifty-percent owner in Swan Records and we used our own acts, which people looked at as a conflict of interest. I always found that amusing because I'm certain that Lawrence Welk, the biggest music publisher I knew, was using some of his copyrights on his show. But we got criticized for it."

As Chancellor records head Bob Marcucci put it, "Any time Dick wanted Frankie Avalon, Frankie Avalon was available."

By *Bandstand*'s twentieth anniversary, Clark reckoned that he'd played 80,000 records, interviewed 5,000 artists, and had presented some 8,000 performers lip-synching their hits.

As it took away the radio audience during those after-school afternoons, the nationwide audience made *Bandstand* a formidable promotion force. Record companies recognized that if they wanted to get an artist into the limelight, there was no quicker way than to get that artist on *Bandstand*. It was generally understood that *Bandstand* would sell records.

By everyone, that is, except for Clark. "I ran a test once," he said, "to prove that you couldn't break a record by playing it if the record just didn't have it. I played a record every day for seven months. It was a record by Tommy Sands, I've forgotten the title. It had all the earmarks of a hit . . . I wrote a letter to myself and sealed [it]. It's still sealed, I never opened it. I enclosed a copy of the record and I wrote, 'Capitol Records, one of the largest companies in the world is promoting this record by this young singer who has several hits, the writers are good, the promotion behind the record is good, there is every indication that the record could be a hit except it stinks. It will not be a hit. However, I will play it every day . . . to prove that you cannot make a record by exposure alone.' And it never was a hit. I ran into Tommy Sands years later and he said, 'I always wondered why you played [that song] every day.' I told him the story. The letter still resides in a briefcase I've got sealed up for posterity. But the important part is that you can't make a record a hit by playing the hell out of it."

On the other hand, he did concede, "Hundreds of radio program directors would have their secretaries sit down and copy what we played, and within days, if not minutes, they would be playing things that we were playing. We would play, in the course of an hour and a half on network television, six, twelve, maybe eighteen records, and so all eighteen of those records would get national airplay, not just on television, but on every important radio station."

The government wasn't convinced. In the early '60s, Clark came under investigation in the Payola hearings that ultimately destroyed deejays like Alan Freed. "Payola was a modus operandi, was a way of life in the golden age of rock and roll, in the '40s and '50s," said Joe Smith, a disc jockey in Boston at the time, though he went on to become president of Elektra Records. "It blew up for a moment in the '60s, when they had congressional hearings. . . . Dick Clark was involved, Alan Freed. Everybody who was a disc jockey of any note was getting something."

"I didn't take payola," Clark countered, "I paid it. . . . Several of the record companies I had an interest in paid disc jockeys to play records. Well, that blew their minds completely because they thought I was sitting there with a closet full of cash. I had moved far beyond that by then. I was an entrepreneur."

His entrepreneurial activities included the record labels, several publishing companies, artist management, a radio offshoot of *Bandstand*, and a slew of live productions that ranged from personal appearances to sock hops (fourteen a week, some weeks) to package concert tours. "We built a horizontal and vertical music situation," Clark said, "which is being done every day today. We published the songs domestically, and abroad, managed the acts, pressed the records, distributed the records, promoted the records. That was the best way I could think of to augment my income, and I did it in a way that I thought was reasonably honest without being overly attentive to my own material. I tried to prove that by a survey which showed that I didn't favor records in which I held a financial interest. The government held otherwise.

"It was a whole political shuck. Most of those gentlemen were up for reelection that year. It was a great way to get headlines. I was a freak attraction."

The hearings did have their ironic aspects. "At the height of being on the griddle," he recalled, "I was asked to procure tickets for the wives and children of six different congressmen to attend the *Dick*

Clark Show. After a slashing session, one of my most unrelenting antagonists caught me in the corridor, wrapped his arm around my shoulder and said, jovially: 'My son here wouldn't talk to me again if I didn't have him meet his idol in person and get his autograph!'"

His testimony did indeed make headlines, and he acquitted himself well, but not so well that the government didn't force him to divest himself of thirty-three of his outside ventures. It didn't take Clark long to rebuild. *Bandstand* continued to be aired every weekday until the summer of 1963. It moved to Saturdays, and Clark moved the show—and all his enterprises—to Los Angeles, where it would be easier to book talent (there were a lot more artists living in L.A. than there were in Philly), and where he could move into other areas of broadcasting and film—as owning music businesses was now no longer an option.

The move marked subtle changes in the show's personality. The Los Angeles teens were different in many ways from the Philly teens, and the dramas of their lives didn't have the daily opportunity to unfold as subtext. It had less of the feel of a neighborhood and more the feel of what it actually was—show business—from the quality and caliber of the musicians to the change in sets.

Beyond that, by 1962, Clark had another sound to exploit, this time a very Los Angeles sound. As the soft-rockin' Philly Sound had become *de rigueur* during *Bandstand*'s late-'50s heyday, the move to California shifted the songs to the '60s' surf sound.

The show did continue, however, to be an institution, and a perennially high-rated one at that. This was more than could be said for most rock television shows. While many of the TV variety shows started to include rock acts—Ed Sullivan being the most notable, showcasing Elvis Presley in 1957 and the Beatles in 1964—shows that solely concentrated on popular music were perpetual ne'er-do-wells in the ratings, especially in the U.S., shows now celebrated in memory and retrospect. The '60s programs *Hullabaloo* and *Shindig!* lasted only two seasons. The '70s program *Midnight Special* in the "nothing to lose" 1:00 A.M. slot proved less than cost effective in its eight years on the air. *Don Kirshner's Rock Concert* lasted a year longer in a similar time slot and using a similar modus operandi.

Shows that had rock as a part of some bigger picture often fared better. Ricky Nelson's musical star rose largely on the fortunes of *The*

Adventures of Ozzie and Harriet, yet as they rose, his music also became central to the plot. *The Partridge Family*, which took the already middle-of-the-road Cowsills and pulled that vision of a family band even further into a pop-rather-than-rock direction, lasted four years and revived the sort of teen-idol worship that had made stars of *Bandstand* regulars like Fabian. Perhaps the most successful venue for rock (and indeed many other genres of live music) was *Saturday Night Live*, which slipped in two segments with their special musical guests between comedy skits with the guest host and in-house troupe.

Of course, the single most successful entity in TV music had to be the Monkees. When producers couldn't convince the Beatles to do *A Hard Day's Night* as a weekly TV show, they created their own group. "What they wanted to do was capture the spirit of the times," said Mickey Dolenz. "Television, very often, reflects a commercial success, especially something that started out as a feature or started out as some sort of social statement or event. It very often does that. What they did was took the camaraderie, the youth and independence of the Beatles, say, and they combined that with the kind of domestic principles of situation comedy, which have always been tried and true, and they cut out all the smoking and drinking and references to sex and drugs and that out of the longhair phenomena—because, if you'll remember, long hair was still considered pretty bad news for the average American, it was still associated with drugs and other nasty things, it was threatening to middle America. So along came the Monkees, with long hair, playing fun kind of music every Monday night, and they were no danger. So the kids said, 'See, Mom. You can have long hair and you still don't have to be an asshole!' If we made any contribution to the social ethic, that is what it was."

Even so, the show only lasted for two years of original episodes.

Clark himself went on to produce much of the music on television. In the '60s, he had Paul Revere and the Raiders host *Where the Action Is*, and produced other shows like *Happening* and *Get It Together*, not to mention non-rock shows like *Swingin' Country*. His annual *New Year's Rockin' Eve* has become a winter perennial. And that doesn't go into his nonmusical enterprises like game shows and films.

In fact, *Bandstand* never pretended to be a rock-and-roll show. If you want to know Clark's personal taste, you need only examine the show's theme music, "Bandstand Boogie," as played by the Les Elgart

Big Band. As he frankly related to Lester Bangs, his interest in young people is sparked by "sheer unadulterated greed. That's a facetious answer; it's mostly true. It's been a very good livelihood secondarily and I would appreciate it if you wouldn't excerpt it and just publish that part. I enjoy it. If I didn't, there's no amount of money in the world could make me do what I do. And let's face it, it's a hell of an interesting way to make a living. You never know from day to day what young people are gonna do next."

Over the course of its long run, *Bandstand* rode the trends of popular music, following them, but, to the show's credit, never all that far behind. They never had the wildest psychedelic bands on the show, but they had Pink Floyd. Bands from Creedence Clearwater Revival to Johnny ("Rotten") Lydon's Public Image Ltd. appeared on the show before it folded its tent in 1989. The show ran continuously for thirty-seven years total, thirty-three with Clark in the driver's seat, making it one of TV's longest running series ever. It continued to go strong for ten years after the advent of its bastard stepchild MTV. From the time it first hit the national airwaves in 1957, *Bandstand* changed the perception and dissemination of popular music.

Elvis Presley Strolls in to the Union Street Recording Studios in Memphis

Sam Phillips owned Sun Records and recording studios on Union St. in Memphis, Tennessee. He recorded and released a host of blues and country music acts. He is often, with the benefit of hindsight, quoted as having said, "If I could find a white person who could sing like a black person, I could make a million dollars." He was almost right.

The studios were a sideline for Phillips, an adjunct to his regional record company, Sun. For a five-spot, you could make an acetate record of anything you wanted. A young truck driver named Elvis Aron Presley walked in to the Union Street studios one day to record his mother's favorite songs for a birthday present. While Elvis was less than enamored with the results, Phillips's office manager, Marion Keisker, was very excited. She thought she had found Phillips another great vocalist. She encouraged Phillips to bring him in for a session, which Phillips eventually did in the spring of 1954.

"In later years," Jerry Schilling, a life-long friend of Elvis's recalled, "he introduced me to Marion and said, 'This is the lady that started the whole thing.'"

Phillips wanted him to record a ballad, and Elvis did his very best to sound like Dean Martin, which was not what Phillips wanted at all. During a break, Elvis, guitarist Scotty Moore, and bassist Bill Black ripped into an upbeat, countrified version of "That's All Right Mama," a blues tune by Arthur "Big Boy" Crudup that was popular in the black clubs on Beale Street. Phillips was amazed. "What in the devil are you doing?" he asked the musicians, who thought Phillips was upset. They mumbled that they didn't know. "Well, find out real quick and don't lose it. We'll put it on tape."

This brings up an important point about dealing with Elvis: As much as he was a real flesh-and-blood person and performer, history has turned him into a creature of myth and legend. Not only is he personally a study in contradiction, so is his history. For example, if presented with the version of events at Sun on July fifth in 1954, Elvis might have looked puzzled. He recalled Phillips calling him up and asking him to record some blues: "I hung up and ran fifteen blocks to Mr. Phillips's office before he'd gotten off the line—or so he tells me. We talked about the Crudup records I knew—'Cool Disposition,' 'Rock Me, Mama,' 'Everything's All Right,' and others, but settled for 'That's All Right,' one of my top favorites."

The next day they taped a similar version of Bill Monroe's "Blue Moon of Kentucky."

Phillips took an acetate of the songs to WHBQ deejay Dewey Phillips, whose nightly program, *Red Hot and Blue*, was one of the most popular in Memphis. "Sam came down [with] these sonofaguns," he recalled. "One night I played the record thirty times, fifteen times each side. The phone calls and telegrams started coming in."

Even then, Phillips was unaware of what he had on his hands. His thought was that his new singer could become a very marketable commodity. He underestimated how right he was. As *Rolling Stone* put it, "Presley signaled to mainstream culture that it was time to let go."

Like so many early rock and rollers, Elvis was born into poverty in Tupelo, Mississippi, the only child of Vernon and Gladys Presley. Vernon wasn't very successful at most of the things he tried doing for a living. Through the first twelve years of Elvis's life, he worked as a farmer, sharecropper, and factory worker. He finally landed a job in Memphis with a paint company. Gladys went to work as a nurse's aide. They still lived in one of Memphis's public-housing projects.

Elvis learned about music in the Pentecostal church, on Beale Street and through the radio. "I'd play along with the radio or phonograph and taught myself the chord positions. We were a religious family going round together to sing at camp meetings and revivals, and I'd take my guitar with us when I could. I also dug the real lowdown Mississippi singers, mostly Big Bill Broonzy and Big Boy Crudup, although they would scold me at home for listening to them. 'Sinful music,' the townsfolk in Memphis said it was, which never bothered me, I guess."

Elvis mowed lawns and ushered at a local theater. While he was fairly shy by all accounts, he was also good looking and had dreams of becoming a movie star. A lot of the money he earned went into cultivating a sense of style, buying his clothes on Beale Street, dyeing, pomading, and even trying curlers on his hair. He earned the nickname Velvet Lips Presley around the Lauderdale Courts federal low-rent housing project and Humes high school. He overcame his shyness enough to sing in one of the talent shows at Humes, and was surprised to find that people liked it. So did he. By the end of high school, his yearbook was predicting that Elvis would become a "singing hillbilly of the road," one of the more truly prophetic yearbook prophesies. The roadway part came quickly after he graduated, when he took a job driving for Crown Electric. He drove up to the studio on Union Street on his lunch hour in one of Crown's trucks.

Elvis was an interesting study in contradictions. Beyond the religious music and the "sinful" blues in his life, he was painfully shy yet a born performer. He found the sound of his voice an acquired taste. Having been warned by Sam Phillips that he was bringing a copy of the acetate to the radio station that evening, Elvis decided that he didn't want to be home when it went on.

"I got hold of Elvis's daddy, Vernon," Dewey Phillips recalled of the evening he first played "That's All Right Mama" and "Blue Moon of Kentucky." "He said Elvis was at a movie. . . . 'Get him over here,' I said. And before long Elvis came running in. 'Sit down, I'm going to interview you,' I said. He said, 'Mr. Phillips, I don't know nothing about being interviewed.' 'Just don't say nothing dirty,' I told him.

"He sat down and I said I'd let him know when we were ready to start. I had a couple of records cued up, and while they played, we talked. I asked him where he went to high school, and he said Humes. I wanted to get that out, because a lot of people listening thought he was colored. Finally I said, 'All right, Elvis, thank you very much.' 'Aren't you gonna interview me?' he asked. 'I already have,' I said. 'The mike's been open the whole time.' He broke out in a cold sweat."

Two days later, Sam Phillips signed him to Sun Records. As "That's All Right Mama" started getting regular play, spreading out from Memphis, Elvis started playing concerts around the South. He worked the unbilled bottom of a lineup headlined by country star Webb Pierce as his first professional show. The matinee performance went poorly, so Phillips advised him to go with the upbeat stuff. He launched into "Good Rockin' Tonight."

Something happened when Elvis started singing the up-tempo material. His knees started shaking and his hips began to move. It was incredibly sexy and the audience wouldn't let him off the stage.

He played a country-and-western–deejay convention and made an amazing impression on the jaded pros in the audience, including people from various record companies. He played the *Grand Ol' Opry* and came to the attention of Colonel Tom Parker, a former carny, who was managing Hank Snow and Eddy Arnold.

Unfortunately for Sam Phillips, Sun Records' distribution did not go farther north than the Mason-Dixon line. And despite the relatively good sales Elvis garnered for Sun, Phillips was short on cash. So the Elvis phenomenon stayed mostly in the South through the first half of the '50s. Elvis and the band got on to *The Louisiana Hayride*. They also got an audition for Arthur Godfrey's *Talent Scouts*, but flying to New York disturbed Elvis to the degree that it threw off his performance and he lost the audition to Pat Boone, the first salvo in one of the great rivalries of the '50s.

In the meantime, Elvis's shows throughout the South caused riots. Parker, in no official capacity, brought the record "Let's Play House," Elvis's first chart record (#10 country), to some northern deejays and suddenly the North discovered Elvis. Parker made it known that Phillips would sell Elvis's contract if the price was right.

"We tried to sign Elvis Presley very early in the game," recollects Atlantic Records Chairman Ahmet Ertegun. "He was a little bit too expensive for us. I offered $25,000. They wanted $45,000. I didn't have $45,000 at that time. Otherwise, we would have gotten him."

RCA Records had deeper pockets. Between the record company and a publishing deal, Elvis was bought into the big time for $50,000, a price on par with the Manhattan Purchase. While it might seem Phillips got the short end of the stick, it gave him several things he needed:

- He owed Elvis close to $5,000 in back royalties, which was part of the RCA deal.

- It gave him operating capital, something Sun had never really had.

- He had begun to acquire a good-sized roster of performers in Elvis's wake. They had come streaming into Memphis. By 1955, he had begun recording artists from all over the South with similar backgrounds to Elvis—poverty, a history in the church, a love of blues and country. "First time I heard an Elvis Presley record, . . ." one of those artists, Jerry Lee Lewis, recalled, "I said, 'Wow, looka right here. I don't know who this dude is, but somebody done opened the door.'"

- He also invested some of this minor windfall into a fledgling chain of hotels called Holiday Inn, which left him comfortable in more than just lodging.

With the RCA deal, Parker insinuated himself into the role of Elvis's manager. Parker never lost his carny edge. He, for example, inducted friends and like-minded business associates into a quasi-organization called the Snowmen's League. Parker proclaimed himself the League's "High Potentate" and had League stationery printed up with expressions like "Snow Jobs for All Occasions" and "Don't Put It in Writing . . . Put It in Invisible Ink."

Parker hooked Elvis up with the William Morris Agency, who took ten percent of everything off the top. WMA quickly got Elvis booked for six performances on the Dorsey Brothers TV show. Suddenly, the sensation started to spread nationwide. It helped send his RCA single "Heartbreak Hotel" to the top of the charts. A phenomenon was born. Sam Phillips had discovered his million, but he discovered it for RCA.

Elvis unleashed a new, postwar breed that had been bubbling under the surface for a while—the American teenager. He was sexy and had enough edge that he outraged parents and preachers. This just made him all the more attractive to teens. Boys started to dress like him and grow fuzzy sideburns. Girls screamed, and more. Where there had been idol singers like Frank Sinatra, the main element was romantic fantasy. When Elvis's hips got to swinging, there was no question where they were aiming. Elvis had liberated the libido of popular music. No longer was it about moonlight and crushes. In the minds of his millions of fans, Elvis meant going all the way.

Yet at home, Elvis read the Bible. He had a mother who doted on him and he was unquestionably a mama's boy, despite his greaser good looks. In a way, this let his female fans have it both ways. They creamed their jeans, but they knew nothing was going to come of it. At least not with Elvis.

Parker tested the market, just to see what it would bear. In perhaps the first merchandizing deal geared to attract this emerging, teenaged power block, he made a deal with a California-based children's merchandiser to create Elvis items that ranged from Elvis bracelets to Elvis typewriters. "Presley products sold more than $30 million in the first year they were on the market," the president of the company recalled. This success further demonstrated the power of the Presley audience.

Elvis imitators started springing up everywhere. Young people were enthralled and parents were aghast at the raw, seemingly unbridled sexuality that he exuded, even over the airwaves. He and his style became permanently entrenched in the American music scene.

"I didn't realize that there was a boy by the name of Elvis who was heavily influenced by the black spiritual music, too," Carl Perkins said. "He was on Sun Records first. When I heard his records, I said, 'Oh, god, I've got to get to Memphis! That's the same music I love to play.'"

Not long after "Heartbreak Hotel" topped the charts, Elvis got what he *really* wanted: Movie producer Hal Wallis invited him for a screen test at Paramount and was so impressed with both the phenomenon, the talent, and Elvis as a person, he signed Elvis to a three-film contract, worth close to half a million dollars. Within nine months of signing with the Colonel, Elvis was a millionaire, and back in 1957 being a millionaire really meant something, especially to someone who, two years earlier, had been driving a truck for less than fifty dollars a week.

In the meantime, every variety show host on television wanted a piece of Elvis. An appearance on Milton Berle's show pulled in 40 million viewers, about a quarter of the population of the United States. Less than six months later, an appearance on the *Ed Sullivan Show* was seen by roughly a third of the people in the U.S.

"He was the hottest thing in show business," marveled Dewey Phillips, "and still just a scared kid."

Things didn't go totally swimmingly, however. A booking in Vegas proved a major mistake: Elvis was a hero of the teenager. Vegas was where their parents went to play. However, it wasn't a total bust. He found his next single there, a version of a Big Mama Thornton blues hit called "Hound Dog."

"What happened was, he knew that record and loved that record," said one of the song's writers, Mike Stoller. "Later, he went to Vegas and heard a lounge act do this eviscerated version, so he did it. At least the lyric wasn't feminine, even if it doesn't make much sense. We weren't too happy with it. It was nervous and the lyrics were changed. Obviously, it's a woman's song."

The song with the flip side of "Don't Be Cruel" became one of the most popular singles in history, selling over 5 million copies. The song's authors, Stoller and his long-time partner Jerry Leiber, are white Jewish men, and many artists and scholars have pointed to this as the epitome of what Steve Chapple and Reebee Garofalo refer to as "black roots, white fruits."

"I just think this black music has been not just used, but misused," great boogie-woogie pianist Sammy Price said. "I'll bet I could go to any black school out there (points through the window toward Harlem) and ask any kid who W. C. Handy was and he can't tell me. That's regrettable, that that history, the source . . . for example, let's take Elvis Presley. Now, I don't know what he did for Big Mama Thornton. I don't think he did anything for her. But she started him out with 'Hound Dog.' But ask someone who Big Mama is, they don't know. But they know Elvis Presley. And they associate him with 'Hound Dog.' That's enough."

What this doesn't take into account is another, often underplayed part of the early Elvis phenomenon: His version of "Hound Dog" not only topped the country and pop charts, but the rhythm-and-blues chart as well. While Big Mama Thornton's might have been there longer (she topped the R&B chart for seven weeks with the song in 1953), the African-American community of the '50s gave Elvis his props. They knew where his roots lay.

None of this could have been further from Elvis's mind, however, as 1957 began to ebb. During the summer, he worked on his first film, a Civil War–era western called *The Reno Brothers*. He sang four songs loosely based on period music. One, a rewrite of the folk song "Ãura Lee" called "Love Me Tender" impressed the producers enough that they chose to retitle the film after it. It became one of the songs he sang on the Sullivan show and topped the charts for five weeks that fall, just before the film came out. It opened in a record-number 550 theaters. Elvis had become a movie star.

While he projected a wild, rebellious persona—more spurred by the public reaction to his performances than anything he actually did—by nearly all accounts Elvis was a determined, charming man with "Southern" manners and deference.

"I think the easiest artist we worked with was Presley," said Jerry Leiber. "We produced him many times. We did not get any credit. . . . We were producers without portfolio, but we made 'Jailhouse Rock,' we made a number of them. We just didn't get our names on the labels because we were not the designated producer. Presley was the easiest in one sense because he was a workhorse. He really could put out. He had no problem doing thirty-five takes if you wanted to. Normally you didn't have to, because he would get it right away. But he could sing all night and all day, and he loved it. He would rather do that than just about anything else."

Even Ed Sullivan, who initially said that he would never have an artist as vulgar and "unfit for a family audience" as Elvis on his show before capitulating to overwhelming popular demand, conceded on the air in 1957 after a sedate performance of "Peace in the Valley" by Elvis and the Jordanaires: "I wanted to say to Elvis Presley and the country that this is a real, decent, fine boy. . . . We never had a pleasanter experience on our show with a big name than we've had with you. You are thoroughly all right. Let's have a tremendous hand for a very nice person." Elvis has this aw-shucks look on his face throughout, but it also refuted every piece of criticism ever hurled his way.

But the song itself was indicative of another contradiction implicit in Elvis. Preachers across the country were condemning him from pulpits (making the teens love him all the more—the reverends had a lot to learn about the allure of forbidden fruit), yet here he was on the *Ed Sullivan Show* singing a hymn. He would leaven his concerts with songs like these. The "scared kid" Dewey Phillips knew was still at work full force when he was off the stage. With strangers and "his elders" he had perfect, boyish Southern manners and charm. Every woman received a polite "yes ma'am," every man a "sir," and once he had made initial eye contact, he would avert his own as a sign of respect.

Yet he also retained his wild streak. Jerry Lee Lewis recalled, "I once went to a party at Jack Clement's house me and Elvis, and we got naked and rode our motorcycles down the street. Buck naked. And this policeman on a horse sees us. It was two-thirty, three o'clock in the morning. It was awful. If anyone would have seen us, they never would have bought another record."

By the end of 1957, Elvis had:

- Made three movies and was starting a fourth
- Topped the R&B chart six times
- Topped the country chart eight times
- Topped the pop chart nine times
- Bought a slew of Cadillacs, purchased a home for his parents, leased a mansion in Bel Air for when he was making films, and acquired Graceland, an estate just outside of Memphis, for all other times

His net worth was in the millions. RCA, the company that said it would never get involved in rock and roll, had established their position as a major force in popular music because of it. At the height of 1957 and Elvis mania, they had to farm out pressings to rival companies to keep up with the sales on his records. Some estimated that Elvis's records accounted for a quarter of all of RCA's earnings.

In late December, his number had come up in the draft.

Paramount asked for and received a short deferment of his induction into the army so he could finish the film he was working on. This started a storm of letters citing preferential treatment, and made the army quite leery of giving Private Elvis Presley any other perks that might make it look like he was a "special" soldier. For that reason, when he was inducted in March of 1958, he wasn't put into the special services' entertainment division, where, arguably, he could have done great things for troop morale. Instead, he went back to his roots, and upon finishing basic training, he became a truck driver once more, or more specifically, a jeep driver, responsible for transporting his platoon sergeant.

During basic training, the fear of treating Elvis like anything special nearly backfired. His mother fell ill. Elvis had rented a house for Gladys and Vernon not far from Fort Hood in Texas, but she became so ill that he wanted her to be near where she knew the doctors and where people knew her. He sent Gladys and Vernon back to Memphis, where she was diagnosed with acute hepatitis. He applied for compassionate leave so he could visit his mother in the hospital. The army hemmed and hawed as Gladys Presley got sicker and sicker, until it became evident that Private Elvis Presley would go AWOL if they didn't let him go. No outcry accompanied his leave, and he got to Memphis a day before his mother died. During the funeral, Private Presley could barely keep on his feet and had to be helped by friends. It took five hundred policemen to control the thousands that gathered for the event.

So in less than half a year, he lost his hair to an army crew cut and his mother to death. In late September, Private Presley shipped out to Germany, where he would be stationed for the rest of his hitch in the army. By all accounts, he was a model soldier. He brought his father and other family members with him and bought a house not far from the base near Frankfurt. While there, he became acquainted with young model Priscilla Wagner Beaulieu, the fourteen-year-old stepdaughter of an air force captain stationed nearby. Perhaps mindful of what had happened to his friend Jerry Lee Lewis a little over a year before when he'd married his thirteen-year-old cousin, he didn't let it go beyond acquaintance. He did send her home, with Vernon as a chaperone, ostensibly so that she could continue her modeling career. He would marry her some eight years later. Vernon, too, brought home a bride, a woman who had divorced a master sergeant in Germany where the two had met.

RCA continued to release records Elvis had recorded at sessions before he went into the army and during leaves. While they didn't come as thick and fast as before, he had eight Top 40 pop singles in 1958 and four more in 1959, including the chart toppers "Don't," "Hard Headed Woman," and "A Big Hunk o' Love." *King Creole*, the film he was making just before he was inducted into the army, became a worldwide hit.

Parker had kept busy as well, keeping Elvis in the spotlight in the press as an exemplary soldier, promoting the absent teen idol. At a 1959 convention for jukebox owners and service people, Parker showed his carny side. "I had my Midget Fanclub there," he wrote to Hal Wallis, "about twenty-five midgets with banners reading WELCOME ELVIS PRESLEY MIDGET FAN CLUB. We stole the exploitation setups there and left town as soon as everyone had seen the midgets."

When Sergeant Elvis Presley was demobilized, two years after his induction, he was a changed man. On the one hand, he seemed surer of himself, less the "scared kid." He also had lost a great deal of his wild streak. It showed in his lifestyle and his choices. While he continued to make records, through the '60s the bulk of them were ballads, most often tied to the films he made. Yet he still couldn't lose the poor country boy inside him. When he was working in Hollywood, he didn't do much besides work and hang out in his home in Bel Air. One of his oldest friends noted sadly, "He's afraid he wouldn't know how to act. And he wouldn't."

Yet, if anything, he became a bigger star because of this. The loss of his hair to the army might have taken a toll, causing a Samson-like siphoning of his sex appeal, but it broadened his general appeal. The girls didn't shriek as much anymore, but their parents didn't turn off the TV either. And many of those girls that had been shrieking in the

'50s were parents themselves in the '60s. The R&B chart appearances became fewer, but now he commanded the adult contemporary (a.k.a. middle-of-the-road) charts. By 1967, Elvis Presley would win his first of three Grammy awards. None of them would be for popular music. In fact, they would all be for Best Sacred/Inspirational/Religious recording.

A very early indication of this is Elvis's appearance on Frank Sinatra's TV show in the early '60s. They do a medley, with Sinatra singing "Love Me Tender" and Elvis singing "Witchcraft." They harmonize at the end, to which Sinatra comments, "Man, that's pretty." This meeting of former teen idols epitomizes his new status. Frank, who had already made the jump, promoted Elvis to the ranks of American cultural institutions.

Toward the end of the '60s, though, Elvis became restless. He did a session in Nashville, recording blues songs like Jimmy Reed's "Big Boss Man" and Jerry Reed's "Guitar Man," both bringing him a little bit closer to his roots.

Parker signed his newly invigorated client to do a television special sponsored by the Singer Sewing Machine Company. Parker wanted Elvis to sing twenty holiday songs and say good night. Elvis, who hadn't performed live in some time, had the itch. Against the Colonel's advice, Elvis sided with director Steve Binder, who had done such a great job capturing the TAMI Show several years earlier. Binder's vision was to show the performance prowess that had launched Elvis to stardom over a decade before. Working with band members from that era, including Scotty Moore and drummer D. J. Fontana, they played the familiar rockers in front of a live audience, to the crowd's obvious enjoyment. These were interspersed with production numbers and several gospel songs. By the end, Binder had hours' worth of material to turn into a one-hour special. When it aired in December, the critics raved, and it was one of the highest-rated musical programs of the year.

Also against Parker's advice, Elvis went back to Memphis early the next year to continue the work he had done in Nashville. It was the first time he recorded back on the old home front since he signed with Parker. Over the course of four days, he cut twenty songs. The album *The Memphis Sessions* brought Elvis back to the top of the charts with "Suspicious Minds." An acclaimed month-long stint in Vegas followed.

By 1970, Parker started complaining that he could no longer

control his only client. Elvis went on tour for the first time in ages, playing stadiums like the Astrodome and arenas like Madison Square Garden, his first ever concerts in New York. The shows were recorded and released on an album.

Parker was not the only one displeased with Elvis. He and his child-bride, Priscilla, broke up after five years of marriage. But Elvis was on a roll. His concert in Hawaii was broadcast live via satellite and seen by over a quarter of the world's population. The double album of the show became his first chart-topping album since the early '60s. It would also be his last.

While his fortunes seemed to be rising, Elvis himself was having trouble. He had become addicted to a variety of prescription drugs. Despite training in karate (he earned an eighth-degree black belt), he looked bloated. In August 1977, several of his former employees released an exposé book called *Elvis: What Happened?* Within days of the book coming out, Elvis was found dead in the bathroom of Graceland.

In death, however, Elvis became immortal. People were buying bits of the carpet in Graceland and alleged vials of his sweat. Yet, while Elvis's death became a windfall for RCA (a lesson they would learn well when it came time to exploit the Jim Croce catalog some years later) and his estate, it opened cans of worms that ultimately had his estate spending more time in court over the next twenty years than Elvis spent in concert over his last decade.

One of the things revealed, not at Elvis's death but at the passing of his father and the executor of Elvis's estate, was just how much Tom Parker was earning from Elvis. Parker, whose initial deal was a very high 75–25 split after paying William Morris ten percent off the top, had raised his ante to between a third and a half of what Elvis earned. In a 1980 report filed on behalf of Elvis's heir, Lisa Marie, Attorney Blanchard Tual told a probate court that Parker didn't tell Elvis anything about his finances. He had no pension and no savings except for a non-interest-bearing checking account that had a million dollars in it at any given time (including at the time of his death). The report noted that Parker made over $7 million dollars in the three years after Elvis passed on, without even an artist to manage. He pointed to the 1973 contract that offered Parker a bunch of side deals for keeping Elvis "in line." Tual charged Parker with conspiracy, fraud, and misrepresentation. "Elvis signing the '73 contract with RCA was the worst decision ever made in the history of rock 'n' roll," Tual said. The contract had netted Elvis a little over a million dollars, in lieu of royalties.

Eventually, the issue was resolved in court. Parker was separated from the Presley estate, his official involvement as Elvis's representative cancelled. RCA paid the estate back-royalties from the deal.

Another problem became whether, when he died, Elvis became public domain. His music was protected by copyright for a number of years after his death (the term is now 70 years; at that time it was considerably less). Yet there was no precedent for protecting his image, likeness, and name. It took the estate over a decade to establish that the right of publicity extended to the estate. That estate now charges a minimum licensing fee of $50,000 to use the Elvis name or likeness for a product. In the meantime, Elvis had turned into an icon of almost religious proportions. People made pilgrimages to Graceland the way followers of Islam make the pilgrimage to Mecca. They created shrines in their homes to Elvis. In Las Vegas, you can be married by an Elvis impersonator. A demonstration of how much of a cultural icon Elvis has become, especially after his passing, came during the finale of the 1986 ceremonies honoring the one hundredth anniversary of the Statue of Liberty, which included 200 Elvis impersonators.

In 1987, Mojo Nixon and Skid Roper paid tribute and lampoon to these thoughts in their underground hit "Elvis Is Everywhere": "When I look out into your eyes out there, when I look out into your faces, you know what I see?" Nixon intones before the song kicks in, "I see a little bit of Elvis in each and every one of you out there." In a way, to any rock fan, truer words were never spoken.

Alan Freed Changes the Name of His "Moondog's House" Radio Show to "The Rock and Roll Show"

Alan Freed earned a first-ballot entrance into the Rock and Roll Hall of Fame largely because he gave the music its name, or at least spread the gospel of rock and roll better than any of its other early acolytes and avatars. But Freed's contribution to the genre is a lot more complex than just giving it a handle. Unlike so many of the genre's founding industrial fathers, Freed genuinely liked and appreciated the music. He knew its roots. He even knew what *rock and roll*

meant. Anyone who had spent time in black neighborhoods knew that "rocking and rolling" meant having sex. Freed probably couldn't have been more amused to hear the phrase coming out of the white-bread mouths of people like Dick Clark (whom he saw as the evil anti–Alan Freed) and Ed Sullivan. In the '50s, Freed couldn't know how prescient he was.

Born into a family with just about enough resources to send him to Ohio State, Freed played trombone in high school and college, working with a dance band called the Sultans of Swing (after a similar band in Harlem). Even in the '30s, he had an affinity for dance music.

After a stint in the army during World War II, Freed went to work for a New Castle, Pennsylvania, classical radio station as an announcer in 1942. After a year, he moved on to become a sportscaster in Youngstown, Ohio, before finding a niche a couple of years later spinning jazz and pop recordings in Akron.

Trouble and Freed were old playmates. The city of Akron told him he'd never work in that town again, barring him from the air for leaving one local station for another before his contract was up. So he moved on to WJW in Cleveland, doing a similar show. "He was always drunk," WJW's morning man Soupy Sales recalled, "but he was on late at night and could always handle it."

The early '50s were still the day of the crooner. Freed, still in his twenties, felt that this disenfranchised anyone who wanted to dance. You couldn't jitterbug to crooners, he reasoned.

Like many younger, white listeners, he found the answer elsewhere on the dial, on the stations geared toward the African-American radio audience. Like so many others, he found this new urban-blues sound exciting. He was invited to Leo Mintz's record store in Cleveland and watched kids scarfing up R&B records. "I heard the tenor saxophone of Red Prysock and Big Al Sears," Freed said. "I heard the blues singing, piano playing Ivory Joe Hunter. I wondered. I wondered for about a week. Then I went to my station manager and talked him into permitting me to follow my classical program with a rock 'n' roll party."

Freed started to spin the program of rhythm-and-blues records during the overnight on Cleveland's WJW on July 11, 1951. Calling himself Moondog, to differentiate himself from the classical program that came before, he kept the mike open most of the time, pounding rhythm on a phone book and ad-libbing comments like "Yeah, daddy!

Let's rock and roll" with the records. His theme song came off a recording by a blind New York street musician, also named Moondog.

"When recordings we had made," recalled Mike Stoller, "like we started with the Robins in about 1954 with songs like 'Riot in Cell Block #9' and 'Smokey Joe's Café,' when they started being played on stations that reached a broader audience, not just an African-American audience, that was about the time that they started using the phrase rock and roll, which is of course a very old blues phrase that has to do with sex. It was around that time that Alan Freed started using it. I know this from stuff I overheard and history. I mean, I met Alan Freed once or twice in New York, but I didn't even know who he was or what he was doing in Cleveland. He, apparently, gave the name rock and roll to all this rhythm and blues music."

The show became a big hit, but no one really had any idea how big until the next March, when Freed promoted a dance concert that he called the Moondog Coronation Ball at the Cleveland Arena, a venue with a capacity of ten thousand. Over twenty thousand people showed up, many of them African-American teens. The overwhelming response caused the show to be cancelled. Freed always pointed to this show with a great deal of pride, especially over the racial mixture of the crowd. Later events proved more successful in actually getting the audience into the hall, and nearly a hundred thousand people reportedly attended one of the several Moondog Balls.

"It's hard to convey to someone today the shock of hearing Little Richard after years of Patti Page," notes John Jackson, author of the award-winning Freed biography *Big Beat Heat*. "It's an experience you can't understand unless you come from that relatively narrow age group."

Freed wasn't the only one reaching out to the younger audience with rhythm. "Those of us who were there, the Freeds, and Hound Dogs, and Joe Smiths, people like us, we really were good," Joe Smith remembered. "We picked the records, we programmed our shows, and made them entertaining shows. People used to love to listen to Howard Miller in Chicago or Bill Randall in Cleveland or Mickey Shore in Detroit or Buddy Dean in Baltimore or George Lorenz up in Buffalo, Hound Dog up there or Hound Dog, there was another one in New York. We were really good. We had these massive records, people pressuring us all the time, offering us everything, and we came up with some terrific stuff. And we really broke the rock and roll. No radio station owner wanted us to play Elvis Presley and Little Richard. No manager. 'Keep it nice with Frankie Laine and Tony Bennett. Don't give us this wild-assed music.' And we all did it, anyway. We just did it. We played that music, we got immediate reaction, and we had it."

In addition to the hard-core R&B, they would also spin songs by vocal groups like the Orioles, the Platters, and the Crows just to break things up. These "slow dance specials" helped give rise to the spread of doo-wop.

Within two years, Freed became too big for Cleveland. When his WJW contract expired, he moved on to the highest bidder, which happened to be WINS in New York. "Two people were responsible for bringing Alan to New York," said promotion guru Juggy Gayles, "and that was George Furness and myself."

"His [WJW] show was syndicated to two or three other markets," notes Paul Sherman, whom Freed would hire as his "crowned prince" when he got to WINS. "For peanuts, I think. The local outlet [in New York City] was a station over in Jersey. Bob Smith, who was the program director of WINS, persuaded Bob Leder, then general manager, to listen to this crazy character who called himself Moondog. Not Freed, Moondog. Well, Smith did a selling job on him and WINS hired Freed."

The deal put him on from eleven to two in the morning, six days a week. He was guaranteed $75,000 a year plus percentages of syndication. By the time he arrived in New York, more than forty stations had signed up to either simulcast or rebroadcast the show. Yet there were problems in the air. Moondog, the musician who had provided Freed's pseudonym in Cleveland, was none too happy about Freed using the name in his own stomping grounds of New York. He sued to prevent that from happening. A $5,000 payoff and a promise to change the name of the show appeased the musician, but now came the problem of what to call the show.

Freed, Gayles, Morris Levy, and manager Jack Hooke had lunch at legendary watering hole P. J. Moriarty's to drink this situation over and sort it out. Someone suggested just calling it *The Rock and Roll Show*. Gayles objected, thinking it was too raunchy for the mainstream. Anyone who spent any time uptown knew what the phrase *really* meant. This might have just delighted Freed all the more. And suddenly this emerging musical-hybrid genre had a name.

Trying to define what rock and roll was, Freed called it "swing with a modern name. Kids are starved for music they can dance to, after all those years of crooners."

"In the beginning whoever played on Alan Freed's show was rock and roll," remembers Atlantic Records Chairman Ahmet Ertegun. "That included Paul Anka and Laverne Baker and all those people, and all the groups, of course. The quartets, the doo-wop singers. They were all considered rock and roll."

The show was so successful in its late-night slot that WINS moved it to early evening. "It keeps us off the streets at night," one teen told the *New York Daily News* during the spring of 1956, "because from six-thirty to nine is the rock and roll party with Alan Freed."

Freed began to augment his income with concerts. Initially, just by announcing it on his show, he could sell out the 6,000-capacity St. Nicholas Ballroom. "It was two of the biggest dances we ever held," recalled Morris Levy, the underworld dean of the New York music business. "The ceiling was actually dripping from the moisture. It was raining inside the St. Nicholas Arena."

By 1956, he could book ten days at the Paramount in Brooklyn and even during vile weather break the house attendance records. And then Hollywood came calling. "An agent, Jolly Joyce, was a go-between for the movie company and Freed," Sherman recalled. "They asked Freed to take a small part in a rock-and-roll movie involving Bill Haley and the Comets called *Rock Around the Clock*. The idea behind all this was that Freed would publicize the movie on his radio show, which was then attracting national attention. Deejays out of town were picking up on whatever Freed did. What Freed played, they played, what Freed hyped, they hyped. So Freed said he'd take the movie part, but he wanted the money upfront. Cash. Instead the movie company offered him a percentage. At first he said, 'no.' But Jolly Joyce, who was a very smart man, said, 'Dummy, take a piece.' They settled for a little cash and a generous percentage. They could have *bought* Freed for $15,000, and instead he made a fortune."

Freed also made a foray into television, running a show not unlike *American Bandstand*. Freed considered himself racially color-blind, and had proved this any number of times. His shows attracted mixed crowds as far back as the 1951 Moondog Coronation Ball in Cleveland. He was one of the first disc jockeys who appealed to teens of all races. So, when Frankie Lymon of the Teenagers ("Why Do Fools Fall in Love?") danced on the air with a white girl, he thought nothing of it. However, segregation still ruled in the South, and the image drove Southern network affiliates into a lathering rage. This was the type of thing they feared from this music above anything else. Within weeks, the show was gone. Freed would later start broadcasting locally on a New York television station.

It wasn't all glory, though. The African-American community thought that it was wrong for a white man to be making a fortune off of black artists and raised the issue often with WINS management. As an independent station, it was harder for WINS to defend itself than a network station with hoards of PR people at need. Then there were skirmishes at a couple of the package tours he sent around the country, which the press hyperbolized into riots, and the district attorneys involved quickly brought charges against the packager—Freed. So when his contract came up for renewal, WINS decided to pass. He was snatched up by WABC.

"No question about it, Al was a very bright guy," said Sherman. "He was a musician himself too. In many ways he was an ordinary guy, but he knew music."

Freed was smart about a lot of things. He didn't know finances, though. At one point, he had so many managers that they owned 120 percent of him.

However, he knew good opportunities when they came up. For many years, his name was alongside Chuck Berry's as the cowriter of "Maybellene." He also was listed on hits by the Moonglows, the Flamingos, and many others. This was not an uncommon practice during the '50s. "We were stupid and got upended in every way," acknowledges Mac "Dr. John" Rebennack about those days. "I would bring my publisher a song and it would come out with two or three other guys' names on it, disc jockeys. Now it haunts me. I own a fourth of a song I wrote one hundred percent of, and three disc jockeys that I never met own the other pieces of it. They're collecting as much as I do for something I did all the work. Plus, I don't get paid. I have to fight for my little one-fourth of that money, because these people do not send you statements, and they do not pay. It's not a good feeling. Most of the people I know in the business are the same story, so it's not that unusual."

To give you an idea how lucrative this could be, every time a song got pressed in the '50s, the songwriters and publishers split two cents. If a record sold a million copies that meant a pool of $20,000 was up for grabs. Beyond that, every time a song got played on the radio or TV, the songwriter would collect a performance royalty from ASCAP, BMI, or SESAC. These were determined by the amount of play, where the song got played, and by the head of the Performance Royalty Organization stripping naked, putting on a black hood, and reading the entrails of a pigeon from a black altar on the roof of the company's office building (okay, the last one isn't true, but might as well be). A hit record could bring in tens or hundreds of thousands of dollars. A standard could keep you in a nice, steady little income for life.

Of course, as a co-owner of the copyright, it behooved you to make it happen as best you could. The more airplay, especially in a major market like New York (not to mention all the places Freed was syndicated), the more the song could make.

There were other, more overt ways of getting records on the air as well. Disc jockeys were often on the receiving end of lavish gifts of cash and merchandise. While there was no law against this generally, it didn't seem kosher to Congress. They had just done boffo box office with hearings about how television game shows were fixed. Now they turned their ears to rock and roll. For many, it was a way to defeat this insurgent music. The only way, some seemed to reason, that anyone would play this music is if someone paid them to do it. They contracted payment and victrola and came up with the word *payola*. Pretty soon, it was as popular a subject as rock and roll itself.

"A guy who will go unnamed, he was the music director up at WINS when Alan Freed was there," muses Joe Smith. "It was a hot radio station. The guy was making $125 a week as the music director. And he was living over on Sutton Place, wearing fancy suits, driving a fancy car, going off to Europe on his $125 a week. The station manager, oblivious to all this, said, 'You're doing a great job. We're going to promote you to the news department and give you $200 a week.' He begged him, 'Please! Don't do that to me!'"

Freed watched Dick Clark testify before Congress. Clark made the congressional questioners look bad. Since he always thought himself smarter and better than Clark, Freed thought he could make Congress look worse. "Alan could be his own worst enemy," Gayles recalled.

"When the payola thing happened, he was taken. He saw what Dick Clark did and thought, 'I'll show him headlines.' He blew his cool and shot off his mouth. He didn't want to hurt anyone. He was a beautiful guy, a genius. He got taken by a lot of people."

His WNEW-TV *Big Beat Dance Party* show was cancelled, and he was dismissed from his show on WABC. "I am no better or worse than any of my fellow disc jockeys," he told his friend, columnist Earl Wilson. "I've never taken a bribe. I would throw anybody down the steps who suggested it. Somebody said to me once, 'if somebody sent you a Cadillac, would you send it back?' I said, 'It depends on the color.'

"What they call payola in the disc jockey business they call lobbying in Washington."

"He had a self-destructive streak," noted Jackson. "He was totally impulsive. That was the difference between him and Dick Clark. Clark was an astute businessman. Freed thought things took care of themselves. . . . His downfall came when he thought he was as indestructible as the music."

Freed sold his house in Connecticut and moved into a home he described as "a nothing house" in Palm Springs. He went to station KDAY, but they wouldn't let him promote as well as deejay, so he briefly went back to New York. When that didn't work out, he went to another home he owned and "couldn't get rid of" in Miami and started spinning for WQAM.

However, records weren't the only things spinning in Freed's life. His drinking was spiraling out of control as well. The Miami job only lasted a matter of weeks.

"Freed suffered," Joe Smith said. "He got nailed because he was the biggest. And it did kill him. In the end, I was lending him money. . . . His house was attached, his salary was attached. He has no money to live on. A few of us would take care of him by taking him to dinner, and doing things like that."

In 1962, the actual payola charges came down. Freed was charged with taking $30,650 worth of bribes. He paid a $300 fine and received a six-month suspended sentence.

By early in 1965, he was dead of uremia and cirrhosis at the age of forty-three. In his brief, meteoric career he'd done much more than give this broad new hybrid of rhythm and blues, country, and pop a broad, generic name. He had brought it to the people, particularly the burgeoning teen audience, offering them music rooted in African-American, Southern, and urban sounds. Until he fell from grace, he was the high priest of pop, and much of the country heard him via his pulpits of radio, television, and the movies. In the last ten years of his life, he helped take rock and roll from "a passing fad" in the wishful thinking of many fans of "the way things were" to a juggernaut, unstoppable to this day.

The Movie "Blackboard Jungle" Comes Out

In 1956, Alan Freed appeared in three movies. While these were early vehicles for moving rock and roll into the mainstream of America, they were not the first.

"There is absolutely no dispute about the first rock and roll film," said Terry Stewart, executive director of the Rock and Roll Hall of Fame. "It was *Blackboard Jungle*."

The late Frank Zappa concurred: "When the titles flashed, Bill Haley and his Comets started blurching, 'One, two, three o'clock, four o'clock rock . . .' It was the loudest sound kids had ever heard at the time . . . Bill Haley . . . was playing the teenage anthem, and it was loud. I was jumping up and down. *Blackboard Jungle*, not even considering that it had the old people winning in the end, represented a strange act of endorsement of the teenage cause."

Bill Haley was an unlikely choice for someone to "endorse" the teen cause. By the time *Blackboard Jungle* came out, Haley was thirty years old, and had been kicking around the music business for nearly as long as most of his new fans had been alive. A chubby guitarist and singer with a spit curl on his forehead, he became the first to find the formula.

Initially, he worked his way through a series of country bands, starting as a pro at fourteen. By nineteen, he was recording with the Downhomers, but after two years of that, he went to Chester, Pennsylvania, not far from Philly, to try his luck as a disc jockey. He wound up forming a new band, the Four Aces of Western Swing, and started recording. Within a year, they had changed their name to the Saddlemen. The Saddlemen recorded for a bunch of labels in the late '40s, including Atlantic. By 1951, they hooked up with Holiday Records. At the record company's behest, they cut a version of Jackie Brenston's "Rocket 88," complete with pedal steel and a boogie bass. Not an R&B record exactly, it didn't reach that audience. Not really a country tune, it didn't reach the Saddlemen's usual audience. However, Haley noticed that when they played the record live, people—especially young people—went nuts, a pleasant change from the usual placid roadhouse audiences.

They dug into the new R&B beat, adding sax player Joey D'Ambrosio. "I got my experience playing rhythm and blues for strippers," D'Ambrosio said. "When I was sixteen, I played the strip joints, playing fifty choruses of 'Night Train' every night. It was the only place you could play that music—with somebody bumping and grinding . . . When I joined Bill Haley, I brought that along with me. He had a cowboy band, and when you put a saxophone with a country band, you're gonna get a different thing—it's gonna change."

That change was evident on "Rock This Joint." The record caught the attention of Alan Freed (still in Cleveland in 1952), who started spinning it nightly. Suddenly, they became a draw on the high school circuit. They lost the bolo ties and cowboy hats, settling for the kind of checked jackets favored by some of the R&B vocal groups of the day. They changed their name to the Comets, a play on Haley's name. Here they tested material.

Haley and his manager had made the fundamental discovery that Freed had made a year earlier—teenagers were the prime demographic to sell music, especially music you could dance to. Rock and roll was all about the rise of the teenager, a demographic that hit astounding numbers in the '50s. Along with that rise came a remarkable amount of disposable income. So, when they got out of the woodshed and cut their next record, "Crazy Man Crazy," it hit #12 in 1953. Rock and roll—R&B played with overtones of country by a white band— had arrived.

By 1954, Decca records signed Haley and the Comets away from the Philly indies with which they had been recording. They cut a tune called "Rock Around the Clock," which hit #23 on the charts in 1954. With that minor major-label success under their belt, they did a thing that became standard for performers over the next ten years—they took an R&B hit—in this case Big Joe Turner's "Shake, Rattle and Roll"—and toned it down for a white, teenaged audience. The result was a top-ten gold record.

"It was crazy," D'Ambrosio remembers. "Everywhere we went, there were a lot of girls and teenagers all over us, tearing our clothes off. It was scary. . . . Movie stars would come and see us. Jayne Mansfield was coming around, and when we were in Hollywood, Tony Curtis and Janet Leigh. They wanted to party with us 'cause we were the group."

On the strength of that hit, the filmmakers of *Blackboard Jungle* ran "Rock Around the Clock" under the film's opening credits. The film's popularity combined with Haley's new-found stature as a teen hero, propelled the song to the top of the charts for a good hunk of the spring and summer of 1955.

While the born-too-early Haley would soon be replaced in the teens' capricious affections by Elvis, this was his moment to shine. Although Haley passed on at the relatively young age of fifty-five, many of the original Comets continue to tour well into their seventies.

However, the lesson of "Rock Around the Clock" and *Blackboard Jungle*, that the rock audience would go in droves to movies that spoke to them, was not lost on either the record companies or the film companies. This was good news and bad news for the burgeoning teen culture. On the one hand, teens glommed onto the film, figuring anything that featured their music must somehow be celebrating them. However, that particular celebration centered on a gang of juvenile delinquents. Thus, a hard-to-break connection between rock and roll and juvenile delinquency was born that exists in many older minds to this day. Many films that featured rock and roll latched on to the *Blackboard Jungle* formula, furthering this perception. For Hollywood, it was gelt by association.

By the next year, the movie *Rock Around the Clock* came out. The film featured Haley as himself and Alan Freed as himself, and related a highly fictionalized version of the Haley story. Freed also appeared in *Rock, Rock, Rock* and *Don't Knock the Rock*, which also had a theme song by Haley and the Comets, and in true Freed fashion had an interesting mix of artists—among them African-American stars Chuck Berry and Fats Domino.

By 1957, Haley's run on the charts and in film fell to the sexier images of Elvis. In the year before he went into the army, Elvis made a bunch of films, including *Love Me Tender*, a Civil War drama, initially called *The Reno Brothers* until they decided that the song would sell the movie would sell the song. They followed suit with *Lovin' You* and *Jailhouse Rock* in 1957. In *King Creole*, Elvis took a role that had actually been written for James Dean.

For Elvis, being a handsome movie star was the goal. Like Sinatra before him, Bing Crosby before *him*, and Al Jolson before pretty nearly anyone, being a musical star became a natural introduction into films.

Some musicians proved to be major screen presences, displaying talent in both media. David Bowie, for example, proved remarkable in his role as the alien who becomes trapped among humanity in *The Man Who Fell to Earth*. Many others merely had the name recognition that helped a movie at the marquee.

Epitomizing another one of the main paths rock would take in the movies is the 1957 *queso classico, The Girl Can't Help It*. Featuring Jayne Mansfield as a no-talent (at least musically) wannabe singer, it also featured *Seven Year Itch* costar Tom Ewell (what was it with this guy and healthy blondes?), along with the musical stylings of rising stars Little Richard, the Platters, Eddie Cochrane, and Gene Vincent—and the established greatness that was Fats Domino. Like so many genre films, the use of rock and roll stemmed from setting the music business as the milieu, a plan that continued through *American Graffiti, Purple Rain*, and *That Thing You Do*, to cite some better examples. As one critic moaned upon the release of *The Suburbans*, a film about one-hit wonders reuniting for a second shot for lack of anything better to do, "Lord, just what is it about rock and roll that so befuddles filmmakers?"

The filmmakers might have had trouble "getting it," capturing the spirit of the new music and teen rebellion on celluloid, but the moguls "got it" the same way as the record executives got it. They made the startling discovery that, unlike the youth of their generally pre–World War II generation, the postwar adolescents had disposable income. Lots of it. And they were willing to spend it on entertainment.

A slew of rocksploitation films started appearing in cinemas and drive-ins across the country. Films like *High School Confidential!, Hot Rod Gang, Let's Rock*, and dozens of others—mostly cheaply made and often with amateur actors—went into general release on the theory that anything that rocked would sell. Most of the time that was true. No one cared about the reviews of an Elvis movie. You liked Elvis, you went to see him. Chuck Berry was in a film? Well, he's the duck's nuts, dad! I'm there!

As energized as the mid-'50s were, the late '50s and early '60s represented a doldrums in the music business in general and in rock and roll in particular. The first wave had broken and the next was gathering steam. In the meantime, what passed for rock started to morph, taking several shapes.

A bright sometime musician, sometime producer, sometime

songwriter, former record store owner, and full-time assembly line worker at the Ford plant in Detroit saw what had happened to R&B in white hands and decided to give as good as he got. So Berry Gordy started recording Caucasian-friendly R&B records that fused the vocal-group tradition with mainstream pop music, a great, rocking backing band, and the most important and ineffable element in the mix—great songs. Motown launched with tunes and talent like Smokey Robinson and the Miracles doing "Shop Around" and "Little" Stevie Wonder's hit "Fingertips Pt. 1."

"A great awakening for me," notes Smokey Robinson, "was when I began receiving letters from white kids who lived in the Detroit suburbs, places like Grosse Point, where blacks couldn't live at the time. And we would get letters from the white kids who would say things like, 'We love Motown. We have all your records. Our parents don't know we have them. If they knew, they'd take them away.'"

Motown also helped promote another big sound that grew out of the vocal group tradition, the girl groups, which launched artists like The Shirelles, writers like Carole King, and producers like George "Shadow" Morton and Phil Spector.

The folk revival of the '60s spawned several hits during rock and roll's downtime, giving birth to the genre's first legitimate superstar, an artist from Minnesota named Bob Dylan. Even he was a rock fan—in his high school yearbook, he said his goal was "to join Little Richard."

Another phenomenon that came about in the early '60s was the Twist. Originally based on a suggestive, 1958 R&B ditty by Hank Ballard and the Midnighters, a former butcher name Earnest Evans turned it into the dance craze of the early '60s. Topping the charts twice over the course of two years, Evans—redubbed Chubby Checker by Dick Clark's wife—did a version that substituted the kind of good, wholesome fun that Clark had come to stand for, neutering the song to popularity.

The other major strain of rock during this period adapted the rocking blues of artists like Chuck Berry and the close harmonies of doo-wop groups like Dion and the Belmonts, the Cadillacs, and the Dells with white, suburban, Southern Californian concerns and sensibilities, like cars, girls, and surfing. The music became known as surf music, and coming as it did from the Hollywood vicinity, it became beloved by the newly relocated *American Bandstand* and the movies, aiding and abetting a wave of teen films called "beach party movies."

These pictures revived the career of *Bandstand* pin-up boy Frankie Avalon. And while the movies were bland and sexless, that more or less was the point. The director of the archetype of these films, 1962's *Beach Party*, William Asher, had cut his teeth directing episodes of *I Love Lucy*. Coming from a TV background, he preferred sex appeal to sex. He also reasoned that after all the rock-and-roll noir that followed *Blackboard Jungle*, people were tired of juvenile delinquents. Avalon and his costar, Annette (the Mouseketeer) Funicello couldn't have been more wholesome and white bread if you'd bathed them in milk.

In addition to the appeal of America's favorite teen couple, the movies offered music. The musical performers were as diverse as the artists climbing the charts. They ranged from the stomping instrumentals of Dick Dale and the Deltones and Motown's young star Stevie Wonder to the bouncy pop of his Motown-label mates the Supremes and the overwrought teen operettas of the Righteous Brothers.

The racial integration in these films and in the charts followed the growing call for integration and civil rights. Both music and cinema reflected changes in society. The growing turbulence of the '60s wouldn't allow for shallowness of the beach party movies nor the one-dimensional vision of the juvenile-delinquent, hot-rodder movie for very much longer. However, there was still one more wave of levity. In 1964, the Beatles took control of popular culture. In addition to controlling the charts, they had one of the most popular films of the year with their screen debut, *A Hard Day's Night*.

Beyond being a lighthearted romp with John, Paul, George, and Ringo, it depicted a band that you could bring home to your mother, but also a band allowed to be the master of its own destiny. The film better solidified just who the Beatles were, or at least who they wanted us to think they were. The film, and the next year's *Help!*, made them even more identifiable both as a band and individuals. The films expanded their personalities and gave them dimensions that the music could not on its own.

It was a lesson readily learned, but not easily imitated. Frank Zappa tried it in *200 Motels* (with Ringo playing Zappa). The Monkees were the prefab reflection of the Beatles, with both their TV show and the movie *Head*. More successfully, though using the band only to recreate the music, is the Who's autobiographical *Quadrophenia*, which is an interesting companion piece with the documentary *The Kids Are All Right*.

Perhaps the best cinematic visions of real rock and roll, however, were provided by the documentary camera of D. A. Pennebaker, who followed Bob Dylan on his 1965 tour, during which Dylan got one step closer to Little Richard-dom, swapping his acoustic guitar for a Stratocaster. The resulting documentary, *Don't Look Back*, is the yardstick against which all other rock documentaries (and indeed all nonfiction films) are measured. Pennebaker also captured the seminal rock festival, filming *Monterey Pop*, with performances by Janis Joplin and Jimi Hendrix, to name just a couple of the many stars at that 1967 event.

That film spawned another genre of nonfiction, music film that emerged with the release of *The TAMI Show* in 1964. Not everyone could get to a concert, nor did every artist get to every place. *The TAMI Show* (TAMI standing for "Teenage Awards Music International," by the way) featured a mixed bag of performers, ranging from James Brown to the Rolling Stones to Jan and Dean to Marvin Gaye, live, in concert, albeit on film. It was successful enough to spawn a sequel, *The Big TNT Show,* two years later.

In the wake of the Beatles, the LP became the chief means of communicating rock and roll to the consumers. In some cases the music was just too big for a two-and-a-half-minute single. Certainly the concerns of the rock fan were larger. LSD became generally available on college campuses and reefer wasn't just for black folks anymore. Rock fans weren't merely "drinking wine spo-dee-o-dee," and the times had become far more tumultuous. The second generation of "teen culture" had morphed into "youth culture." In this context, *The Blackboard Jungle* seemed tame.

Of course, Hollywood was there to exploit the change. The same company (American International) that introduced the beach party movie offered the 1968 film *Psych-Out*. Starring Jack Nicholson and Bruce Dern, the film portrayed the scene in Haight-Ashbury. This and other films culminated in the powerful, massively successful *Easy Rider*.

"After *Easy Rider*," said Peter Biskind, author of *Easy Riders, Raging Bulls: How the Sex-and-Drugs-and-Rock-and-Roll Generation Saved Hollywood*, "young filmmakers could do anything they wanted."

But *Easy Rider* did much more than make stars out of Peter Fonda, Dennis Hopper, and Jack Nicholson. It also made stars out of Steppenwolf, and the soundtrack made the filmmakers and record companies a fortune. The album went gold, as did "Born to Be Wild." The filmmakers and record companies (many owned by the film companies by this point) learned another point of symbiosis—songs sold movies sold soundtrack albums. Suddenly pop stars battled to record the theme songs to James Bond films. It brought them exposure that radio alone could never offer. If you wanted to break a song or an artist, one way was to get their music into a movie, as EMI proved in the early '80s.

"I'd like to see Bobby McFerrin do something from a big movie," Jack Satter, former VP of Promotion for EMI-Manhattan Records, said when confronted with taking the singer's eccentric a cappella album to a pop audience. "That's the vehicle that really exposes a lot of these sort of left-of-center records that you never think will get a shot. I even reflect on when *Dirty Dancing* started to break. I hadn't heard the song, but there was another name from out of the past, Bill Medley, and I thought, 'Wait a minute, what's this all about?' Because there's another artist, who would ever have thought he'd have another hit? So you never know. You have to keep an open mind to everything. You never know when you might catch a left-field instrumental, even."

Satter did place a song from that Bobby McFerrin album into a film. While the film was not one of the biggest successes of its time, it provided enough impetus and exposure to the song "Don't Worry, Be Happy" to launch it to the top of the charts.

One of the biggest strengths of the movies involves their ability to allow us to live vicariously through what happens on the screen. For a while we're all bigger than life. "We want to deliver the impression of dropping in on someone else's world," said Chris Hegedus, Pennebaker's partner in film and life.

So, while only half a million people got to personally experience Woodstock, maybe a thousand times that many got to live it via the film. Similarly, the single death at Altamont at the hands of the Hell's Angels in charge of security eclipsed the three who died at Woodstock, though they didn't die violently, and more important, they didn't die on film. Not that the Maysles Brothers hoped to capture anything but music at Altamont. "The original thought was that we would go there and film the event and just see what happened," said Al Maysles, "but right from the beginning we had an idea that something out of the ordinary was going on there."

In the '70s, other means of exploiting cinema projects became popular. Cable TV and home video offered these movies an aftermarket and another means of recouping revenues spent on film projects. So, a rock film like *Eddie and the Cruisers*, that bombed at the box office, actually became a moderate success as people who wouldn't go to a theater to see it caught it on cable, and then went out and bought the soundtrack album.

As filmmakers born in the '50s and raised on rock grew up, several things happened to rock on film. The movies began to exhibit a greater understanding and empathy for music. Acclaimed filmmakers like Martin Scorsese and Jonathan Demme felt compelled to make concert films of favorite bands. Scorsese, who earlier in his career had edited *Woodstock*, was introduced to Robbie Robertson, who wanted to capture The Band's final concert for posterity. "I couldn't resist," said Scorsese. "Music is as important to me as cinema. Almost . . . Robbie was the force behind *The Last Waltz*, but he had gotten someone as crazy as he was to shoot it—me. We kept daring each other."

Similarly, Jonathan Demme saw Talking Heads on tour, and admired the way the show built from one person on stage to a nine piece band. While everyone else in the audience saw a concert, Demme saw a film with everything but the film. "There's David Byrne thinking very cinematically once again in terms of designing a stage show," Demme said. "He wanted the kind of drama and the suggestion of character and the suggestion of narrative that's kind of inherent in the way the band expanded right before our very eyes, the way the set built to a certain look, and then changed and then went into a series of dramatic lighting interpretations. He wanted the show to feel like a movie. And it was even in the back of his mind that it would be good to make a movie of it, but the work, in terms of just mounting a show, prevented him from pursuing the movie idea. That's where I came into the picture, because I saw the show, saw that it was a movie waiting to be filmed, contacted him in perfect Haitian style—I knew a guy who knew a guy who knew David Byrne—we met. I told him that I didn't want to tamper with anything, that my goal as a director was to capture for a movie audience what it was like to see the show. I didn't want any interviews, I didn't want any cutaways to the audience, anything that would distract from the opportunity to get lost, to literally get lost inside this show, as one does with the best films."

It became "the thing" to have a filmmaker follow a star act around for the purposes of documenting events like the making of an album (Wilco's *I Am Trying to Break Your Heart*) or a tour (U2's *Rattle and Hum*), with varying degrees of success. However, in most cases, even if the film failed at the box office, the album and home video would often make the project profitable.

By the mid '80s, films were made to capture both the real and fictional stories revolving around rock. Films like *The Buddy Holly Story* and *La Bamba* captured the stories of seminal rockers Buddy Holly and Richie Valens to considerable acclaim. *American Hot Wax* told the thinly fictionalized story of Alan Freed.

They even started to get it right in fictional films. *The Commitments* captured the spirit of a rock band in its early stages. Filmmaker Alan Parker cast musicians rather than actors in the key roles. "I didn't want to cheat the music, so obviously I had to look for musicians," he said.

The Ramones' *Rock and Roll High School* captured both the spirit of the '50s rocksploitation films it was sending up and the anarchic spirit of late '70s punk as well. *Almost Famous* captured the essence of traveling on tour with a more mainstream band during essentially the same period.

Perhaps the film to get it "rightest" was the amazing, heavy metal, documentary parody *This Is Spinal Tap*. A dead-on spoof of the music business, heavy metal, and even documentary films, the movie became a cult classic, and the fictitious band comprised of actors and comedians took on a life of its own, still recording satirical rock records nearly two decades after the film wrapped.

As rock became the soundtrack to more and more of our lives, it also became the soundtrack to more and more films, even films that had nothing necessarily to do with rock. It could evoke whole eras or even deep personal feelings for boomers and postboomers, offering filmmakers an emotional shorthand in relating to their audience. Anyone who had lived through the Vietnam conflict, either at home or on the battlefield, could relate to the musical cues in *Apocalypse Now*. Any yuppie could sing along to the soundtrack to *The Big Chill*.

Beyond offering (at their best) that kind of cultural resonance, using rock in movies also generated an additional revenue stream to help a film's bottom line. For any piece of cinema with an expensive soundtrack, a "music from and inspired by" the film album was guaranteed to follow. Placing songs in films became a big, lucrative business.

As rock "grew up," many documentaries attempted to make sense of it. PBS broadcast a twenty-hour spectacular attempting that in a grand, organic sweep. Most tried to make sense of it in smaller bites. *The Great Rock and Roll Swindle* and the follow-up piece *The Filth and the Fury*, for example, helped demystify the Sex Pistols.

While the hit rock-and-roll movies made since 1955 are documentable, the misses are legion. Filmmakers still tend to use rock (and other forms of popular music) as a crutch more than a plot device, as a gimmick rather than an organic part of the whole, and as a source of revenue rather than a source of entertainment. When rock was new and naïve, filmmakers could get away with this. As it has gained experience, such use more often elicits cynicism.

From the Transistor Radio
to the Cassette
to the Compact Disc

There's a telling moment in the movie *Men in Black* that speaks volumes about the music business. Tommy Lee Jones is taking new recruit Will Smith through the room of extraterrestrial original patents that fund their clandestine operation. He picks up a small disc and says, "Well, looks like I'm going to have to buy the 'White Album' again."

Despite what the record companies seem to think, over the last two centuries technology has powered the music marketplace, not the other way around. From the player piano to the DVD burner and iPod, it has ultimately always been the music business that has had to adjust to the new technology.

So, when economists and sociologists ask the question, "Why 1955?" in terms of the musical groundswell that spawned rock and roll, they cite things like young people in the '50s buying rock and roll as "symbolic goods," greater disposable income, the economic difficulty in maintaining a "big band," the type of popular music that preceded rock. But Bob Goodale of the Internet company Ultrastar has an answer that seems to work better. He points out that the mid-'50s saw the introduction of the portable transistor radio. "Without transistors, no portable radios; without portable radios, where would rock have gone?"

In the '50s, American culture became peripatetic in unprecedented ways. With the rise of the suburb, Americans relied on their cars to get to work (or to a mass-transportation hub that would get them to work), get to the store, get to school and to take out dates. In the mid-'50s, relatively small, inexpensive radios—as compared to the tube-type behemoths that preceded them—began to appear in cars throughout the world. Music was becoming portable. And as young people were using the car more and more, so was rock and roll. It became the cruising music of choice, the sound of young America on wheels.

By 1957, it became the sound of young America's pockets as well, when the second generation of battery-operated, portable transistor radios started arriving on these shores from Japan. Introduced some years earlier by Texas Instruments, the first portable, pocket-sized transistor radio sold for close to $50 in 1950s money, which would be like paying $400 now—not so outlandish, as "early adaptors" are apt to pay that much for a new piece of entertainment technology. "A lot of brand-new electronic machinery gets bought because it's new," former Tower Records chief Russ Solomon held. "It's just new, people buy it. That's their hobby. But that doesn't create a mass market."

So the TI unit was way too expensive for your average, or even above average, sixteen-year-old. The Japanese units sold for a lot less. Now, the music could go with you anywhere. You could even get an earphone, so that no one else had to hear it—useful in class or in the bedroom after lights out. Many listeners heard Alan Freed's late-night shows while lying under the covers with an earphone in their ear.

Of course, the portable and car radios had one major drawback—someone else got to program the music. You could change the station, but you were always at the mercy of the deejay. In part, this is what made that time the golden age of rock radio—the disc jockey was king, gatekeeper, and older sibling who clued you in on "the good stuff." "They were referred to as the golden age of rock and roll," Joe Smith concurred, "but it's like, did the people in the dark ages know they were living in the dark ages? We didn't know it was the golden age. I was playing Presley and Little Richard and Orbison and all those people, running against the establishment."

While rock-and-roll radio had become so popular, or perhaps because rock-and-roll radio had become so popular, some car companies tried to put portable phonographs into cars. These experiments proved disastrous—they skipped along, destroying the listening experience as well as the records themselves. So, if you wanted music in a car, you had to rely on the radio.

It would be some ten years before the solution to this problem arrived. William Lear, inventor of the Lear Jet, devised the 8-track. To allow his flying vehicles continuous music, he took the sort of tape loops in a cartridge that radio stations used for music and advertising and devised a tape head that would move so as to fit four stereo channels onto a tape. This created several problems. If the tape or the heads fell even slightly out of alignment, you'd hear a weird shadow sound from other channels. Also, because of the time constraints, sometimes the head moved in the middle of a song, breaking up the piece like the old 78 rpm albums would.

Another limitation of the 8-track was as much a limitation of the times. Very few people had the equipment to record them. Around this time, the record business made a remarkable discovery. It had actually started when the glass and lacquer disc gave way to the LP. The powers in the record business found out that there's gold in the attic. Having a formidable catalog gave a company the ability to sell it again and again in different configurations and different formats. With the 8-track, they didn't even have to worry about that. People would buy the same music twice—an album for the house and an 8-track for the car. Some companies even packaged them like that, offering a break in price when you bought both.

For all its eccentricities, the 8-track caught on. By 1966, all Ford cars offered an in-dash 8-track unit. A year later, Chrysler and GM followed suit. From 1966 until the early '80s, the 8-track was the mainstay of tape portability. The format didn't totally fade away until very late in the decade.

Similar to Edison's intentions, when Phillips conceived of the compact cassette tape, they thought of it as a device for dictation. Certainly, the slow tape speed and high-frequency hiss didn't make the unit compatible with music. However, a lot of people went out and bought portable tape recorders so they could tape their friend's records or shows off the radio. This got a boost when Ray Dolby devised a way of defeating the high-frequency hiss in the late '60s, first using reel-to-reel units, and by 1970, translating the reel-to-reel technology to cassettes.

Initially, this format became a home-based means of entertainment, but soon higher-line cars started replacing their 8-track units with the smaller, more reliable, less temperamental cassettes. By the mid-'70s, even inexpensive stereos had a cassette component which made recording albums or creating personal "mix tapes" for the car or friends fairly easy.

So now people could create the music for their driving experience. Creating mix tapes of various themes or favorite songs was time-consuming, but it was also fun. No longer were you at the mercy of the disc jockey and radio. If you wanted to hear anything, no matter how obscure, and had access to a copy, you could tape it and listen to it in your car.

In 1979, the cassette reached the height of portability when Sony introduced the Walkman. A stereo-cassette unit with headphones, the Walkman offered consumers near–stereo component quality on the go. Once again, the record companies got the opportunity to sell through both their catalogs and to sell duplicate units of current "product," as the record manufacturers were apt to call the prerecorded music that they put out. Individual music fans could create their own personal soundscapes to take with them anywhere they wanted. The only thing that the Walkman made difficult was sharing that experience. Technology had turned music from something historically communal to something intensely personal.

Digital audio was beginning to make serious waves in the late '70s as well. Ry Cooder released *Bop 'til You Drop*, the first all-digital album, in 1979. Yet, after the process of recording and mastering digitally, it still had to be cut by a lathe to press the record. "We shouldn't have had tape to begin with," Les Paul argues. "We shouldn't have been gouging out records either. The first lecture I gave at the Audio Engineering Society, I said, 'With all those bald heads I'm looking at out there, you'd think that you guys would get your act together and stop plowing into a disk, to gouge a record out like a farmer with an ox. It's stupid to have a needle tracking in that machine. You haven't come any farther than what Edison handed you, and it just doesn't make sense, that you guys really ought to get out there and step into the new world.' At that time, tape had just come out, and I said, 'Tape is no better. Tape scraping over those heads and shedding and all the problems that you have with tape, tape is stupid, it's wrong. It's the best thing that we have today, but why don't we get to the new world, and that is go to light.' That's on a tape from around 1950 to the Audio Engineering Society."

Despite this, the reign of tape had begun. By 1983, cassettes were outselling LPs. A lot of people, nonetheless, continued to buy LPs and record them on their own cassette machines for play in the car or Walkman. And another tape for the friend who might like this. And a few tracks for a mix tape . . .

This coincided with one of the biggest dips in the history of the music business. Needing something to blame so stockholders wouldn't blame them, record manufacturers came up with the slogan "Home taping is killing music." "Right now," songwriter and head of the Songwriters Guild, George Weiss, said in the early '90s, "there are approximately 667,000,000 albums on tape, unauthorized."

"Our founding fathers recognized [that] the purpose of copyright is not to enrich authors at the expense of consumers, but rather it is to benefit society as a whole," countered Ruth Rodgers of the Home Recording Rights Coalition. "Home recording practices have nothing to do with commercial retransmission of signals, unauthorized commercial reproduction of content, or other acts of 'piracy.' Home recording and piracy should not be confused."

The means of legitimizing the practice of home taping of music and the parameters in which it was allowed came from some very unusual sources: the video companies and the Supreme Court. When Sony introduced the Betamax, home—as opposed to professional—videotape recorder, several movie and television companies sued to get the units removed from the market, claiming that by creating a machine that could copy copyrighted work Sony was infringing on intellectual property. Sony countered that making a noncommercial copy of a TV show or a film for personal purposes was fair use. The courts upheld that. Suddenly, it became clearly legal to make copies of copyrighted material for your own personal use.

What they couldn't accomplish judicially, the music industry tried to accomplish legislatively. After introducing several proindustry bill amendments starting in 1981, Senator Charles Mathias introduced the Audio Home Recording Act in 1985. The timing couldn't have been better, as the record industry had come up with another way of selling through the catalog, using Paul's admonition about looking toward light. Phillips had come out with a means of transferring digital information to a disc read by a laser. Now Cooder's album only left the digital domain when it hit the amplifier of whatever was playing it. Music could be digitally recorded, mixed, mastered, encoded, and played back.

Some artists, particularly Neil Young, argued that this might improve fidelity, but it really didn't improve the sound. Many found the effect of digital recording cold, thin, and sterile. Many were willing to "submit" their sound to the vagaries of analog distortion to get the sonic warmth provided by the analog equipment. Beyond this, many highly placed engineers had questions about the fidelity of the compact disc. "Analog records are extremely accurate animals, especially on the outer bands of the record," noted famed mastering engineer Bob Ludwig. "They have a wider response than compact discs do. The response of the cutting system—the specification is within 1 dB from 10 Hz to 25,000 Hz. If you are playing it back with a *calibrated* cartridge on a good system, you will indeed yield that kind of accuracy. I mean, the most subtle changes, like the slightly higher resolution between a butterfly [European] two track and an American two track is actually translatable to a disc, and can be discerned. There's hardly anything you can do that won't get picked up by a disc, especially in the outer bands."

Still, the compact disc had myriad advantages. If handled correctly, it was virtually indestructible, as virtually nothing touched the surface of the disc to play it. Where the rubric held that you should never play a vinyl recording more than once a day to let the grooves "recover" from the pressure of the stylus, you could play a CD endlessly without any deleterious effects—at least not to the CD.

The new format caught the public's fancy, especially when the price of hardware fell. "We knew that CDs would become the dominant format when we first saw a CD player in 1982," said Don Rose, the founder of Rykodisc, the first CD-only record company. "Not that we were any geniuses, but we just happened to stumble into something at a time when we were open-minded enough to allow its potential to sink in. We realized there was a potential for a lot of material to be reissued on compact disc, a lot of significant music that had more or less saturated its viability in the analog market."

Once again, the moribund record business could "sell through" its catalog. They weren't too subtle about it, and initially they weren't too careful, either. "I walked into a record shop and saw one of the Doors records on CD," recalled the Doors' producer, Paul Rothchild. "I said, 'What?!' Took it home and listened to it, and it was abysmal. It had been taken from a minimum of fifth-generation master, perhaps even eighth-generation cassette running master. It was noisy, distorted, obscene."

"The first few CDs of Elton," said Elton John producer Gus Dudgeon, "that came out were dreadful. They were just terrible because they basically didn't understand what they were doing. They looked for the loudest peak and set it up, and go have another cup of tea and watch a TV program while it ran off, and come back and do the other five albums. I spent hours on each of them."

The compact disc came at a time when the bottom had begun to fall out of the industry. This was a reflection of the takeover staged by corporations that saw the money being made in popular music. What they didn't account for in their accounting was the creative element, and the chilling effect answering to stockholders had on that element. By the late '70s, the business had slowly stopped breeding career artists and began spinning off one- or two-hit wonders. This, of course, didn't help with any sort of long-term view of the business, and the opportunity to sell everyone the "White Album" again was something the business welcomed. "I understand why Elektra did it," Rothchild continued. "It's like 'Let's put the stuff out on CD.' To them it's just a manufacturing process. The order is find the Doors' masters and transfer them to CD. The complexity of such a simple instruction as 'Find the Doors' masters,' they don't know what they're looking for, because practically every box they touched was marked 'Master.' There would be hundreds of boxes marked 'Master.' So I'm sure, out of despair, whoever the transfer engineer was took a box, listened to it, said, 'Well, this sounds like the Doors' music,' and used it."

Digital technology also developed a new means of making home copies. Sony created a version of the digital audiotape recorder that had helped make *Bop 'til You Drop* (and so many after it) a reality for home use. Since many of the record companies were already just divisions of hardware manufacturers (Sony owned Columbia and Epic records, for example), they saw this as a natural extension of the business. For the creative community, it was another story. "When you tape something [on a regular, nondigital] home taping machine," said Weiss, "you are degrading the original. . . . The copy is not so hot. . . . But with digital audiotape, forget it. You buy a compact disc, put it into this machine and nothing touches each other. It's all electronic information that is being sent from one side to the other. Nothing is being degraded and the [tape] is not a copy, it's a clone. It's exactly as good and as authentic and with as much fidelity as the original . . . this DAT machine is just going to devastate us: copy, copy, copy! Clone, clone, clone!"

Relief came from Congress. In 1992, the lawmakers passed a bill that put a two-percent royalty on the digital audio recorders, a three-percent royalty on the tapes. This money would go into a pool that would be distributed to recording artists on the basis of sales. This also applied to later technologies for digital recording, the digital compact cassette and the mini-disc. In passing the bill, Congressman Carlos Moorhead of California suggested that home taping cost the music business around a third of its annual revenue.

The move slapped a Band-Aid on the problem. However, as the music business would discover sometime later, first aid like that just isn't enough when you're bleeding from an artery.

Chapter 9: 1955

Chuck Berry Records
"Maybellene"

There's an interesting section of the "Million Dollar Quartet" recording with Elvis, Jerry Lee Lewis, Carl Perkins, and Johnny Cash. They jam for around eleven minutes on one song. That song is Chuck Berry's "Brown-Eyed Handsome Man."

Elvis had added Berry's "Maybellene" to his show while still on Sun. The attraction was simple. As much as Elvis was the white guy with the black sound, Berry was the black guy with the white sound. Just like the white kids were running around the dial to find R & B they could dance to, Berry would listen to the *Grand Ol' Opry*. Where Sam Phillips would say, "If only I could find a white boy with that black sound," the head of Berry's record company, Leonard Chess, would say, "If Chuck Berry were white, he'd be bigger than Elvis Presley."

"Chuck had this style of music he was playing that was really catchy to me," said Berry's long-time collaborator, Johnnie Johnson, whose boogie-jazz piano work became almost as important to Berry's sound as Berry's own hollow-body Gibson electric guitar. "A black guy playing hillbilly music. I thought, 'This would be something different if I could get him to do this one night for me.' That one night became twenty-eight, thirty years."

Berry was a performer who forced his time to come. America had started to come to grips with its African-American citizens in a revolutionary movement, the likes of which the country had not seen since the Civil War. In 1954, the landmark Civil Rights decision *Brown vs. Board of Education* enforced desegregation of the nation's schools. A year later, Rosa Parks would refuse to go to the back of a Montgomery, Alabama, bus, starting a year of strikes that eventually desegregated the city's transit system. In between, Chuck Berry released "Maybellene" and sent it to the top 5 in *Billboard*. In the long run, it's tough to say which struck a bigger blow for the cause of civil rights in America.

Not that Berry was all that interested in the political aspects of what he was doing. He mainly wanted to make money. "Rock and roll accepted me and paid me, even though I loved big bands," Berry said. "I went that way because I wanted a home of my own. I had a family. I had to raise them. Let's don't leave out the economics. No way."

Anyone who has any doubts about his love of big bands need only listen to Berry's cover of Bobby Troup's "Route 66" on the *New Juke Box Hits* album. Rife with horns and even a pedal steel guitar, and powered along by Berry's guitar and Johnson's muscular boogie piano, it could have been recorded ten or fifteen years earlier and still would've sounded comfortable on the charts.

Unlike so many of the white stars of early rock, such as Carl Perkins, who learned about the blues and how to play the guitar in the cotton fields, Berry was born into a relatively affluent family that he proudly recalled as living in the best of St. Louis's black neighborhoods. He was the fourth of six children. His father was a carpenter. Like so many of his contemporaries, he was split between the church's music and blues, boogie-woogie, big-band jazz, and country.

Coming up in a good family in a good neighborhood didn't curb his mischievous streak. At eighteen, he was arrested with some friends for armed robbery and wound up in reform school.

While in reform school he started to take singing seriously, joining a vocal group. When he got out, he bought himself a professional guitar and began sitting in with bands around St. Louis. "In East St. Louis at that time," Johnson said, "everything was open twenty-four hours a day. He was playing at a club about two blocks from where I was playing. My band would always finish first, so we could go and listen to the group he was playing with. They would be playing around three, four o'clock in the morning, and I'd be done by around 12:30. I couldn't sit in with him because they didn't have a piano player, but I'd go up and listen."

As fate would have it, New Year's Eve, 1952, one of the musicians in Johnson's band got sick. Johnson started calling around to find someone to fill in. On short notice. On New Year's Eve. "I don't care how bad you are," Johnson said, "somebody wants you for New Year's Eve. Especially when on every corner was a club in East St. Louis. Anything that can whistle good's got a gig."

As it turned out, Berry was available and sat in with Johnson's band that New Year's Eve. They played Johnson's set, but Berry brought his country edge to Johnson's urban boogie-woogie. Johnson enjoyed the sound as much as he thought he would, and he recognized the potential of this hybrid in terms of the East St. Louis clubgoing audience. A good sound is a sound that works.

Johnson was, and continues to be, one of the finest blues pianists ever to crack his knuckles and attack the 88s. Just listen to the piano behind "Sweet Little Sixteen" and you can hear that. But Johnson had his problems. He didn't like to fly, he drank some, and he had a terrible fear of the microphone. So it became natural for Berry, who had insinuated himself into a full-time job with Johnson's trio, the house band at the Cosmopolitan Club in East St. Louis, to front that band. The next step was that the group became the Chuck Berry Band.

In 1954, Berry started seeking a life beyond St. Louis—something Johnson didn't even really care to explore one way or another. Berry took a tape and got an audience with his idol, Muddy Waters, a country bluesman from Mississippi gone electric in Chicago. Berry had a brief conversation with Waters. "Chuck went to see Muddy, and walked up to him after the act and said, 'Look, I have a band. I have music. Where should I go?' Muddy said, 'Go see Chess,'" said Marshall Chess, son of company founder Leonard Chess.

Waters had recorded for Chess Records since the company started, giving the company its first hit with "Rolling Stone." Through marketing savvy and an immigrant drive that sent Leonard on car tours through the South, selling records and finding talent, they built the company up to a fair-sized force in "race music," while building up a strong catalog of songs through their publishing company, ARC Music.

"In a way," Marshall Chess added, "Muddy was an immigrant, just like my father. Muddy came from a farm where you made fifty cents a day. He came to Chicago, just like my father, and what's an immigrant's big dream? To make money."

This was something Berry could get behind as well. He was pushing thirty and knew that something had to break for him soon. He played the songs for Leonard Chess. One song, "Ida Red," was based on an old country fiddle tune that Berry had juked up with a boogie beat together with his distinctive guitar and Johnson's brawny barrelhouse piano. "My father listened to it and said, 'You've got something here that's different, but I don't like the lyrics. Come back with some new ones.' One week later, he came back with 'Maybellene,' and my father instantly recorded it."

Very soon after that, Chess was headed to New York, so he had a couple of white-label copies of the record made. A white-label copy was just that—a copy of the record without any label copy. "I took the dub to Alan [Freed] and said, 'Play this,'" Leonard Chess said. "By the time I got back to Chicago, Freed had called a dozen times, saying it was his biggest record ever."

Suddenly, Chuck Berry found himself duking it out on the charts with Elvis Presley, both artists fighting for position on both the pop charts and the R&B charts. And suddenly, race became just a little bit less meaningful in America.

Over the years, Chess developed a reputation beyond their musical legend. The record company had a less savory celebrity in terms of how they dealt with their artists. Etta James recalled:

> I came from St. Louis stranded in the snow one weekend, and I went to Jackie Wilson who gave myself and a girl I was traveling with bus fare and hotel money to go to Chicago. That was the closest place. I remember going to Chess Records and Leonard Chess had a check on his desk. He said, "I want you with Chess records. You will be really good. I'll get you out of the deal with Modern. We'll do this and we'll do that." And I thought to myself, "This looks really good." This looked like a real company compared to what I had left in Los Angeles, with those Hollywood guys out there. And he said, "Let me show you what my artists get," because I was kind of looking, I could see there was a check there. They had been talking to Chuck Berry earlier that day. He lifted this check up to me and it was for ninety some thousand dollars, and it was made out to Chuck Berry and Allan Freed.
>
> So he put me on his label, paid the balance of the money that Modern Records wanted. I stayed there in a private hotel. He paid the rent and all that. I started my show-business life, living in a private hotel where you could cook. Other entertainers were there, like Curtis Mayfield. Everybody lived in this one hotel. We used to put all our money together, get some food and cook it. I remember us putting together and not having much, just enough to get some cornmeal. And I learned that whenever you get hungry, if you've got enough money, you get some yellow cornmeal and you get some sugar. You can always get some sugar somewhere, even if you have to walk into a McDonald's someplace, and steal some of the sugar. Take sugar and cornmeal and fry it. Boy, is that good. Then, if you've got enough money, you get a little syrup. I remember we ate that for two days.
>
> I had one hit record, "All I Do Is Cry," and then I had "Stop the Wedding," and then I had, "My Dearest. . . ." They were going in layers. So, it was about a year later, when it would be time for me to receive some royalties, I went down there. I was rubbing my hands together. And he showed me the hotel bill, the full year, the money he had paid Modern Records to settle out. He handed me the statement, and I knew I was going to look

down there and see a nice fat figure. Being young, and not caring about that kind of stuff, the only thing I used to do—and the other artists, if they admit it, they know that that's what they used to do, too—is read the tops of statements, and then go straight down to where the money is. You didn't even read the other part. So, I was going through this, and I said, "I don't want to know about any of this. What does the bottom say my check's going to be?" And I go down and I looked and I saw that it was written in red. And I said, "$14,000! All right!" And Leonard said, "Hold it, hold it." I just looked like, wow that's really good for me. But he said, "Don't get all bent out of shape." And I was kind of confused, like what is he saying that for. And he says, "Look Etta, don't worry about what that says. What do you need." Now, I'm really confused. "Here's what I need, in big red numbers. Wait a minute. You're saying I don't have this coming?" "Hell no, you don't have this coming," he said. "You owe me this." I went, I just met this guy, how could I owe him all this money? I went over all these charges, and they didn't mean jack either. And he said, "Just tell me what you need."

"If I'd gotten paid for record sales and royalties and writer's royalties that I'm entitled to without having to go get an attorney to go catch some of these suckers, I wouldn't have to work when I didn't feel like going," Bo Diddley concurred. "Everybody that you talk to who came from Chess Records will tell you, almost like a broken record, the same thing. We got ripped! It's bad, man. I appreciate Chess Records giving me the opportunity to become Bo Diddley and do all the great things I've done, but I don't appreciate being ripped off because I had to trust them with the money that comes in and they have to pay me. I ain't got shit. I've been waiting all these years like a good Samaritan, thinking that one day I'll look in the mailbox and say, 'Oh, wow! There's a check in here that will make my pockets look like footballs.' It never happened. You dig what I'm saying? I'm very upset about it. They made a pit bull out of me, with an extra set of teeth. Is that bad enough? They poked at me and poked at me and made me an evil dude."

"I get paid for everything that I do now. When I was with Chess, I did not get that," Koko Taylor, who had a mammoth hit with "Wang Dang Doodle" in 1966, agreed. "I don't have any bad feelings, though. I only have good feeling about Chess, because one of the greatest things that Chess ever did for me was recording me. They gave me my first break by recording me. Then, when they did 'Wang Dang Doodle,' and it turned out to be such a great hit, that's the tune that started me on my way. Even today, 'Wang Dang Doodle' [is] one of the main attractions of my concerts anywhere I go. So, in that respect, I really appreciate and I'm deeply honored that they did that much for me. It's not always the money."

"They were in it, but they didn't know the business," Willie Dixon, one of their preeminent songwriters, arrangers, and producers said of the Chess brothers. "They were in it because they had the people around them that knew the business, and they handled the business end of it. He never got involved in any of my property things. In the first place, I've always been a guy who was afraid to trust people."

Berry, however, was so successful and savvy that Chess couldn't take advantage of him that way. They did, however, take his song publishing and foist cowriters on him. He spent close to a decade recovering these copyrights with his attorney during the '70s and '80s. "The feeling of being ripped off," said Berry, "I found out about that later. When I discovered I didn't get the entire credit for something I created when I should have—that's a disappointment. That was the biggest disappointment, and it was more than one incident."

The naturalness of his sound, his smooth wordplay, his revolutionary beat, all camouflaged another element of Berry's creativity—his songs were a calculated attempt to reach his audience. Berry regarded what he did strictly as entertainment. He created strictly for the amusement of his audience. "(To me, art) was drawing," he noted. "To sing was not art. . . . I grew up thinking art was pictures until I got into music and found I was an artist and didn't paint."

"Everything I wrote," he added, "wasn't about me, but about the people listening."

Instead, he was a thirty-something-year-old man celebrating one of rock and roll's most enduring and endearing elements, eternal youth. He sang of girls, cars, and school. He reached out to and connected with the teen audience in a way no other artist did. Bill Haley could ape their language ("See You Later, Alligator") but Berry helped create it ("motorvating," "Too Pooped to Pop") and actually seemed to speak it. As opposed to Haley, who was just about the same age, and like Dick Clark, Berry always seemed ageless—the trim, brown-eyed, handsome man.

Berry certainly wasn't the first African-American artist to do well on the pop charts. Fats Domino predated him; Louis Jordan and any number of stars from the '40s had pop hits. Nat "King" Cole was crooning his way to mass acceptance; the Mills Brothers, the Platters, even Duke Ellington, Eartha Kitt, and Cab Calloway. But Berry was an Elvis-like sensation, and in his wake followed more—by 1957, the Top 20 had been visited by the likes of Frankie Lymon and the Teenagers and Little Richard.

It was Lymon who would get Alan Freed thrown off network TV by dancing with a white girl—to the horror of stations all over the South. Little Richard was something else again. Even wilder than Jerry Lee Lewis, you could *feel* the dichotomies of Richard Penniman's personality in his music. He wanted to preach, but knew rocking would be way more lucrative. "My mother had twelve kids," he said, "and I had to do something to help out my family. So, I put blues and boogie-woogie together and made rock and roll."

While it's questionable whether he "made rock and roll" (Berry, Presley, Domino, and Haley were there before him), he did strip the country out of it, speeding up R&B with prominent electric guitars and a piano as muscular yet way less controlled than Johnnie Johnson's. His howls and barely contained sexuality were shocking in 1956, and that's just what teens wanted. This was rebellion you could dance to.

Through the end of the '50s, Berry had duckwalked his way into the Top 10 with songs like "Rock and Roll Music," "School Days," "Johnny B. Goode," and "Sweet Little Sixteen." Berry's relatively short creative period ('55–'59) left a high-energy burn on the face of popular music. Any time anyone played a double-stop on the guitar, it was a "Chuck Berry lick." Like Elvis, he brought together country and blues sensibilities into a pop package. In contrast to Elvis, because he was black, Berry was both more controversial and legally vulnerable.

In the '50s and even the early '60s, the issue of race was far more incendiary than it is today, but also far more underground. A movie like *Do the Right Thing* would never have gotten made and would have been burned before it was distributed (possibly along with its creator). So here was this attractive, successful musician, getting heard by every teenager in the world, writing about "Sweet Little Sixteen"! Many white leaders, already threatened by rock and roll, found this particularly insidious—it was their worst nightmare come true—young white girls screaming and throwing clothing at a black man.

Berry, however, was a generally careful man. He invested his money in real estate, including one of the first integrated clubs in Missouri. In 1959, he brought a girl home with him from Texas. It turned out she was underage. He claimed that she came willingly, and that he brought her to work as a hat-check girl at his club and to teach him Spanish so he could write some songs in the language and capture yet another burgeoning audience. It took two trials and nearly four years, but in 1962 Berry was convicted of violating the Mann Act (transporting minors across state lines for immoral purposes), and sentenced to two years in a federal prison.

In the meantime, the music business had begun to deal with this upstart music. For one thing, the FCC started banning songs for being too suggestive. Then the powers at the major record companies reasoned that maybe they couldn't control a Chuck Berry or a Leonard Chess or a Little Richard musically, but they could undermine them. This was not a new technique at all, but it became increasingly pervasive—they created chart duels for cover versions. Traditionally, the version with the most money behind it won (and still does). Consider:

- The McGuire Sisters' 1954 cover version of "Goodnight, Sweetheart, Goodnight" made the pop Top 10 while the Spaniels' original was relegated to the R&B Top 5.

- Bill Haley and the Comets topped the charts with their version of "Shake, Rattle and Roll," while Big Joe Turner's version topped the R&B charts but didn't cross over.

- The Crew-Cuts' version of "Sh-Boom" topped the pop charts while the Chords' version stalled at #5.

Then there were Georgia Gibbs and Pat Boone.

Gibbs first broke into the charts as a big band singer. In the four years before rock and roll clocked in, she had already landed seventeen Top 40 hits, including a gold-selling #1 record of an eviscerated tango called "Kiss of Fire." In early 1955, she took LaVerne Baker's #14 pop hit, "Tweedle Dee," and sent it to #2, selling over a million copies of her whitewashed version. Then she took Etta James' "Roll with Me,

Henry," a banned answer song to Hank Ballard's already "scandalous" "Work with Me, Annie," changed the title to "Dance with Me, Henry," and topped the charts, scoring another gold record.

"My version was banned from the air because I said 'roll.'" Etta James laughed in retrospect. "Can you imagine? What would they have done to Prince in those days? They would have burned him at the stake! Johnny Otis called me and said, 'Your record has been banned from the air by the Federal Communications Commission.' Then he started explaining to me about Georgia Gibbs' version and all. She had made a version called 'Dance with Me, Henry.' They said, 'Look at you. You wrote this song, and Georgia Gibbs comes out and sells four million copies.' I was really mad at her, but shortly after that, I understood. I started getting royalty checks, and I realized it was a blessing for her to record the song. Georgia Gibbs did her version, and then Bud Abbott and Lou Costello did a movie. I remember that movie. Every time I went for a ride and saw the marquee, I thought that was pretty cool."

In 1955, Pat Boone raced his version of "Ain't That a Shame" up the charts against Fats Domino's original version. Both records went gold, but Domino's side stalled at #10 while Boone's side climbed to the top. It would not be his last trip there.

Pat Boone was everybody's all-American. He was on the radio in Nashville by the time he was ten, and emceed a radio teen talent show at seventeen, moving over to the TV side when TV was introduced to Nashville. He went to college—first in Nashville, then in Texas—studying to become a teacher and singing for tuition. He married his high school sweetheart, the daughter of country legend Red Foley. During his sophomore year, when they discovered they were going to have a child, he auditioned for *Ted Mack's Original Amateur Hour*, which he won. These TV appearances landed him a record contract. He thought he'd be singing ballads, but wound up doing rock and roll. His first song, "Two Hearts" became a minor hit. He nearly didn't cover "Ain't That a Shame," because he had problems with the song's grammar.

Boone became the king of the R&B cover. His version of "At My Front Door" bested the original by the El Dorados by ten chart positions; his take on "I'll Be Home" sold over a million copies and went to #4 while the Flamingos' version stayed on the R&B charts. During the first half of 1956, he made a cottage industry of Little Richard, making hits out of both "Tutti Frutti" and "Long Tall Sally." The *New York World Telegram and Sun* summed him up best: "The public—a sizeable portion of which considers him a heaven-sent antidote to the excesses of most rock and roll singers—wants him as often as they can get him." Through 1962, that was pretty often. He had ten gold records, a host of Top 10s, had made movies and hosted a network TV show by then.

The period 1960–1964 is generally considered the doldrums of early rock. The lament went that Little Richard (who retired from rock, the first time, the day after *Sputnik* launched and went into the clergy) had joined the church, Elvis had joined the army, Jerry Lee Lewis (who married his teenaged cousin) was in disgrace, and Chuck Berry was in jail. On Chuck's release from jail, he found a new world facing him. On the other side of the Atlantic, a bunch of rabid fans who happened to also play in bands had recorded scads of his songs.

"If you wanted to give rock and roll another name, you might call it Chuck Berry," former Beatle John Lennon once said. "I've lifted every lick he ever played," added the Rolling Stones' Keith Richards. "Berry's the gentleman that started it all, as far as I'm concerned."

So, while the Beatles and the Stones were having success with his older tunes, Berry managed to land three songs in the Top 40 in 1964: "Nadine," "No Particular Place to Go," and "You Never Can Tell," which got yet another life during the infamous twist-contest sequence in the 1994 film *Pulp Fiction*.

But Berry had come out of prison a much more ornery person. He stopped recording new material by the mid-'60s and dismissed his band, claiming that he could make more money without having to worry about the drinking habits of those who were playing with him. He would tour alone with his guitar. The promoter was expected to provide a band and cash in advance—extra if you wanted him to do the duckwalk. During these shows, he took great pleasure in trying to befuddle the band. "Chuck doesn't tell you what he's going to play, what key he's going to be in or anything," his longtime sideman Johnson said. "By the time the band stumbled upon what key he's in, he jumps off into something else."

With an all-star pickup band in London, in 1972, he recorded a live concert. The show included a prurient little ditty called "My Ding-A-Ling." This song became his first and only chart-topping hit in 1973.

Nor were Berry's legal problems behind him. In 1979, he served another 100 days in prison for tax evasion. In 1990, he was accused of drug possession, child abuse, and surreptitiously videotaping women as they used the restroom in a St. Louis restaurant. He pleaded guilty to the drug charge, receiving a six-month suspended sentence. By 1994, he had settled with the women in the videos.

In 2000, Johnnie Johnson finally sought his due. He filed a lawsuit claiming that he cowrote most of the early Berry hits. As this book went to press, that issue had yet to be settled.

Despite all of Berry's legal foibles, however, musically he was incredibly influential. "Chuck opened up a lot of doors for a lot of people," Bo Diddley said. "He sent a lot of people to the bank."

Buddy Holly Crashes

Don McLean's memorial of February 3, 1959, as "the day the music died," never really washed. The music lived. Something way more basic died. That was the day the postwar children, the "teenagers," first lost their innocence and their sense of immortality. Many of the shocked faces in homerooms and cafeterias the next day were little younger than Ritchie Valens, who was seventeen when his meteoric career crashed in a snowy cornfield in Iowa.

Also on the plane was J. P. Richardson, a prominent Texas disc jockey and songwriter, who had a novelty hit the year before with "Chantilly Lace." He also created a body of some sixty-five songs, including the award-winning country hits "White Lightning," "Beggar to a King," and "Treasure of Love," as well as Johnny Preston's chart-topping hit "Running Bear." All became hits after his death.

But the most notable person on the plane was Charles Hardin Holley, better known to family, friends, and fans as Buddy Holly. Starting in 1957 with his chart-topping hit "That'll Be the Day," Holly set about rewriting the still young rules of rock and writing up a whole bunch of new ones that would last until today. In his eighteen months as a hit recording artist, he put together a body of work that changed rock and roll. He also became rock and roll's first genuine martyr, partly because of the way he died and partly because of the unfulfilled promise of his work.

By 1957, rock and roll had survived, thrived, and grown for two years. Clearly, the fad had legs, and wasn't going to pass any time soon. The process of chewing up and spitting out talent had already begun, and many singers had their hit and went on with their lives (or didn't) by then. This was what made the Winter Dance Party Tour of the frozen Midwest that winter a pretty remarkable bill. Among the five acts performing on the ticket, nearly twenty Top 40 hits could be counted. The major act that survived, Dion and the Belmonts, had their biggest hit, "A Teenager in Love" the following spring. The fifth act, aspiring teen idol Frankie Sardo, has become less than a footnote in pop-music history, one of the acts that got chewed up and spat out.

During the winter of 1959, Ritchie Valens was riding high. He had already had two hits, a minor proto-surf California rockabilly number called "Come On, Let's Go" and a monster, #2 gold record with his puppy-love ballad to a girl he hadn't even managed to get on a date, "Donna." His new hit, a juiced-up version of an old Mexican folk song, "La Bamba," was beginning to rise up the charts as well, the first certifiable Spanish rock-and-roll hit.

J. P. "The Big Bopper" Richardson was one of the few extensively published disc jockey songwriters who (unlike Alan Freed) actually wrote most of the music with which he is credited. Before 1956,

Richardson was best known as an on-air personality on KPRM, a radio station serving the area of Texas that bordered Louisiana. In fact, one of the promotional stunts he pulled involved racing a fellow disc jockey from their area of Texas into Louisiana—Richardson by car, the other in a speed boat along the inland waterway. The other deejay lost and had to push Richardson through town in a wheelbarrow. In another promotional stunt, Richardson stayed on the air, live, for over 122 hours straight, setting a record at the time.

His songwriting came along as a challenge. In those days, many radio stations were programmed more like TV stations. That's how Alan Freed could have a classical show, and then become Moondog and start spinning R&B. In the case of Richardson, one of the shows on his station featured a live country performer. One day Richardson was kidding with the singer, saying anyone could sing country. The singer challenged him to prove it. Richardson did, eventually cutting several tracks for Mercury Records, including "White Lightning." While Richardson's version didn't go anywhere, subsequent versions by Richardson's friend and homeboy George Jones topped the country chart and even broke pop.

Richardson's "Big Bopper" persona came about because of this also. Most of the time, Richardson spun country, but like Freed, Joe Smith, and so many other deejays of the period, he became enamored of rhythm and blues and suggested spinning a show to the station manager. Since Richardson already had several shows, and since his generally laid-back demeanor wouldn't go over with a youth-oriented R&B show, he became the Big Bopper, a jive-talking, rhyming, wild man. "That was a pretty naughty kind of music for its day and J. P. wanted to be just on the edge of smutty with everything he did," said Jerry Boynton, one of his fellow announcers. "He believed there was great humor in touching on the very edge of smuttiness."

"Chantilly Lace" was something of an accident. In 1958 song-writer Ross Bagdasarian, who wrote Rosemary Clooney's big hit "Come On-a My House" with his cousin, playwright William Saroyan, started playing with his tape recorder. He discovered that when he recorded himself at half speed and played it back at regular speed, the effect was pretty darn funny, kind of like prolonged exposure to helium. He used it in a novelty hit called "The Witch Doctor" (and would practically institutionalize it with his "band" the Chipmunks). Sheb Wooley used a similar technique for his chart-topping novelty hit "Purple People Eater." Richardson brought them together, and when efforts to get someone else to release the song failed, he cut his own version and released it on a local label. On the way to the session, the head of the label reminded him that the song needed a B-side. On the drive to the studio he came up with the rough idea for "Chantilly Lace." Needless to say, the B-side became a much bigger hit than the A-side. Early in 1959, he was still riding high on the hit.

Easily the biggest star on the tour, Buddy Holly had already topped the charts and become an acknowledged hit artist. By all accounts, Holley (he lost the *e* with his first recording contract) was a good student, the "King of the Sixth Grade" in his hometown of Lubbock. His family was musical, and by high school, Holly could play banjo, mandolin, and guitar, which he did in a "western bop" duo with his friend Bob Montgomery. One of the artists Buddy and Bob opened for during this time was a Sun-era Elvis Presley. Seeing Elvis convinced Holly that he had a future in rock, and he'd better get on the stick or get left behind. He bought a Stratocaster and was one of the first artists to really expand the tonal vocabulary for the solid-body electric guitar in a rock context.

By 1956, he had signed up with Decca in Nashville and was recording rockabilly sides, including the wonderful "Midnight Shift." When they didn't work out commercially, he regrouped, quite literally, putting together a band that called themselves the Crickets. With this band he solidified the face of the rock and roll band for a long time to come, the dual guitars, bass, and drum lineup that still prevails in rock bands today.

Holly found a studio run by Norman Petty in Clovis, New Mexico, about ninety miles from Holly's hometown of Lubbock, Texas. Instead of charging by the hour, as was—and still is—the norm for studio time, he charged by the song. This allowed Holly the leisure to experiment and get the sound he wanted. An acolyte of Les Paul, he already knew about close miking and sound-on-sound recording. "Clovis is ninety-one miles from here," noted Lubbock-based Holly historian Bill Griggs. "It's on Mountain Time. Buddy and the band used to play a game called Beat the Clock, driving so fast they would arrive earlier than they left."

"Holly and the Crickets camped out at Petty's studio for days at a time," added musician, songwriter, and pop musicologist Marshall Crenshaw, "using it as a combination laboratory and playground. They were the first rock and rollers to approach the recording process in this manner."

Working this way, they rerecorded one of the songs that fell with a thud during the Nashville sessions. Petty became their manager, and started shopping the tapes. Strangely enough, they took the work to Brunswick, a division of the company that also owned Decca. Taken from a key line in the John Wayne film *The Searchers*, "That'll Be the Day" slowly scaled to the top of the charts, selling millions of copies.

Over the next year, Holly and the Crickets had about half a dozen more solid hits. Yet the band discovered that they weren't getting any richer, at least not in ratio to their growing popularity. Holly demanded an accounting from Petty, and when he didn't get one, he fired him as his manager. The Crickets didn't want to split with Holly, so he separated from them as well. He may well have been looking for an excuse, as he had fallen in love with the receptionist from his music publishing company in New York, and wanted to move to be near her. He took up residence in the bohemian central that was Greenwich Village in the 1950s. There, he and his new bride, Maria Elena, née Santiago, set up house. Very soon afterward, she was expecting a child.

Petty, however, still held the lion's share of the money, and getting to it would be an arduous task. So Holly signed on for a tour with a band of "New Crickets" that included Waylon Jennings on bass and Tommy Allsup on guitar.

"It was crazy, daddy—the goings-on Friday night at George Devine's Million Dollar Ballroom," wrote a tongue-in-cheek Joe Botsford of the *Milwaukee Sentinel* of an early stop in the tour. "Nearly 6,000 young people turned out to hear such rock 'n' roll stars as Buddy Holly and the Crickets, Big Bopper, Dion and the Belmonts, and Ritchie Valens. If you haven't heard them, you haven't lived, man . . . Backed by the Crickets—two young guitarists and a drummer—Buddy Holly rocked his beanpole figure on stage, clutched his little guitar against his loud red coat and jerked his way through 'Peggy Sue.' His voice was scarcely audible over the raucous guitars, but he itchy-twitched in grand style, and that's what the kids wanted."

The ill-conceived tour had the five acts gallivanting all over the

Midwest in midwinter. The temperature hovered in the twenty-five-below-zero range. "We had to burn newspapers in the aisle [of the bus] to keep warm," said Allsup.

Nor was this the kind of bus we currently associate with a musician touring, full of luxuries and amenities. The bus the musicians traveled on for hours throughout the frozen tundra of the Midwestern winter was basically a school bus. An old one. That broke down several times. In fact, before the stop in Clear Lake, Iowa, the bus had broken down, the heat had failed, and the drummer was hospitalized with frostbite. Holly filled in on drums for Dion and the Belmonts' portion of the show, then strapped on a guitar for his own set while the Belmonts' Carlo Mastrangelo took over the kit for Holly. "Dion says, 'Can you imagine that he'd be playing drums behind us?'" recalled Fred Milano of the Belmonts. "So I went over to Buddy and said, 'Did you ever think you'd back up Dion and the Belmonts on drums?' And he said, 'No, what a great thing.' He felt the same way we did."

By the time the tour hit Clear Lake, several things were going on. Richardson had a bad cold and wanted to try and sleep it off. "He held the record at the time for staying awake the most hours," said Milano. "So we'd kid him, 'What do you mean, you're tired?'"

Holly's supply of clean clothing was running dangerously low and he, too, yearned for a good night's sleep, as opposed to a ten-hour, overnight bus trip to North Dakota. So, before the show, he chartered a plane. He figured he could get to Fargo in two hours instead of ten, get eight hours of sleep, and still have some time to get his laundry done.

The show itself went well. Jennings recalled, "It was a real up night. Everybody was rocking."

When the show was over, Valens called his mother—same as every night. Holly called Maria and had someone hold the phone while he played and sang for her, as usual. While Holly had booked the plane for his band, apparently Valens got Allsup to agree to toss a coin for the seat. Allsup lost. Richardson prevailed on Jennings to give up his seat. Perhaps they rolled dice for it. As Jennings would later recall to Richardson's son, "Your daddy was a good ol' boy and a hell of a crapshooter."

When Holly found out, he told Jennings, "Well, I hope that old bus freezes over." Jennings called back, "Well, I hope your plane crashes." The plane did.

"Never a week goes by I don't think about it," said Jennings.

Rock and roll was still young and, as far as the gatekeepers were concerned, barbarous. Many local newspapers didn't cover the crash at all, preferring to cover Senate Majority Leader Lyndon Baines Johnson receiving the Heart Association's Heart-of-the-Year Award from President Dwight D. Eisenhower. In American cities it was news, but not big news. It was, of course, a major topic of the day on the rock-and-roll radio shows. It even made the television in New York. That was how Maria Elena found out. "I turned on the TV and heard that he had died. I couldn't take it in."

Two days later, she miscarried.

The band was incommunicado, traveling that wide expanse of the Midwest and trying to get some sleep. "We were on the bus," Milano said. "We didn't know what happened until two o'clock the next afternoon when we got [there]. It was a shock. A heartbreaker. Then when we called home, everyone thought we were dead, because that's what had been reported on the radio."

"At first I couldn't believe it," added Allison, a long time friend of Holly's. "We thought the whole thing was a mistake."

Fan reaction was similar. "That's one of our heroes who fixed," Griggs recalled thinking. "That's not supposed to happen when you're a teenager."

"I think maybe we didn't realize until later just how critical that moment was," noted New York radio legend "Cousin" Bruce Morrow, who was on the air that night, "because I don't think we realized until then how important the music really was. We didn't realize that rock 'n' roll was already becoming a family member and this was the first death, the first loss. That's why the impact—emotional more than the musical—is so strong today."

In the best and most callous show-biz tradition, the show went on. "We had to make a decision," said Milano, "whether or not to play that night. Frankie Sardo, us, Wayon Jennings, and Buddy's guitar player, Tommy, got together. Everybody agreed that Buddy and the others would want us to play."

It became a career-making night for a local fifteen-year-old. Robert Velline had a duck's-ass haircut and a rock quartet. He also had tickets to see the show that night. Instead, he wound up performing both with his band and at the front of Holly's band. They would do it again three years later in a recording studio. By then Velline had scored a handful of hits on his own, including a Top 10 cover of the Clovers' "Devil or Angel" and a gold, chart-topping, Brill Building ballad called "Take Good Care of My Baby" under the name Bobby Vee.

The real tragedy of the event, of course, was the loss of all that potential. Holly had just finished producing Jennings' first solo project, "Jole Blon." He knew his way around a recording studio, and was absolutely fearless about recording. His own new projects included work with strings and a session with R&B sax-giant King Curtis. There's no telling where he might have gone.

As big an influence as Berry is, so is Holly. His format of two guitars, bass, and drums set the format for the British invasion. The Beatles worshiped him to the point of parodying his band's name. John Lennon also cited Ritchie Valens as an influence on the band, and pioneering rock journalist Lester Bangs proclaimed Valens' "La Bamba" one of the deep roots of punk.

The tragedy provided a windfall for many. Clear Lake holds an annual event on the third of February. Tourists also come to see the place where the music died. "It fills every hotel and motel room in a twenty-mile radius," said the head of the local chamber of commerce, noting that rooms were often booked a year in advance.

Eventually, Maria Elena also began to reap the benefits of being the widow of a star who would eventually sell over 40 million albums. While she claimed, "I'm not rich, rich," she became the benefactor and protector of the Holly estate, maintaining her name even after remarrying "for reasons of the estate."

Valens' family left their home in Pacoima and did a pretty fair approximation of a disappearing act. In the wake of the tragedy there have been stamps and memorials, plaques and exhibits, and movie bios of Holly and Valens. Holly was a member of the first group of artists inducted into the Rock and Roll Hall of Fame.

There have also been reissues and lawsuits, settlements and skirmishes. One of the biggest Buddy Holly fans on the planet, Sir Paul McCartney, found out that Petty was having deep financial problems and bought his Holly publishing interests. Since then, at least the publishing royalties have been paid on time.

Every year, McCartney throws a party on September 7 to mark Holly's birth. Ironically, it was after attending one of these soirees in

1978 that Keith Moon of the Who died of alcohol-induced asphyxiation. By then, however, death and rock-and-roll were at least on speaking terms. The deaths of Jimi Hendrix, Janis Joplin, John Lennon, Ricky Nelson, and on and on, while shocking, did not feel like a violation. You can lose your innocence in that way only once.

Chapter 11: 1963

Beatlemania

That's a look of surprise and joy on Paul McCartney's face just after he'd received a certificate from BMI certifying "Yesterday" as the first five-million-performance song in history. The performing rights organization translates that to 250,000 hours of US radio and TV play. McCartney gratefully accepted his award in his UK recording studio. (Photo: BMI/David Koppel)

The story has been told and retold to the point of folklore. In the seaport town of Liverpool, in the North of England, John Lennon started working in a variety of skiffle groups as he made his way through grammar (high) school during the mid-'50s. In 1956, he met Paul McCartney, three years his junior, and they started playing together.

"My dad was a musician," said McCartney. "He had a little band in the '20s called the Jim Max Band. Because of him, I knew many of the songs that the old crowd knew. John, too. One of John's favorite songs was 'Don't Blame Me.' People . . . never associate him with the kinds of songs his mum taught him. His mum was a musical lady. She taught him banjo chords."

While many didn't see this, one of their contemporaries, Pete Townshend of the Who, did. "The Beatles, to me, belong to the other era," he said. "You know, the Beatles belong with Johnny Mercer and Rodgers and Hart, they're from that, they straddled that era. They became something rock and roll later on. I know that it's sacrilegious to some people to say this."

McCartney introduced Lennon to a friend of his, George Harrison. "George's relationship with me," Lennon would recall, "was one of a young follower and older guy. . . . I was already an art student when Paul and George were still in grammar school."

Harrison was an acolyte of Scotty Moore, Chet Atkins, Carl Perkins, Chuck Berry, and Buddy Holly. "George Harrison once told me, 'Man, I heard the lick from "Matchbox" and I said, 'That's it! That's what I'm going to do, I'm going to play,'" Perkins, who met the group in 1964 recalled. "I just don't hear it. I never thought I did anything on the guitar or anything in the business that merited lasting or especially enticing some young pickers to say, 'I want to play like that.'"

All three of them liked Holly and Berry and a wide variety of American rock and roll and rhythm and blues that came across the Atlantic with the sailors docked in port. With this musical common ground, they formed the Quarrymen (after the Quarry Bank grammar school they attended), which, a few personnel changes later, became the Silver Beatles.

In 1960, they answered the call of the Reeperbahn in Germany, where bands could earn a nice piece of change, but had to play between eighteen and thirty-five sets a week. The Silver Beatles, and many other Liverpudlian bands, would go back and forth between the burgeoning club scene at home and the madness of the Reeperbahn. They did all kinds of gigs, from playing in strip clubs to taking up residence in the Cavern, a club underneath a warehouse.

"They were doing songs we'd grown up with but were scared to do," said one of their Liverpool contemporaries, Billy Kinsley of the Merseybeats. "You didn't do Chuck Berry or Gene Vincent songs."

They became a popular club attraction in both Liverpool and Germany. One of the artists they met on the Reeperbahn was a local Liverpool celebrity, Tony Sheridan. Sheridan had earned the nickname "the teacher" among the Liverpudlian bands, and had opened for Gene Vincent and Eddie Cochrane. He took the Beatles in as his backing band at a recording session where he cut Mersey-style skiffle versions of "My Bonnie (Lies Over the Ocean)," "The Saints Go Marching In," and several similar tunes (frequently available on one of the all-time-great budget-bin albums). This session spawned a German single which became a sought-after commodity among Sheridan and Beatle fans in Liverpool.

It was not something the regular distributors were bringing with them, being a German import and all, so record merchant Brian Epstein, who ran the grammophone department in his father's furniture store, was unaware of it. However, after numerous requests for the record, he went to the Cavern to see what all the fuss was about. "It struck me that there was more than local patriotism in it," he said. "As soon as I heard them I thought they had something. I felt they were great. And I liked them, liked them very much indeed. I liked them even more offstage than on."

Epstein agreed to manage them. However, he soon discovered that what played in Liverpool would not necessarily go over in London. As the purveyor of the "largest record selection in the North," as his store proudly proclaimed, he had lots of connections with the record companies. Every single one of them turned the Beatles down. Twice. One company said that they weren't interested because "guitar bands are on their way out."

They were finally picked up by EMI. In 1962 they put out their first single, "Love Me Do," which sank like a stone. However, their second single, "Please Please Me" caught fire in the beginning of 1963, and suddenly a phenomenon that had been local to the north spread to the entire country. England was infested with Beatles.

While the Beatles had had the musical goods since the Reeperbahn days, and Lennon and McCartney were developing into one of the best songwriting teams ever, there was more to the adoration. They had a look, they had an attitude. When Epstein had met them, they were wearing leathers. Once an aspiring dress designer, Epstein helped them reinvent their look, giving them haircuts that looked something like the historic tonsures of Benedictine monks and dressing them in lapel-less jackets. Between the sound and their spontaneous wit and intelligence, they became the object of desire of thousands of English schoolgirls, but the Queen Mother liked them too.

Even serious music critics were beginning to sit up and take notice. The London *Times* music critic (that's all he's identified as) talked about their "chains of pandiatonic clusters" and "the major tonic sevenths and ninths built into their tunes and the flat submediant key switches." He continued, "The virtue of the Beatles' repertory is that, apparently, they do it themselves: Three of the four are composers [and] they are versatile instrumentalists. . . . The other trademark of their compositions is a firm and purposeful bass line with a musical life of its own."

Lennon certainly agreed with the latter part. "Paul was one of the most innovative bass player[s] that ever played the bass, and half the stuff that's going on now is directly ripped off from his Beatles period. . . . He is a great musician who plays the bass like few others could play it."

The New Statesman proclaimed, "The Beatles are an agreeable bunch of kids, quite unsinister (unlike some American teenage comets), with that charming combination of flamboyance and a certain hip self-mickey-taking, which is the ideal of their age group. . . . They are probably just about to begin their slow descent: the moment when someone thinks of making a film with a pop idol normally marks the peak of his curve. In twenty years' time nothing of them will survive."

The correspondent from *She* disagreed. "We'll have to watch out for John and Paul's long-term progress as song writers. If *that* keeps pace with the times, then there's no reason why the Beatles shouldn't be top of the charts in the 1970s."

As their fame rose, they toured England, opening for one of their idols, Roy Orbison. Orbison recalled that he was lucky he even got on stage at night. "After their fourteenth or fifteenth encore," he said, "Paul and John grabbed me by the arm and said, 'Yankee go home.' They then asked me how they could make it in the States and I told them, 'Dress like you're doing, keep the hair, say you're British, and get on a show like the *Ed Sullivan Show.*'"

They wanted to break in the U.S., but Capitol, the U.S. arm of EMI, didn't want to be bothered. English groups had historically tanked in the U.S. The U.S. exported rock and roll. Their first U.S. recordings came out via one-offs with more astute independent record companies, forcing Capitol's hand to release "I Want to Hold Your Hand." To the company's complete astonishment, it shot to #1, and stayed there for seven weeks, and went gold. Swan Records put out "She Loves You," which replaced "I Want to Hold Your Hand" on the top of the charts for another two weeks. Beatlemania had hit the States with the force of a British tsunami.

On February 9, 1964, with two #1 singles under their belt already, they took Orbison's advice and went on the *Ed Sullivan Show*. Two days before, they checked into the Plaza Hotel in New York, one of the fanciest hotels in the world. When word got out, the hotel was besieged by hundreds of girls. The band had to hire a security agency to help the stodgy hotel maintain some sense of decorum. The hotel only knew the members by name (that was how they registered) and knew also that they were "financially responsible."

That Sunday, some 73 million Americans watched them on TV. It was one of the watershed events (*turning points*, if you will) of rock and roll. For those who were too young for Elvis, it was a defining moment. It sent more people learning to play the guitar than any single happening before or after. Suddenly, everyone on two continents wanted to be a Beatle.

The Beatles' arrival in America couldn't have come at a better time for them or America. While people often portray popular music as moribund at the time, that's way too easy and not really accurate. On the East Coast and spreading westward, the noveau-folk-music movement had taken hold and generated a focal point in a young

Minnesotan in Manhattan, Bob Dylan. On the West Coast, the Beach Boys and friends spread the gospel of the surf. In Detroit, the Motown sound had once again started to change the way people perceived "black music" by giving it the patina of pop. So for every novelty like "Sukiyaki," "On Top of Spaghetti," and "Tie Me Kangaroo Down, Sport," for every MOR ballad like "Blue on Blue," there was "Wipe Out," "Pride and Joy," "Just One Look," "Blowin' in the Wind" and "Surf City."

None of this, however, was causing the full-blown hysteria of Elvis in the mid-'50s. The nation was still in shock from the Cuban Missile Crisis and the assassination of President John F. Kennedy. The country was about due for a good scream, both metaphorically and physically, and the Beatles provided the impetus.

By the end of the year, the Beatles had taken America by storm. They placed nineteen singles into the Top 40, including seven chart toppers that spent a total of twenty-two weeks at #1. Four of those singles went gold. Their names graced eleven albums on the album charts, including such unlikely ones as *The Beatles vs. The Four Seasons* and interview discs.

It also caused many to reassess the Beatles. For example, the same journalist who, in covering "the siege at the Plaza," described a Beatle as "a British rock 'n' roll singer who looks like an old English sheep dog and bays like an American foxhound" seemed to reconsider his position several months later on their return to the U.S., discovering what the U.K. media already knew. "The most important thing they have going for them is not their music but the fact that they are charming, funny fellows. The teenagers have said this all along and an older public is discovering it now, principally through their movie *A Hard Day's Night*."

The film was a masterstroke and cemented the Beatles' place in pop culture. When everyone expected the run-of-the-mill rock-sploitation flick, the Beatles gave a glance at their mettle, temperament, and John's art-school background with the film. The movie captured the madness of life as a Beatle and was funny. In director Richard Lester, they found a truly simpatico creative partner. Lester himself had been a musician, singing in vocal groups in college, bumming around Europe playing his guitar and the piano for meals and lodging. He had already made a couple more routine rock films, but more important, he had worked on Peter Sellers' *The Mouse on the Moon*. He combined all those sensibilities and the Beatles' own innate charm into a film that became a major hit, and not just with hysterical teens. The kids came for the music, but the humor won the parents over. The universal consensus became that the Beatles were okay in every sense. The soundtrack album sold a million copies in four days. The phenomenon became even more huge.

Suddenly the record companies—who took a year to shed conventional wisdom that English music didn't sell in the U.S.—started signing up English acts by the dozen. "[In] the early '60s," said Ahmet Ertegun, "it didn't take a genius to see that, first with the Beatles, the Rolling Stones, and the Who, these were very, very new and important openings toward rock and roll. We didn't have those artists. I had to get into that area. We couldn't just sit by. Besides, I love that music."

During 1964, the Dave Clark Five, Dusty Springfield, the Searchers, Billy J. Kramer and the Dakotas, Peter and Gordon, Gerry & the Pacemakers, the Animals, Manfred Mann, the Zombies, Herman's Hermits, and the Rolling Stones all broke through to the U.S. Top 20. Not only had the Beatles won over the hearts and minds of America, but they invited their friends to come in on their coattails.

To help promote his band, Andrew Loog Oldham, manager of the Rolling Stones, whispered in someone's ear about a rivalry between the bands. Indeed, they did seem—on the surface—to speak to different sides of the youth conflicts that had started in the early sixties between arty youth called mods and the more earthy rockers. During a press conference scene in *A Hard Day's Night*, the Beatles were famously asked which side they were on, to which Ringo replied, "Neither. We're mockers."

"That was wholly a press thing that someone started," said Starr, "and once it got started it just went on its merry way. There was never any bad feeling between us and the Stones. We used to hang out a lot. John and Paul had written that first song ("I Wanna Be Your Man") for them in the early days. We went to see them when they were first playing clubs."

Brian Epstein, in addition to refining the band's image, refined the way rock and roll did business. Coming from a retail background and a family that had run businesses in the North of England for several generations, he had business savvy, but he also had a streak of honesty unusual in the business end of rock and roll. He genuinely wanted to look out for his artists. By the spring of 1964, he represented eight groups. "I want to be able to influence and help personally the people that work for me—I want to help them realize themselves, give the best they can. I believe I can help them. . . ."

One of the ways he helped them (though it would ultimately hurt them) was with the ingenious idea of taking the group public. He floated a stock issue for the group's intellectual property, an idea a quarter century ahead of its time. Within two years, the stock had quadrupled. "In three or four years, we could be has-beens," Lennon said as the issue floated, while the group was on location in the Bahamas filming the follow-up to A *Hard Day's Night*. "I want to be a has-been with money."

Having money and the ear of the Queen Mother brought on something that the English regarded as outrageous and scandalous at the time. When the Queen's Honors List came out late in the spring of 1965, the names John Lennon, Paul McCartney, George Harrison, and Richard Starkey (Ringo's given name) were on it as new members of the British Empire. This was yet another step toward respectability.

It held them in good stead when they went to make their next triumph, playing the Budokan in Tokyo, the stadium that the Japanese had built for the martial arts competitions during the 1964 Tokyo Olympics. The venue had not become the concert venue it is now, but the fact that the Beatles had just been honored by the Queen helped grease the negotiations between English and Japanese diplomats that followed the announcement of their intention to play the concert. Japan has never quite recovered. By the end of the 1990s, they were still the number two market—behind the U.S. but ahead of the U.K.— for Beatles' memorabilia. In the Roppongi district—Tokyo's answer to der Reeperbahn—perhaps a dozen Japanese Beatle bands, many of whom don't speak a word of English and sing phonetically, can be heard in clubs like the Cavern (which has branches in several other Japanese cities) and Abbey Road. Plans are afoot to open the first John Lennon museum as part of a new 35,000-seat venue about an hour out of Tokyo.

The Beatles' dynamic was starting to change with success. George Martin once described the Lennon-McCartney songwriting partnership with this image: "Imagine two people pulling on a rope, smiling at each other and pulling all the time with all their might. The tension between the two of them made for the bond."

"Gradually, things changed," Martin adds. "The boys went into their little spheres and there was more rivalry brewing between John and Paul. In truth, they were never great collaborators in the sense of sitting down and writing together."

"There were three ways John and I would write," McCartney said. "We would sit down with nothing and two guitars . . . that was writing from the ground up. 'She Loves You,' 'From Me to You,' 'This Boy' were all written that way. Another way of writing was when one of us had an idea . . . and we'd both sit and write together. 'Norwegian Wood' was like that. . . . The third way was when one had an idea, and we weren't going to be seeing each other for a week, and the idea was just too hot to stop. . . . It always got a bit more bizarre when the two of us got going."

The writing and the relationship became strained, even more so when the band decided—against McCartney's wishes—to stop playing live after their third tour of the U.S. John had made an offhand statement to a British journalist that the Beatles were more popular at the time than Jesus. This sparked protests and picketing at their shows. That was one reason Lennon, especially, wanted to get off the road. Another was they really didn't need it. For most bands, even—perhaps especially—today, playing live is the only place they make any money, especially if they don't write their own songs. The Beatles did write their own songs, and by their midtwenties they were all comfortably well off. John had other interests he wanted to explore, including acting and writing books. Harrison had discovered the vast Indian community and its music, and had started to learn to play the sitar and learn about Hinduism.

All these interests and tensions manifested themselves in their post-*Help* album, *Rubber Soul*. It had George playing the sitar, adding a thoroughly exotic tone to the song "Norwegian Wood." It also had the flat-out ballads, "Yesterday" (on the English version), "In My Life," and "Michelle," songs with beautiful melodies but absolutely none of the Beatles' rock edge.

It was followed by the landmark *Revolver*, with songs like "Eleanor Rigby," which eschewed rock instruments entirely in favor of a string octet; "Tomorrow Never Knows," which used Harrison's sitar, treated guitar, overdubs and some of Ringo's most inspired drumming to chilling effect as Lennon sang verses from his own nightmares and the Tibetan *Book of the Dead*; "Got to Get You into My Life" with its full-blown soul horn section; Harrison's scabrous classic "Taxman," and the beautiful "Here, There and Everywhere." It was the album that changed everything in rock and roll, an experiment that helped push rock a quantum leap farther than anything before it. It tacitly—and perhaps, with songs like "Dr. Robert," less than tacitly—espoused the use of drugs, one of the first mainstream records ever so influenced by hallucinogens. The two most amazing things about *Revolver*, though, were how well it held together and that it produced two hit singles, though that was becoming less and less important as the album-oriented "underground" radio on the FM dial played nearly every track. More than any other album, it defined rock and roll as an art form and defied anyone to argue about it.

If *Revolver* announced this new direction, their next album confirmed it. "I remember hitting upon this idea," McCartney recalled, "and saying to the group, 'Okay, for this one album, we won't be the Beatles. This is going to be our safety valve. We're going to think of a new name for us, a new way of being, a new way of recording, everything fresh, and by the way, I've written a song about something called Sergeant Pepper's Lonely Hearts Club Band.' We agreed we weren't the Beatles anymore. When we went in to make the record it wasn't 'John' singing on this or that track. It was anyone John wanted to be. And it was quite good. We did stuff on that record that we had never done before."

Indeed, they did stuff that had never been done before at all, at least not in the context of rock and roll. It was one of the first albums to flow entirely from a concept. "*Sergeant Pepper* is called the first concept album," Lennon said, "but it doesn't go anywhere. All my contributions to the album have absolutely nothing to do with this idea of Sergeant Pepper and his band; but it works 'cause we *said* it worked, and that's how the album appeared. But it was not as put-together as it sounds, except for Sergeant Pepper introducing Billy Shears and the so-called reprise. Every other song could have been on any other album."

But what songs! "Lucy in the Sky with Diamonds" practically invented psychedelic rock. "A Day in the Life" incorporates elements of musique concrète (one of the things the *Times* critic accused them of all those years ago), music hall, and beat poetry. Even Ringo on "A Little Help from My Friends" is classic. If *Revolver* threw away the rule book for what you could do on a rock record, the Beatles output after it rewrote that book, and *Sergeant Pepper* was the first chapter.

As if they needed any more publicity, in the wake of such an astounding (and popular) achievement, around this time the rumor started spreading that Paul had died in a car accident. The stories grew and became so pervasive that novelty songs were written about it, it was parodied in *Mad* magazine, debated in a mock TV trial presided over by F. Lee Bailey and even in a *Batman* comic. All manner of evidence was posited:

- Paul looked straight out from the album of *Sergeant Pepper* because it was a cardboard cutout.
- The cutout held a black English horn.
- On the back cover, Paul has his back to the camera.

This went on for several more albums until Paul finally felt it necessary to answer these rumors. He had been on his estate in Scotland. He confirmed that he was very much alive, but "if I were dead, I'd be the last to know."

Their next musical adventure proved that even the Beatles' misfires were brilliant. *Magical Mystery Tour* was a television special that was way too spacey to be pop and too cheesy to be really hip. However, once again, the music was brilliant. "Penny Lane" found Paul really digging into personal memories, as did John in "Strawberry Fields Forever," both referring to landmarks of their Liverpool youth. "All You Need Is Love," "Hello Goodbye," and "The Fool on the Hill," each pushed the songwriting and/or studio production envelope just a little further.

Several things happened that drove the wedge between the Beatles deeper. One was meeting Maharishi Mahesh Yogi. The other, almost on the same weekend, was the death of Brian Epstein. Suddenly they had lost the rudder on their professional lives and had, almost on a whim, entrusted their spiritual life to someone they barely knew. By this time, even more than in the early part of the decade, anything the Beatles did was newsworthy. Their trip to India to meditate with Maharishi Mahesh Yogi was covered extensively. The experience left a bad taste in Lennon's mouth, which was reflected on the group's next album, *The Beatles*, a.k.a. the "White Album." Another tour de force, unlike *Sergeant Pepper*, this sprawling two-album set was a mess, but a beautiful one, with one of Harrison's best songs, "While My Guitar Gently Weeps." Even Ringo wrote a neat little tune, "Don't Pass Me By." This album was one of their first to feature major (though unbilled) guest artists; Eric Clapton plays, as does Nicky Hopkins. It is evident, however, that this band is losing cohesion. "George and I," said Ringo, "were sort of . . . not lost in the shuffle, but there were other priorities besides getting our names forward."

Business was taking its toll also. In the wake of Epstein's death, the group signed on with American business manager Allan Klein, against Paul's judgment. Additionally, one of the major stockholders of Northern Songs sold out, and suddenly John and Paul were no longer the majority stockholders in their own publishing.

John had also left his wife and child, again to the shock and concern of Paul. He had met Yoko Ono, a transplanted Japanese conceptual artist and painter. She started teaching John about a lot of the artistic theory that he both seemed to know intrinsically and began learning in art college before the Beatles had taken off.

As a result of all this, the Beatles were not getting along at all. They were worried about their songs and, for the first time in their careers, they had serious concerns about the business of being the Beatles. They shelved their next project, *Let It Be*, temporarily. Martin didn't think it was even worth mixing. "They were not happy days for the boys," Martin recalled, "and the result was not their best record. John was insistent that it should be a 'live' album and would not let me do any editing, any overdubbing, or any other instruments."

Eventually, it fell into the mad genius hands of Phil Spector, who tinkered with it slightly, adding his characteristic level of "three minute symphony" bombast to several tracks. "When I heard the eventual disc," Martin mused, "the only person more surprised than I was Paul. . . . It turned into the most un-Beatle album ever to be issued."

In the meantime, the group put together their swan song, *Abbey Road*. Ironically, Harrison has two of the best songs on the album, his standard, "Something" and the beautiful "Here Comes the Sun." It also had Lennon and McCartney powerhouses like "Come Together," "You Never Give Me Your Money," and "Because." Starr's charmingly silly "Octopus's Garden" is also a high point. The side-two suite is inventive and contains the fitting epitaph for the band—"In the end, the love you take is equal to the love you make."

"When you talk about the Beatles' influence," said Jack Hues of the '80s pop group Wang Chung, "when we were sort of growing up with them, what was impressive about them, and what's very rare with rock bands now was that they progressed musically from the early 'I Want to Hold Your Hand' rather than just progressing with their image. They progressed musically and they got more and more into expressing themselves in a musical way. 'Strawberry Fields' and 'I Am the Walrus' and George Martin scoring their stuff like 'She's Leaving Home' are really major achievements and something that really hasn't been attempted since. *Sergeant Pepper* and the "White Album" are real high points of that ability to write music, and their image being a secondary thing. It's all exploratory in a very good way. That is an influence and a model."

"Lennon and McCartney are to popular music," said '90s British soul star Terence Trent D'arby, "what Bach and Mozart represented in the annals of the vocabulary of what we call classical music."

"The Beatles' myth," said producer Don Was, who worked with Ringo in later years and did music for the Beatles biopic *Backbeat*, "is a lot more important than what they were like in reality. The myth, for someone my age, is very important. Here are these heralds of freedom. These are the guys who made the statement to me, you can wear your hair the way that you want to, you can live your life the way that you want to, you can turn your guitar up as loud as you want to. Don't let anyone tell you what to do with your life."

The most remarkable thing about all the Beatles is that, after six years of scuffling, the recorded creative output of the group, with all its growth and change, was accomplished in just eight years. "I was amazed it lasted so long," Martin maintained. "It was 1962 when I started with them, and we made the last record in 1970. That's a hell of a long time for four people to live in one another's pockets."

"John and I as writers, and the Beatles as a whole," said McCartney, "we were virtually an impossible act to follow."

"The whole Beatles thing," said Lennon, "was beyond comprehension."

"It was a magical mixture," Harrison agreed, "and it had something to do with a higher fate, but I can't explain why it's moved the world so much. . . . Sometimes I wonder whether I was really a part of it or whether it was all a dream. . . . This is a wonderful form of pension fund, and it's nice to see that it's still making people happy."

The band broke up shortly after *Abbey Road*, though they took a while to announce it. Nearly all the former Beatles acknowledged that they were just not as good apart as they were together. People wanted more, but there was just too much acrimony. McCartney formed a new band called Wings and had some extraordinary success. It seemed as if Harrison had bottled up all his creative energy, and his first post-Beatles recording was the epochal three-disc *All Things Shall Pass*. At least in the beginning, the most successful former Beatle turned out to be Starr. He also was the only one that everyone in the band seemed to get along with. "They all worked with me," he said. "We were all doing things for each other, still. On the *Ringo* album, everyone is on it but none of them were in the same room at the same time. John would come down and George would come down and we went to England and recorded Paul. Paul was doing solo stuff, I played with him. John did solo stuff, I played with him. George doing his solo stuff, I played with him. I seemed to be like the connection."

Lennon made a few post-Beatles albums, then took a ten-year hiatus from the rock wars. He was recording his first new music in ten years in 1980 when he was shot by a deranged fan. Suddenly all hopes of a reunion fell by the wayside. "As far as I'm concerned," Harrison said, "there won't be a Beatles reunion as long as John Lennon remains dead."

But there's dead and there's dead. After twenty-five years of antipathy among the former band members, managers, and record companies, by 1995 everything was settled. The Apple Corp. they started after the sale of Northern Music was an ongoing concern and so, even after twenty-five years of not getting along, they still were in business together. Harrison had had a recent scare with cancer. The previous year a two-record set of the group's performances at the BBC in the prehistoric sixties became the third-fastest-selling record of the year. The billion records that the *Guinness Book of World Records* asserts they had sold by 1985 had probably grown by another fifty percent. So they finally got back together to sort through the bits and pieces of tape that they had in the archives. To this endeavor, John's widow,

Yoko Ono, offered a pair of John's unreleased demo tapes, him singing a couple of songs she felt would be appropriate for the Beatles. And so, in 1995, along with the music on the first *Anthology* set, there was new Beatles music.

The song was produced, not by George Martin, but by Harrison and Starr's friend and producer Jeff Lynne. "Jeff Lynne was surprised," said the group's long-time press agent Derek Taylor, "at how fast they got into it, considering the three of them hadn't really played together for a long, long time. But they always did know how to do it."

The single hit the Top 10 and went gold. All three *Anthology* albums topped the charts. Clearly, people were still interested, twenty-five years on, in the Beatles' musical legacy. "When people see me, they see a Beatle," Harrison said some thirty years after the band broke up and shortly before he, himself, succumbed to cancer. "As far as I'm concerned, that was a long time ago."

Bob Dylan Goes Electric
at the
Newport Folk Festival

One can only wonder what the audience members at the
Newport Folk Festival were expecting that July day when they gathered in the field to see Peter, Paul, and Mary and others on this high-
light night of the festival, with Bob Dylan as the star attraction. Dylan
had already set off the first salvo of his metamorphosis into a rock-

and-roll performer half a year earlier with the release of *Bringing It All Back Home*. About a week before the Newport Folk Festival, a Bob Dylan single hit the streets, a Dylan single unlike anything he had ever released before. While the album *Bringing It All Back Home* had a rock feel, when "Like a Rolling Stone" came out just before Newport the fans who had been following Dylan for the last four years felt he had slapped them across the face. The Woody Guthrie purism had vanished. In its place were electric guitars and a Hammond organ. To his fans, it was blasphemy!

Yet, earlier on in the day the audience had been entertained by sets from the definitely and unapologetically electric Paul Butterfield Blues Band. That group's guitarist, Mike Bloomfield, had played on "Like a Rolling Stone."

Though it was evident that many of his old fans felt betrayed, Dylan gained a whole new following with this bold break from the folk tradition. Though even Dylan is not sure where his songs come from, it is evident that he was contemplating this break for a while, and had been a rock fan for even longer. "I had about three days off up there to get some stuff together. It just came, you know. It started with that 'La Bamba' riff."

Another departure for Dylan was that the song was recorded specifically to be released as a single. Yet the finished recording of the song was over six minutes long, and Dylan refused to cut it down to the traditional three-minute length. Despite this, the song came close to the top of the charts, and remains the biggest Bob Dylan single to date. Throughout that spring and summer, the Byrds' version of his "Mr. Tambourine Man" also rode the pop charts, peaking at the top in June. It was not Dylan's first foray as a writer into these depths or heights. Besides topping the charts with "Blowin' in the Wind"—at the time Warner Brothers fastest-selling single ever—Peter, Paul, and Mary had taken another Dylan song, "Don't Think Twice, It's All Right" into the Top 10 two years earlier.

However, until that day in July of 1965, the Newport crowd had regarded Dylan as "one of theirs," a folkie purist, one of "Woody's Children." His set a year earlier had caused unprecedented excitement at the usually staid event. His 1965 set had sold out the day of sale in hours.

Even his notes for the festival program were cryptic and borderline surreal, the adventures of Horseman and Photochick trying to escape "a thousand angry plumbers all in chrome suits," while "The dykes have broken down [and] . . . started beating everybody up and putting them in closets." Not your usual biography.

But then Dylan had never been your usual performer, and being cryptic was a way of life and art for him. He started, however, in quite an ordinary way for a musician who went through his teen years in the mid-'50s. "I always wanted to be a guitar player and singer," he said. "Since I was ten, eleven or twelve, it was all that I did that interested me."

Dylan was born Robert Allen Zimmerman in Duluth. After his father survived a bout with polio that left the formerly very physical man crippled and in pain for the rest of his life, the elder Zimmerman moved his family in with his mother and went into business with his brothers who were electricians in Hibbing, a town in Minnesota's Iron Range. Dylan's father ran their retail outlet.

Throughout high school, young Robert played guitar in a variety of rock-and-roll bands. His stated goal in his high school yearbook was to play rock with Little Richard.

After graduation, he went off to St. Paul to attend the University of Minnesota. However, he spent more time playing coffeehouses in the area's bohemian district (every city had one), dubbed "Dinkytown." "I was singing stuff like 'Ruby Lee' by the Sunny Mountain Boys, and 'Jack O' Diamonds' by Odetta," he said, "and somehow, because of my earlier rock 'n' roll background was unconsciously crossing the two styles. This made me different from your regular folk singer. . . ."

He became immersed in the folk movement. This many-pronged effort reached out to people, seeking songs from people in areas like Appalachia, then playing them for eager audiences. The beneficiaries of the movement included country blues singers like Big Bill Broonzy and Huddie "Leadbelly" Ledbetter, songcatchers—people who would go up to the mountains to find songs in their most isolated and pure form—like Alan Lomax, ethnic artists like the Clancy Brothers, and people with a guitar and a talent for reaching an audience, like Woody Guthrie. During the '40s, the folk movement had developed a focal point with the Almanac Singers, which included Pete Seeger and Guthrie. They would play union rallies and college campuses and did very well until the '50s wave of anticommunist hysteria enveloped the nation. Seeger went on to have hits with the Weavers, recording pop versions of Ledbetter's "Goodnight, Irene," Seeger's own "Kisses Sweeter Than Wine," and many others.

After a bit over a year, Zimmerman decided that Dinkytown had earned its name and he had learned all that he could there. He headed off by thumb, with a suitcase and a guitar, to New York, with stops in Wisconsin and Chicago, among other places. He got to New York in time to visit Woody Guthrie in the hospital as the elder statesman of the folk movement lay dying of Huntington's disease. They became friends. By that time Zimmerman had learned a vast number of Guthrie's songs.

He became a local legend, playing clubs and getting to know the people. Audiences were charmed by his acoustic rock-and-roll presentation of folk music. He played harmonica on a session for Harry Belafonte, opened shows at Folk City. A *New York Times* copy editor and sometimes music critic, Robert Shelton, caught him opening one night at Folk City and raved about him in the "Gray Lady." The next day, he played a session attended by A & R legend John Hammond, who signed Zimmerman on the spot to Columbia Records. The young artist also hooked up with manager Albert Grossman. He changed his name to Bob Dylan, after the poet Dylan Thomas.

His first album, *Bob Dylan*, had a couple of songs he wrote and a batch of folk songs. He had been signed, after all, as a folk singer. One of the songs on the album is a version of "Man of Constant Sorrow," the song that would make the Soggy Bottom Boys famous in the 2000 film *O Brother, Where Art Thou? Bob Dylan* sold . . . poorly, perhaps five thousand copies initially.

At this point, Dylan would claim, "Things were changing all the time and a certain song needed to be written. I started writing them because I wanted to sing them . . . one thing led to another and I just kept on writing my own songs."

He added, "If I didn't have a song like 'Masters of War' to sing, I'd find a song like 'Masters of War' to sing. Same thing with 'Times They Are A-Changin'.' If I didn't have a song like that, I'd go out and look around and I'd search until I found one like that, you know?"

His next set, 1963's *The Freewheelin' Bob Dylan*, established him not only as a songwriter but as a spokesman for the intelligentsia. With songs that remain standards, like "Masters of War," "Hard Rain's

A-Gonna Fall," and "Blowin' in the Wind," the album became a classic of the folk movement, as Dylan was already beginning to grow
out of the constrictions of folk. Additionally, Peter, Paul, and Mary,
who were also Grossman clients, started charting with his songs. They
would tout Dylan, to whomever would listen, as one of the most talented young composers and performers out there.

Many artists were beginning to realize this, both in the U.S. and
abroad. "Before I started to write, there was Bob Dylan," said the
Who's lead guitarist and chief songwriter, Pete Townshend. "I mean,
Bob Dylan started recording in '62. So, we made our first recording in
'64, and I wrote my first song in '62. And I think I started to write
because of hearing Bob Dylan, not the Beatles, Bob Dylan. And I think
that I obsessively referenced my own work, to him and to Brian
Wilson, even today. For me the three leading writers are probably
Dylan, Brian Wilson, and then Ray Davies, because he, Ray Davies,
gave me an English way of doing an American thing."

In the space of one album, Dylan had moved from being a folk
singer to being a protest singer, penning songs that the civil rights
movement took to its bosom. This rankled Dylan. "I don't do anything with a sort of message," he said. "I'm just transferring my
thoughts into music. . . . Don't put me down as a man with a message.
My songs are just me talking to myself."

Yet he got deeper and deeper into socially conscious music with
his next albums, *The Times They Are A-Changin'* and *Another Side of Bob
Dylan*, both released in 1964. These introduced songs like "Chimes of
Freedom" and "Only a Pawn in Their Game" into the musical lexicon.
But *Another Side* also had original love songs like "It Ain't Me Babe"
and "All I Really Want to Do." It had been less than a year and Dylan
was ready to move on. So he brought John Sebastian, John Hammond,
Jr. (a more-than-fair blues guitarist), Will Lee, and a host of other
studio rockers to make *Bringing It All Back Home*. He toured through
England, acoustic, and still got called a sellout.

So when he got to Newport, he had already moved several steps
from the "purer faith" of folk music. After selling only five thousand
albums as a folk artist he had gone to plan B, and that found him back
to his earliest roots, playing rock with an electric guitar and a band.
"They booed. There's no doubt about the fact that they booed," said
band member Al Kooper, but he has never been quite sure that it was

about either the rock, as most suppose, or even the sound that found the instruments drowning out Dylan's voice. "The reason they booed is because he only played for fifteen minutes and everybody else played for forty-five minutes to an hour, and he was the headliner of the festival. They were feeling ripped off. Wouldn't you?"

Peter Yarrow, of Peter, Paul, and Mary, who had brought Dylan the composer to the attention of the pop music world with their rendition of "Blowin' in The Wind," came backstage to find out what was happening. He was told by the concert's promoter that Dylan was going back to get an acoustic guitar. It wasn't a retreat, however. According to Al Kooper, they had only rehearsed the three songs.

Dylan, on the other hand, was ready for anything. "I wasn't surprised by the reaction I got in 1965 at Newport," he said. "Going electric was a natural progression. I had been hanging around with different people, playing different material in small gatherings and at other festivals. Newport got more media attention because it was larger than the other festivals. The way people reacted was nothing I could have prepared for, but by that time I knew pretty much what I was doing onstage."

The audiences kept booing. Kooper describes a concert in Forest Hills shortly after Newport as dramatic to the point of being like a gothic novel. "Before the show we had a meeting and Bob said, 'Hey, anything could happen out there. Just ignore whatever happens and keep playing. It could be a circus out there,'" Kooper recalled. "The crowd just booed through the whole thing. . . . But the most humorous part was that 'Like a Rolling Stone' was already at the top of the charts. So they sang along with 'Like a Rolling Stone'—and then they booed."

The audience continued booing all the way through England. While he cut his next album, *Highway 61 Revisited*, with the "Like a Rolling Stone" band, many of them were already members of the Paul Butterfield Blues Band, an ongoing and touring project. Dylan found another band called Levon and the Hawks for the English and subsequent tours through '65 and '66. "That tour was a very strange process," said the band's guitarist Jaime "Robbie" Robertson. "You can hear the violence, and the dynamics in the music. We'd go from town to town, from country to country, and it was like a job. We set up, we played, they booed and threw things at us. Then we went to the next town, played, they booed, threw things at us and we left again. I remember thinking, 'This is a strange way to make a buck'. . . . The only reason tapes of those shows exist today is because we wanted to know, 'Are we crazy?' We'd go back to the hotel room, listen to the tape and think, shit, that's not bad. Why is everybody so upset?"

"They certainly booed," Dylan nearly laughed. "I'll tell you that. . . . They just about done it all over the place. . . . I mean, they must be pretty rich to go someplace and boo. I mean, I couldn't afford it if I was in their shoes."

What Dylan realized was that he had become bigger than folk music—bigger in terms of what he could say, bigger in terms of how he could say it, and bigger in terms of who he could reach. Indeed, he had become bigger, by 1966, than popular music—Dylan was part of popular culture. "Popular songs are the only art form that describes the temper of the times," he said. "That's where the people hang at. It's not in books. It's not onstage. It's not in galleries."

Renowned "beat" poet Allen Ginsberg threw in his two cents on the subject and noted, "It was an artistic challenge to see if great art can be done on a jukebox. He proved it can."

Dylan effectively had ushered in the era of folk rock. In the long term, the electric Dylan gave rock and roll a new lyrical sensibility and license, a freedom to take creative control and control creatively. When he was sidelined for eighteen months after a motorcycle accident, some of his peers took that over. During the period of his recovery, the Beatles made *Revolver* and *Sergeant Pepper*, the Rolling Stones *Their Satanic Majesties Request*, and even the Beach Boys had created *Pet Sounds*. "I didn't know the studio like those guys did," Dylan said, "I didn't really care to."

This would build up to a point where, later in his career, he would complain, "I started out when you could go in the studio and record your songs and leave. I don't remember when that changed, but I found myself spending more time in the studio doing less and less."

But that was actually part of what made Dylan great. His songs continue to speak for themselves. "My songs are different from anybody else's songs," he said. "Other artists can get by on their voices and their style, but my songs speak volumes, and all I have to do is lay them down correctly, lyrically, and they do what they need to do."

Through his comeback with his "Nashville period," which produced hits like "Lay, Lady, Lay," and more rocking affairs like the live *Before the Flood* and the classic *Blood on the Tracks*, Dylan proved that he was an artist to reckon with. Beyond that, he maintained such a high level of songwriting, it kept him in the limelight well into the late '70s. Even lesser albums, like his soundtrack to Sam Peckinpah's *Pat Garrett and Billy the Kid* had triumphant songs like "Knocking on Heaven's Door." He found interesting accomplices as well. In 1978, a song called "Sultans of Swing" featured the remarkable guitar work of Mark Knopfler on a song that sounded oddly Dylanesque. Dylan brought him in to record the first album in another "phase" of his career, a brief exploration of Christian themes that began with *Slow Train Coming*.

Dylan gave rock and roll a new vocabulary, a new list of subjects, beyond school and girls and cars, that could be the fodder for rock and roll. He took the medium he loved so well and stretched it beyond where anyone thought it could go. "The way Elvis freed your body, Bob freed your mind and showed us that just because the music was innately physical did not mean that it was anti-intellectual," offered Bruce Springsteen when he inducted Dylan into the Rock and Roll Hall of Fame. "He had the vision and the talent to make a pop song that contained the whole world. He invented a new way a pop singer could sound, broke through the limitations of what a recording artist could achieve, and changed the face of rock and roll forever."

Before Dylan, rock and roll might have come to a point where there was just no more to express. By the '90s, he felt that way about many things, including himself. "The world don't need any more songs," he said. "They've got enough. They've got way too many. As a matter of fact, if nobody wrote any songs from this day on, the world ain't gonna suffer for it."

He added, around the time of his 1997 set *Time Out of Mind*, "I don't think there's anything among this particular set of songs to overshadow what I've done earlier."

However, every phase of Dylan's shined a light brightly on other artists doing similar things, either before or inspired by him. His folk period brought heightened levels of popularity to the likes of Dave Van Ronk and even brought a new generation to the music of Woody Guthrie. Nearly every folk musician covered Dylan.

While Chuck Berry and Buddy Holly were the prototypes, Dylan virtually invented the modern concept of the singer/songwriter, creating a movement of musicians with their own songs and acoustic guitars. Artists from James Taylor to Rickie Lee Jones to John Mayer acknowledge their fealty to Dylan.

His move to rock issued a poetic license to every rock musician who followed. Certainly the Beatles felt Dylan's influence, as did the Who. Jim Morrison and the Doors' poetic pretensions might not have existed if Dylan hadn't created that door and opened it to a world of subjects beyond girls and cars.

This became especially important around 1966 with the escalating U.S. military presence in the conflict in Vietnam. The drafting of more and younger soldiers into that conflict helped to create a context for their musical peers to pen songs of opposition, from angry polemic to acerbic sarcasm.

Dylan's fusion of country music with rock and folk sensibilities opened the door to country rockers from the Eagles to the Allman Brothers. Much of the early '70s Southern California scene, including the music of singer-songwriters Joni Mitchell and Jackson Browne, was at least informed by Dylan's work.

In his wake, however, a passel of artists have been tagged with the career-threatening appellation "the New Dylan." The earliest was probably Phil Ochs. The mantle and albatross was passed to the shoulders of artists ranging from Steve Forbert to Ryan Adams. Why should we need new Dylans when the old one remained active and creative into the new millennium? One of the few artists to survive the mantle, Bruce Springsteen, might have answered the question during his speech inducting Dylan into the Rock and Roll Hall of Fame: "To this day, where great rock music is being made, there is the shadow of Bob Dylan over and over and over."

Paul Williams Launches "Crawdaddy!" Magazine

It always seemed ironic that Mark David Chapman, murderer of John Lennon, came to the scene of the crime with a copy of *Catcher in the Rye* in hand. Many writers cite Allen Ginsberg, Jack Kerouac, and William Burroughs as influences, but J. D. Salinger's treatise on what and who are phony has done more to inform rock criticism than perhaps any other book, musical or not. Holden Caulfield was even a critic:

The band was putrid. Buddy Singer. Very brassy, but not good brassy—corny brassy.

Few critics from any period, in any genre, could make it any clearer how they felt about the music or why they felt that way.

With the advent of the Beatles and Bob Dylan, the borders to which rock and roll could aspire stretched, allowing the music to make an appeal to the brain as well as the body. By the mid-'60s, the time was right for people outside of making the music to try and start to make some sense of it, to separate the good from the bad, the authentic from the phony, what they liked from what they thought was trash. It came time for people to develop an educated opinion of rock and roll and start writing about it.

Dave Marsh, one of the veteran members of the rock journalism fraternity, once said that he learned more from rock and roll "about life and how to live it and what it means, because so much of the stuff in school was fabricated and predigested and false when you got out there in the world." Holden Caulfield woulda been proud.

Of course the music trade magazines had already taken big-time notice of rock. *Billboard* and *Cashbox* had been around for years covering the music business—trying to predict what would sell, what would go over well on the radio, tracking trends, charting changes. Their big assets, however, were their charts tracking the sales and radio play of the hits. They were a scorecard for the business—a #1 record in *Billboard* was a major coup and meant money for all involved. Of course, their job was not to deal with music on any basis, excluding what would sell and sound good on the radio. Most of the features in the trades have always tended to be laudatory "puff pieces," especially where artists are concerned. The reviews historically don't deal with any sort of critical evaluation beyond whether this song will work on what format, or into which bin the retailer should put that particular record.

By 1957, the magazine publishing business started to try and capitalize on both the burgeoning teen market and that market's music, rock and roll. *Sixteen* magazine, oriented toward teenaged girls, launched in 1957, running stories and lots of pictures about rock stars, especially the young male ones. The depth of the musical and artistic content, however, usually was limited to the artists' favorite colors. One of the better of the fanzine bunch, *Hit Parader*, actually ran the occasionally substantive article along with pictures and the magazine's stock in trade, song lyrics.

The "underground press" also got started in the '50s, with the *Village Voice* as its standard bearer. Started more in response to the mainstream media's conservative slant during an era of McCarthy red-baiting, the weekly's underground, liberal mandate extended to its coverage of arts.

Many of the first writers to try to make some critical sense out of rock and roll came from other musical disciplines. The *London Times* writer, for example, who tried to discuss the Beatles in terms of "submediant switches from C major into A flat major and to a lesser extent mediant ones (e.g., the octave ascent in the famous 'I want to hold your hand') . . ." had a pretty serious music theory education, and didn't care who knew it or who could understand what he was saying about the band. Certainly the Beatles didn't.

Others, like Robert Shelton, came at it from the point of view of a musical avatar and advocate. A copy editor at the *New York Times*, Shelton would occasionally get pieces of music criticism published. His beat was folk, blues, jazz, and country—music the *Times* deemed inconsequential enough not to need a full-time critic (as opposed to Broadway or European composed music). One of Shelton's hangouts was Gerde's Folk City in Greenwich Village, where he saw a very young Bob Dylan perform in the fall of 1961. Proclaiming that, "there is no doubt that he is bursting at the seams with talent," that one notice proved pivotal in Dylan's career. It was a notable instance of how important the press could be in bringing an artist into the public's eyes and ears.

In 1965, Shelton observed, "There are many categories of rock 'n' roll from the 'Spector sound,' to the 'Chicago sound' and the 'Rebelation sound' of the Lake Charles area of Louisiana. But knowledgeable persons in pop music think the strongest element of American rock 'n' roll now, musically and financially, is the 'Detroit sound' . . . issued by the Motown record company." This helped to legitimize all those sounds in the minds of the New York cognoscenti.

On the other side of the country, Ralph Gleason started writing about popular music for the *San Francisco Chronicle* early in the 1950s, when popular music included big bands, certain country stars, and crooners. Gleason took popular music very seriously, and his tastes were exceedingly catholic. During the '50s, you could find interviews with Hank Williams, Elvis Presley, Fats Domino, and any number of jazz musicians who came through the Bay Area.

Suddenly rock began to develop the kind of critical criteria that informed jazz and classical music, ushering in the age of pop music journalism and rock criticism. This gave the music a level of gravitas that it heretofore didn't have, creating commentary on the culture.

This seriousness developed more quickly in the U.K. than in the U.S. For one thing, England had the venerable *New Musical Express*, already a decade old as rock slipped out of its infancy in the '60s. It became largely a rock paper, appropriate as rock was the new music of the day. Like the trades, these papers were weeklies and kept right on top of trends, but unlike the trades, they did it critically. Their approach only grew more critical as time progressed.

Into this environment, a couple of college dropouts and serious rock fans took note of the music journalism environment. Paul Williams was a freshman at Swarthmore College, just outside of Philadelphia. At seventeen, he was already a veteran of the science fiction fanzine scene. He was writing a column for one of the new folk magazines that had joined *Sing Out!*, *Broadside*, and the short-lived *Folking Around*, in addition to having a rock-and-roll morning show and a weekly blues program on the college station. He was trying to glean some information from one of the *Sixteen* magazine–style fanzines when he had a revelation: "I read that two of my favorite bands, the Yardbirds and the Rolling Stones, had got their start playing in a club in Richmond, Surrey, England, called the Crawdaddy Club," he recalled, "and it hit me in a blinding flash that it was now time to start this rock and roll magazine I'd been thinking about, and that it should be called *Crawdaddy!*"

Taking his cue from the folk magazines and from the time-honored jazz publications like *Downbeat*, *Crawdaddy!* featured substantive, meaty reviews. On the cover of the first issue, he took a quote from *Music Echo*, one of the English "inkies"—the weekly music tabloids like *NME* and *Melody Maker*—from a band that had just returned from a U.S. tour where they discovered, "There is no musical paper scene out there like there is in England. The trades are strictly for the business side and the only things left are the fan magazines . . ." This established his agenda, though for a one-man operation, a weekly schedule soon proved unrealistic.

Initially the magazine, in the best science fiction fanzine tradition, was mimeographed and stapled together. Williams hawked it for a quarter at record shops, bookstores, and newsstands from his college base in Philadelphia through New York City to his home base in Boston. After three issues, Williams dropped out of Swarthmore and moved back to the Boston area. There he hooked up with a Brandeis student named Jon Landau, who started writing regularly for the magazine. By the seventh issue, the magazine was a year old and now located in an office in Greenwich Village, New York. People were starting to pay attention. The *Village Voice* dropped by the magazine's Sixth Avenue office behind a musical instrument shop. They found the magazine promising. "The reason for its promise," they wrote, "[is] that it fills a gap. Up to now people interested in the r&r scene have had to read either the trade or fan magazines. . . . *Crawdaddy!* is for people who dig rock 'n' roll as an art form."

Ralph Gleason weighed in, in his *Chronicle* column, calling *Crawdaddy!* "the most interesting publication in the U.S. covering the rock scene . . . it is devoted with religious fervor to the rock scene. . . . Interestingly enough, the quality of the magazine matches the dedication of its contributors, both in writing and in analysis and thoughtful speculation."

In the eighth issue of *Crawdaddy!*, Williams published something that became an early manifesto of rock criticism. Initially a paper for a college course on aesthetics at Stonybrook College on Long Island, just outside of New York City, Richard Meltzer's "The Aesthetics of Rock" was one of the first nationally published mainstream articles to look at rock and roll from an academic as well as classically artistic point of view.

"We were part of a literary movement that combined counterculture aesthetics, politics, a love of the arts," noted a later *Crawdaddy!* editor, John Swenson, "and a sense that the world we lived in was heavy flux, and that visionaries might well chart an optimistic if not utopian future out of it all. Multinational corporations had yet to take over the entertainment business, which meant that label management and A&R people in the music world, and producers in the film world were sensitive to the necessity of artists making self-consciously artistic statements rather than mass-market product. Sports, science fiction, avant-garde classical music, comedy, and alternative energy proposals were all part of the intellectual mix. Most of all, we had fun."

The import of what *Crawdaddy!* was doing had not escaped notice. On the West Coast, Jann Wenner, a disciple of Ralph Gleason, was very much paying attention. His creation, *Rolling Stone*, wasn't the first magazine in San Francisco giving serious coverage to rock; that honor would go to the *Mojo Navigator News*. Nor was his the first magazine to have national aspirations—clearly *Crawdaddy!* did, although Williams didn't have the publishing acumen to know how to go about it initially. Similarly, several other magazines started in the wake of *Crawdaddy!,* including the short-lived but incendiary *Cheetah* in New York. Many of *Cheetah*'s cast and crew went on to form the nucleus of the *Village Voice*'s post-1970 music coverage team—Bob Christgau and Richard Goldstein, in particular.

What *Rolling Stone* had was the one-two punch of the charming and disarming Jann Wenner at its helm and the venerable and knowledgeable Ralph Gleason providing the intellectual wind for its sails. "I was writing a column for the *Daily Californian* when I was still in school at Berkeley," Wenner recalled. "That was also where I met Ralph. . . . He sort of took me under his wing, this schleppy kid who didn't know much about anything. Ralph saw what rock 'n' roll was about, and he saw it before anyone started writing seriously about it. He saw the value and the joy in rock 'n' roll. . . . I couldn't have started *Rolling Stone* without him."

Beyond that, Wenner had a bigger idea. For *Crawdaddy!* and its ilk, rock may as well have existed in a vacuum. Wenner saw *Rolling Stone* as a rock magazine, but a rock magazine that dealt with its subject in the broader context of popular culture as it related to . . . Jann Wenner. As he said in his editorial in the magazine's first issue, "*Rolling Stone* is not just about music, but also about the things and attitudes that music embraces."

In a way, he fused the sensibility of *Crawdaddy!* in terms of taking rock and roll as a force that was not going away or easily dismissed with the underground weeklies that sprouted up in the wake of the *Village Voice*. His mandate was not to cover rock and roll, it was to cover and codify rock-and-roll *culture*. This was the key difference between *Rolling Stone* and the rock-and-roll magazines.

This key difference—of covering rock and roll in terms of the broader popular culture and popular culture in terms of rock and roll—appealed to a lot of the writers who seriously covered rock and roll.

One of the first to sign up was Jon Landau. Greil Marcus joined the staff as reviews editor.

In 1968, *Creem* Magazine started with a similar agenda to that of both *Rolling Stone* and *Crawdaddy!*, with a couple of important differences. For one thing, the tone of both *Crawdaddy!* and *Rolling Stone* tended toward such seriousness that they bordered on, if not crossed over into, self-importance. *Creem* recognized that, yes, rock and roll is important, but at its heart is a joyful core, and often the things that got taken so seriously by others, the artists themselves had intended as *witty* and *fun*. *Creem* tackled its subject with both a sense of humor and a sense of adventure. The second issue even featured a cover by cartoonist R. Crumb that had "Mr. Dreamwhip," an ambulatory aerosol can, spraying ardent young ladies with whipped . . . *Creem*. "It not only covers rock authoritatively," noted Bob Christgau in the *Village Voice*, "but it is unquestionably the funniest magazine in America."

Ironically, the Crumb cover came about for the most prosaic of reasons. "Mr. Crumb needed money for a clap shot," offered Tony Reay, the first editor of *Creem*. "I offered him fifty dollars for a cover drawing (Barry [Kramer, *Creem*'s publisher,] fought hard to reduce it to $30). *Zap Comix* were just beginning to get national distribution in head shops across the country and he had just done the Janis/Big Brother cover for Columbia. I paid the money just for the use of his name. . . . I didn't care if he drew monkeys in a barrel—and actually, neither I nor Barry were that impressed with the results."

By 1970, pop music criticism had developed a voice—several voices, in fact—and even spawned several "stars" in its own right. *Creem*'s agent provocateur Lester Bangs used the magazine's largely open format to write creative death threats to James Taylor and ten-thousand-word paeans to Iggy and the Stooges that delved deeply into the aesthetics of not only rock, but popular culture in general. "Along with editor Dave Marsh," wrote Greil Marcus, "[Lester] discovered, invented, nurtured, and promoted an esthetic of joyful disdain, a love for apparent trash and contempt for all pretension."

Marcus himself brought historical acuity, an academic's rigorous reality check, and a love of language to the party. Marsh brought a fiery mix of passion and commitment to the idea that if the music maybe couldn't change the world, it could change your mind. Jon

Landau wrote prose that often reflected the intensely personal reaction engendered by public art.

And what they wrote had an effect on the music that few people anticipated. Jon Landau wrote an elegiac piece about his twenty-seventh birthday and how seeing Bruce Springsteen and the E Street Band reaffirmed his reason for living and chased away his musical ennui. He saw his rock-and-roll past in his rearview mirror, and he "saw rock 'n' roll future and his name is Bruce Springsteen." Springsteen, an artist whom Columbia was just about to give up on, got a new lease on his career from that little quote. When he got stuck putting together his third album, he brought in Landau to break the creative logjam. Landau has been in his corner since, eschewing writing about rock for helping in its creation as the manager of Springsteen and a host of other artists.

As the '70s wore on, the "counterculture" aesthetics began to seem hopelessly archaic, and a lot of music criticism had to face up to that. By 1972, the most obvious causes of the counterculture—Richard Nixon and the war in Vietnam—had both wound down to their inevitable conclusions, losses both. Madison Avenue had won, the consumer culture was making America (and much of Europe) famous. Sure, America was still, de facto, a racially segregated country, and the gap between the rich and the poor would keep growing. But this was after a decade of national trauma that started with the Kennedy assassination (or maybe the Cuban Missile Crisis) and ended with Watergate. It took us through the defoliation of large chunks of Southeast Asia, the death of vast numbers of nineteen-year-olds, the great majority of them poor and black, and campus unrest. Los Angeles, Detroit, Newark, and Harlem, with large areas of charred real estate, looked like the urban versions of Laos and Cambodia. America and much of the rest of the world was tired of all of it. Even if you wanted to protest, no one wanted to listen to you do it.

So, musically, the disaffected listened to heavy metal, the affected listened to progressive rock from England like Yes, the Moody Blues, and King Crimson, the heavily affected latched on to glam like David Bowie and T-Rex, the unaffected mellowed out to the Laurel Canyon singer/songwriter collective, and the lucky and knowledgeable listened to Parliament and Funkadelic. On the one hand, rock had branched out in so many ways that it *needed* knowledgeable people to help folks make sense of it all. On the other hand, the corporate cooptation of the music business had begun in earnest, and anything that flew under radio's radar got stiffed in the stores. Some managed to sell if a Lester Bangs or a Robert Christgau championed them, if just enough to get by.

As the culture changed, as rock and roll changed, so did the music's coverage. Seeing how well magazines like *Rolling Stone* and *Creem* were doing, most of the major newspapers hired on a staff rock writer, or if they could get one, a multi-purpose music writer who could write cogently, if not intelligently, about rock, R&B, and jazz.

Rolling Stone continued on its merry way. Lester Bangs and Dave Marsh from *Creem* both graced its pages. Part of the magazine's success came because it never claimed to deal with the counterculture. When money got tight, it was able to show investors its potential for huge sales on the newsstand and through advertising. *Rolling Stone*'s principles always regarded it as a business and treated it as such. So, if the magazine espoused Wenner's liberal mainstream politics (it ran a cover story on George McGovern), it also espoused pop music (enough to run a cover with David Cassidy naked). To stay where the media lived, Wenner moved the entire operation to New York shortly before its tenth anniversary.

Nor was rock and roll *Rolling Stone*'s sole purview. (Cassidy, after all, was way more a television star than a music star.) They did cover stories on groupies, legal prostitution, narcs, drugs in the army, Abbie Hoffman, Dennis Hopper, Meher Baba, Muhammad Ali, Marvel Comics, and Tricia Nixon. "The music became less newsworthy and interesting," said Wenner. "There was a slump in the record business, including the creative end of it, so there wasn't all that much to write about. Music just wasn't much fun anymore."

The Sex Pistols and the enormous wake of musical energy that trailed behind their media-driven commotion changed that. Suddenly, music once again had energy and excitement. Whether or not you liked punk and the "new wave" that followed it, it made for interesting copy. "In the summer of 1977, *NME* and others of its ilk were gleefully reporting the latest antics of the Sex Pistols and the 101 other punk groups," wrote York Membery. "Barely a week passed without the Pistols' Johnny Rotten or Sid Vicious doing something outrageous, and the circulation boom kept everybody satisfied."

"[In] 1976 and 1977 . . . the Ramones and CBGB's in New York City and the Sex Pistols in London," wrote Marcus, "would take the name [Lester Bangs] had given it: Punk."

However, as punk shortened song length, it also abbreviated rock criticism. Those critics who continued to write found that the amount of space they were allocated had shrunk. While the *Village Voice* would still publish a 2,000-word review on occasion, no one, not even *Creem*, would give anyone, even Lester Bangs, the latitude to write 10,000 words on one album, no matter how brilliant those words were. By the '80s, there were more magazines covering more records and saying less and less with each successive issue.

In April of 1982, Bangs was found dead in his Fourteenth Street apartment, a victim of taking a powerful painkiller while in the throes of the flu. He was thirty-three years old. His death marked the beginning of the end of serious rock criticism. People would imitate his habits, but few could imitate his intellectual acuity, his beat, stream-of-consciousness style, and his amazingly circuitous, antilogical way of coming to a point. Certainly no one could do them all.

Magazine publishing changed radically in the '80s. In the movie *The Big Chill*, the pop culture journalist played by Jeff Goldblum describes his job as giving people all the facts that they want to read in the time it takes to take a dump. The advent of magazines like *Spin* initially seemed promising. However, they, too, limited critique to 300 words or less. While rock songs might have stretched the limit of the three-minute single, music journalism had become the realm of short attention spans. Often, a barely rewritten press release or bio would serve as an article on a band. As a publicity executive at one of the major record companies used to tell his writers, "Imagine you're writing an article that begins that the artist you are writing this bio about is playing the local amphitheater. Your bio starts the second sentence."

As the music changed and branched out, new periodicals became very genre specific. Both the music and the media covering it became little communities. Fans of heavy metal wanted to read heavy metal magazines. Folk fans wanted to read about their music in their magazines. The new popular music of the '90s (although it grew up in the late '70s and '80s), hip-hop, spawned some of the most popular magazines—*The Source* and *Vibe*. Noted producer Quincy Jones, who pioneered *Vibe*, called his new periodical the *Rolling Stone* for the hip-hop generation. While *Rolling Stone* covered hip-hop, it refused to jump into any one genre, continuing its mandate to cover the culture as a whole. "It's flattering saying he's doing a version of *Rolling Stone* for another audience," Wenner told CNN. "That's great. I think he's done a good job and I'm flattered he uses *Rolling Stone* as a role model."

Beyond all that, many younger critics got into the field so they could hang out with rock stars and get free records from the record companies. A lot of the magazines paid minimally and didn't mentor their writers along. Many of these writers didn't write bad reviews for fear of their record lifelines getting cut off. Many of the places they wrote for didn't care. "There used to be forums for great writing," noted *Chicago Sun-Times* critic Jim DeRogatis. "There used to be give-and-take between the press, the recording artists, and fans. Now the press has allowed itself to be coopted by the industry, and the result is a proliferation of the three-star review. It's Pablum."

By the turn of the millennium, however, another problem entered into the equation. Long-time *Washington Post* music writer Richard Harrington, a music journalist since the late '60s, was demoted. It was alleged that he was too old to cover his beat. "Rock criticism," noted *New York Times* critic Jon Pareles, "is the only job where people would question . . . if you learned to do your job better as you did it longer."

Even the veterans, however, wonder at the efficacy of rock criticism in the new order. "Do you think there is still time for rock to develop a set of critical criteria?" Dave Marsh asked. "It is a project long abandoned at the journalistic level, so far as I can see; developed only as a more or less explicit form of white supremacist class snobbery at the fanzine level; and turned into an aspect of sociology at the level most hostile to discussing actual music at the academic level. I wish there were some hope of putting something together but alas, I despair."

Ahmet Ertegun Signs Cream—"Rock and Roll" Becomes "Rock"

By the mid-'60s, rock and roll had not disappeared as so many in the '50s predicted it would. Instead, it became a genre. As this happened, people stopped perceiving the music as one monolithic movement. Different strains of the music began to branch out of the main stem of rock and roll, and eventually the "and roll" part of the genre's name fell away. Jerry Wexler proposed that when the "and roll" went away, the music became big business.

"The significance of the term *rock and roll* has changed over the years," agreed his former employer, Ahmet Ertegun. "Now, it almost includes everything. There are so many different types of rock and roll now."

As they did with so many things, the Beatles helped set these schisms in motion with albums like *Sergeant Pepper*. Up until this point, as Pete Townshend put it, "Albums were what you got for Christmas. Singles were what you bought for prestige. It was the whole recreation of the local dance hall cum discotheque in your own sweet front room."

So part of the transition from *rock and roll* to *rock* had to do with the music changing, or perhaps enlarging, its focus. Where once the sole purpose of rock and roll was dance music, albums like *Revolver* and *Pet Sounds* asked, or even demanded, that you *listen* as well.

There were three key components to this. One was the schism between the Beatles' fans and the Stones' fans that grew into actual riots in England between two factions known as mods and rockers. Mods, epitomized by groups like the Who, dressed in outrageous clothes and tended to be fairly middle class, to cast a wide sociological net. Rockers, more the Stones' crowd, tended to be earthier, working class, and loved the purer strain of rock and blues espoused by Alexis Korner, the Blues Busters, and, of course, the Stones. The Beatles avoided that altogether.

The British blues movement became a growing concern in the mid-'60s. In the wake of Alexis Korner's Blues Incorporated, a straight-ahead blues band that grew out of the '50s trad jazz scene, rose groups like the Stones—many of which played with Blues Incorporated at one time or another—and John Mayall's Blues Breakers. Mayall formed his band in 1962. "It was a novelty at that time," said Mayall, "British white guys playing the blues. That's what made the splash."

The Breakers served as an incubator for great British rock through the '60s. The Blues Breakers rhythm section of Mick Fleetwood and John McVie spun off into their own (initially) blues band, Fleetwood Mac. Guitarist Eric Clapton went on to greatness, first with the Yardbirds, then as part of the triumvirate Cream.

"I latched on to Eric Clapton," Ahmet Ertegun said with no small amount of pride. "Robert Stigwood and I heard Clapton together for the first time and I said, 'Well, that is an artist I want!' And so we recorded Cream."

Other former Yardbirds included guitarist Jeff Beck, who moved on through the Faces to a remarkable solo career, and Jimmy Page, who went on to spearhead one of the most influential bands of the '60s and '70s, Led Zeppelin.

"The reputation I won in the last days of the Yardbirds in the States," Page said, "certainly helped launch Led Zeppelin in the beginning."

"The first recordings of Led Zeppelin," Ertegun adds, concerning another one of his second wave of British invaders, "were important landmarks in the history of Atlantic records . . . that was the beginning of our white rock-and-roll history."

Cream and Led Zeppelin started off playing the blues, and like the Who, everything they played, they played LOUD. This inspired scads of other bands who heard the volume but missed the fact that Page and Clapton were virtuosos at their instruments.

"Led Zeppelin!" said Klaus Meine from German heavy metal veterans the Scorpions. "That I think was the main influence. Zeppelin was the best band."

Groups that capitalized on the volume like Black Sabbath, Grand Funk Railroad, and Steppenwolf gave voice to the aggression that members of the "age of Aquarius" who weren't necessarily Aquarian had begun to feel during the late '60s. "Heavy music like ours," said Black Sabbath guitarist Tony Iommi, "gains a lot of the weight from volume."

While Black Sabbath's first three albums might have given the music its shape, Steppenwolf's anthemic "Born to Be Wild," brought to the fore in the monstrously successful film *Easy Rider*, gave this new branch of rock its name—heavy metal.

Another element of the transition from *rock and roll* to *rock* was the proliferation of drugs, particularly hallucinogens like psilocybin and

LSD, espoused by '60s philosophical and cultural gurus, from de-robed Harvard professor Timothy Leary to South American philosopher Carlos Castaneda. An entire movement of rock grew up around drugs in the 1960s, and the groups that fell into this psychedelic sound covered a broad swath of rock, from the bluegrass-informed, extended improvisations of the Grateful Dead in California to the electronic soundscapes of Pink Floyd in London. These main branches of the tree grew their own branchlets as well.

"A lot of music," renowned producer George Martin said, "has been created in the past few years by stoned people for stoned people, but I do not think it has elevated our music. I know that if I had been on drugs I could never have got *Sergeant Pepper* together."

Actually, a lot of the musicians associated with psychedelic music didn't actually *do* the drugs. In Pink Floyd, for example, "Roger's and Nick's largest indulgence was alcohol," the group's guitarist David Gilmour said of bassist Roger Waters and drummer Nick Mason, and added, "mine and Rick's [Rick Wright, keyboards] might have involved an occasional reefer. But . . . we were nothing like our image. I'm not sure Roger's ever taken LSD—it certainly wasn't on our menu after [original guitarist and songwriter] Syd [Barrett] left. We've never got away from that reputation, though, not to this day."

The California group Iron Butterfly fused the volume of the Who and the roving musical ethos of Pink Floyd. Their 1967 hit, "In-A-Gadda-Da-Vida," ran seventeen minutes, taking up a full side of the album of the same name. The song became a staple on the new FM, progressive, underground radio stations that were coming along at the time (putting on a seventeen-minute track gave the deejay time to go to the bathroom without risking dead air). The song caught on with listeners and became a big hit, eventually selling 4 million copies in the U.S. alone.

What tied this all together toward the end of the '60s was the introduction of a new level of recording and musical sophistication. Guitarists like Clapton, Beck, and Page married their passion for rock and blues with a practiced technique that brought the music up to a new level. Les Paul's eight-track studio began to spread out. Before that, most studios ran on three tracks—a left track, a right track, and an extra track for overdubs. As the eight track proliferated and even expanded to sixteen and twenty-four tracks, musicians and producers could do more with that virtuosity in the studio.

Many of the groups that started to take advantage of the studio in that manner began as blues bands. The Moody Blues, for example, started off playing blues, and had a big hit with a bit of blue-eyed, British R&B called "Go Now." However, personnel changes in the band changed the band's direction. "Blues is American," said bassist John Lodge, "and I found it very difficult for us. We could mimic what was happening in America, and we could get off on it, and we could play it and enjoy it, but it really wasn't what we wanted to do with our own music."

"I always loved rhythm and blues," adds one of his bandmates, guitarist Justin Hayward, "but the time that I was playing it I always thought we were not all that great at it. Denny [Laine, guitar and vocals] had a very good rhythm-and-blues voice. He had that sort of crack in his voice that he could do it. There was another band on Decca called Ten Years After who used to do it great. So much better than us. So what we had to do was develop our own style and do our own thing that was unique and that we were comfortable with and that expressed us."

This new way to express themselves came on a silver platter in 1966, shortly after Hayward and Lodge joined the group. Their record company wanted to introduce a new kind of stereo recording process, and wanted a rock group to record Dvořák's "New World" Symphony with an orchestra. The Moody Blues said they were excited about recording with an orchestra, but they wanted to use their own material, and said they would create their own suite based on the flow of a day. The album, *Days of Future Passed* was not an instant success in America, taking five years before it hit the U.S. charts. It was, however, a hit three separate times in England.

"We were 'underground,' 'psychedelic,' what was the other word?" Lodge mused. "'Progressive.' Right. Great word."

"Progressive" rock started to make serious inroads on the scene in the early '70s, especially in Europe and particularly in England. Often playing for an audience impressed by the virtuosity of the musicians involved, these groups featured players that might have come up in the all-pervasive blues scene, but explored their other chops. Keyboard players like Gary Brooker of Procol Harum recalled their early classical training. Brooker extrapolated Bach's 18th-century "Air on the G String" with 14th-century poet Geoffrey Chaucer's work and came up with an archetypal late-'60s piece of progressive rock, "A Whiter Shade of Pale."

Another classically trained pianist, Keith Emerson, who had some success in England with a band called the Nice, joined forces with bassist Greg Lake from another of the English progressive bands, King Crimson, and drummer Carl Palmer from a third progressive English group, Atomic Rooster. Together they formed a progressive supergroup of sorts, Emerson, Lake & Palmer, creating a fusion of classical and rock that included "covers" of composers like Mussorgsky and Tchaikovsky played with full orchestration by just the three musicians.

One of the key tools in this was the synthesizer, particularly the Moog. This totally electronic instrument, with tones triggered by a pianolike keyboard, allowed musicians to create full string sections or entire orchestras with a little work on the devices' Byzantine controls. Emerson's arsenal of keyboards used to include a grand piano (that, in a feat of stagecraft and flashiness, would flip upside down in the air), an organ (which, in another bit of showmanship, he would climb into), and a bank of synthesizers, which would surround him on three sides.

Some bands with similar roots to those of the Moody Blues and Led Zeppelin, like Deep Purple, managed to offer up their own flares of occasional brilliance. By the end of the '60s and the beginning of the '70s, rock musicians were making musical statements, both on record and in the press, that would have seemed blasphemous even a few years before. Jon Lord of Deep Purple wrote a suite for orchestra and rock band that the band performed and recorded with the Royal Philharmonic in 1969. "I remember that with absolute, pure clarity for some reason," said Deep Purple bassist Roger Glover. "There's always been a classical bent to our work. I love classical music myself."

"I'm very interested myself in scoring orchestral music," said Jimmy Page. "The frequencies and scope within a band, especially building up banks of guitars, aren't too limited. There's just so much more that can be done with an orchestra, though—the variety of sound—it's a totally different approach."

Years later, Pete Townshend would echo this after a couple of pretty satisfying experiences working with orchestras: "Somebody says, 'Oh, you know, what Sting does, or Paul McCartney does, or Paul Simon, or Pete Townshend does when they're a bit bored with their old rockers is they hire an orchestrator and an orchestra and mastur-bate in front of it.'"

By the '70s, the use of orchestra and strings were fairly common-place on rock records. Billy Joel's "Ballad of Billy the Kid" and "Scenes from an Italian Restaurant" used tasteful orchestration that helped turn them into formidable pieces of classic rock.

Other musicians brought heavy jazz chops to the party. Bill Bru-ford, drummer for the band Yes, was far more influenced by Art Blakey than John Bonham. "I thought," he said of the time, "I was joining a jazz band."

Similarly, a young band from Holland called Focus fused key-boardist and flautist Thijs Van Leer's classical training with the heavy, virtuosic rock and jazz chops of guitarist Jan Akkerman. Yet for all that, they are still mostly remembered for "Hocus Pocus," a novelty song from their second album that was so weird it went Top 10 in the U.S. "We were sitting in this castle pretty high in the sky, I can tell you that," said Akkerman. "And there are no mountains for hundreds of miles. Holland is flat. Flatter is impossible. We were kind of weird, spaced out. We had this line, with these chords in the middle. So we said, 'Why don't you yodel, man?' Because he used to yodel with this cabaret group before. This is how it happened. He yodeled himself into the Top 10. . . . The yodeling part was kind of a send-up. The kiddies, or course, remember only the yodeling. But there's a whole pile of music after that."

By this time, jazz musicians who had eschewed rock the same way people in the '20s had ignored jazz—at their peril—began to explore it. Miles Davis, one of the heroes of postbop, "cool" jazz, started working with younger musicians with rock, R&B, and jazz chops, essentially creating a cooler version of jazz fusion.

This caught the ear of a couple of songwriting jazz and blues fans from the New York area. While more interested in jazz and blues than rock, per se, Walter Becker and Donald Fagen started playing their own version of rock with wry lyricism and jazz chord changes. Using a rotating group of studio players, they called their project Steely Dan (after a particularly nasty piece of steam-powered hardware in William Burroughs' *Naked Lunch*). "We both looked for some alternative to the culture we were brought up in," said Fagen. "We found it in black music, jazz and blues, and so on. . . . I'm bored with repetitive, very simple harmonies."

Several bands started to incorporate horns and jazz chops into their sound. One group, Chicago, made elaborate horn charts the centerpiece of their sound. Blood, Sweat and Tears grew out of a New York group built by former Dylan sideman Al Kooper and members of the Blues Project. They brought on horns, as well. "From the very beginning there was a concept for the band that included more of a jazz orientation and more experimentation," said the group's drummer Bobby Colomby. "I wanted something that had a little more power to it, a little more edge, and a little more improvising. You had people like Randy Brecker, Fred Lipsius, and David Halligan; we had an opportunity for the guys to display whatever talent they had."

After a few years of working like a "real" band, including touring and the like, Becker and Fagen took the Beatles' road and became, for the better part of three decades, a studio-only organization. Because of this, they were able to explore what Page described as "banks of guitars" and other instruments, using the growing potentials of the recording studio. By the early '70s, studios had as many as forty-eight tracks available for an artist. This allowed records to be built very carefully and discretely.

"Multitrack recording does not get you better sound," opined George Martin. "It only postpones the moment of truth and then you have to decide what your mix is going to be. I use sixteen-track quite a lot because I have all these facilities . . . but I would be quite happy with less. Sorry to repeat myself, on *Pepper*, but I think it is worthwhile mentioning that this was done on a four-track."

With the luxury of all the sonic space provided by 16, 24, 36, 48, and 64 tracks available (now with digital recording, the number is even greater), bands began to take forever in the recording studio, attempting to make their records sound as good as possible. One major band spent close to eighteen months, nearly nonstop in the studio, making an album. The album did well, but most people goggled at the studio bills they ran up.

"You have to realize that by the time the second month rolls around, you're not looking forward to it anymore," said Todd Rundgren, an artist who went solo in the '70s, scoring both hit records and remarkably complex and satisfying albums as an artist and a producer. "You're supposed to be creating pleasurable and meaningful stuff, and what happens is it's the last thing in the world you want to do, is go into the studio and go through that grind again. I don't comprehend it myself, but I guess the ends justify the means. If anyone does that and manages to get the sales, that's fine."

Many American acts used this as their guideline, however. They needed to spend the time in the studio. They used it to create. Rock started to move away from something that was essentially live being captured in amber (or on vinyl) to becoming something that was built in the studio, and then had to be rehearsed to go out on the road.

As rock progressed, it developed a "nothing-is-shocking" ethos. It became a mission, a *raison d'être* of certain rockers, to challenge listeners' notions of normal. English vocalist David Bowie did it through use of makeup, costumes, personas, and staged androgyny. The New York Dolls did it by juxtaposing beefy hard rock with costumes that included dresses, high heels, and purses. Michigan's Stooges did it with raw rock and a lead singer, Iggy Pop, who would roll around in broken glass. KISS, a standard-issue hard rock band from New York, came upon the idea of outer-space costumes and circus makeup, along with circus stunts like fire breathing during the course of the show. Alice Cooper put on ghoulish makeup, wore a snake on stage, and used props such as a guillotine.

Staging became an important element of rock shows. For most bands, it wasn't enough just to get onstage and entertain. Wanton destruction had long been a hallmark of the Who's onstage finale, but in the late '60s they also added elaborate light shows, as did many bands. Several venues, like the Fillmore, had in-house light shows as well.

"Our genius lighting designer, John Wolfe," Townshend recalled, "used to do this thing with a laser. He used to create a laser ceiling display, and what he would do with it is lower it ever so slowly. So what you felt was happening to you is you felt you were going up in the air. A lot of people have said to me, you know, 'When you were singing, "Listening to you I get the music," I started to fly off the ground.' A few people have said that to me and I've just got to get this sense that was what was happening. Actually, in *Tommy* the first thing that you saw was six great big klieg lamps reflected on the audience for that blinding effect that took you out."

As the '70s continued, the number of groups proliferated, as did the number of genres and hybrid genres. People were no longer into "rock." They liked "country rock" like the Eagles or "swamp rock" like Creedence Clearwater Revival or "progressive rock" like Genesis or "pop rock" like Elton John, ad infinitum. Geographic areas spawned "sounds" like the "Boss-Town" sound or the Southern California sound—some of it the organic manifestation of what Billy Bergman and Richard Horn termed "recombinant do-re-mi," but mostly used as marketing tools.

"Unlike the '60s," wrote Ira Robbins in a beautiful summation of the post-Woodstock era, "rock fans in the '70s were forced to endure talentless nobodies with little interest in music beyond fame, fortune and drugs. . . . Along the way we survived glam/glitter, heavy metal, fossils that wouldn't quit, power pop, all the ghosts of rock 'n' roll past . . ."

From Monterey Pop
to Woodstock to Altamont:
Innocence Found and Lost

Woodstock organizer Michael Lang

"There was a place called the Tin Angel," recalled Ververt Turner, oft-quoted protégé of Jimi Hendrix. "In the afternoons, we would drive in and sit there together. Jimi would write on napkins, draw pictures and write songs and tell me about the music business and the world and song ideas, like his concepts for Gypsy Suns and Rainbows. Lollapalooza was a concept that Jimi was talking about back in 1968, having under one tent this kind of big circus thing that

155

would come to town, kind of camp outside, and set up for a week at a time. It would be multimedia. That was the concept."

By the summer of 1969, Jimi might have felt that concept had somehow been realized. It seemed like he went from one festival to another that summer—Newport Pop in California, Denver Pop at Mile High Stadium, Woodstock. Little wonder, then, that he conceived of a rock-and-roll caravan.

Summer has meant music festivals, however, for many years. As early as 1934, classical music lovers in the Berkshires started to book concerts with the New York and Boston orchestras. Some years later, these concerts had a full-time home at Tanglewood. In 1954, Boston-based club owner George Wein began presenting jazz festivals in Newport, Rhode Island, about equidistant between New York City and his home base. They ran every year between '54 and '71, with the exception of 1961.

"Jazz had become a bad word with the riots in 1960 at Newport," he noted about the event that spurred the 1961 cancellation. "I had to work very hard to overcome that. I did work hard."

What saved him was the emerging merger of pop music and folk music. The Newport Folk Festival became as important as the jazz festival. "Rock saved me," Wein conceded.

By 1967, rock and roll had transcended a fad. It was, even by the most conservative estimate, a dozen years old, and still growing strong. Not yet a full-blown cultural phenomenon, it was the sound of the youth of the Western world.

That a powerful youth culture developed at this time is not surprising. The number of people between the ages of fourteen and twenty-four nearly doubled over the course of the '60s. That age group made up fully a fifth of the world's population by 1969. From the Reeperbahn to Bleecker Street, from Hyde Park to Haight Ashbury, this was the biggest generation of young people the world had ever known, the leading edge of the postwar "baby boom," and it was beginning to assert itself culturally. Elvis, Chuck Berry, the Beach Boys, the Beatles all became touchstones of the emerging youth culture, but they were only the beginning.

The political tides were changing as well. The biggest scare many in this generation had known—and only the older ones at that—was the two weeks when the world went into alert status as the Soviet

Union tried to ship missiles into Cuba, less than one hundred miles from the U.S. This helped renew the fear and loathing of communism that had fueled the McCarthy hearings of the '50s, this time directed to *international* communism. By the mid-'60s, the "salami theory"—that you take a little slice of communism here, a little slice of communism there, and suddenly half the salami, i.e., the world, has "gone commie"—had led America into a new fight that divided the northern and southern halves of an Asian nation into "free" and "communist" regimes—Vietnam. Now, those late teens born in the wake of World War II and Korea faced a war of their own. By 1967, the U.S. government had shipped out nearly half a million young American men to that strip of Southeast Asia. Most of them couldn't even find it on a map. By the end of that year, tens of thousands were either killed or wounded there.

If the real estate they fought over seemed remote, the reasons they went over to fight in the first place were as opaque as the mud in which they fought. Images of the carnage came into every American household with the morning paper and the evening television news. A great many of the young men saw this potential future and felt helpless against it. On college campuses and in major cities, the youth with the most to lose started protesting the war and rebelling against the middle-class lifestyle that they identified as causing it. This had a polarizing effect on America. Many young men burned their draft cards and hightailed it to Canada, where they would stay—some until the late '70s when President Jimmy Carter declared amnesty for draft evaders, some never to return again. Still others went to jail to avoid the war. One of the most famous opponents of the conflict, heavyweight boxing champ Muhammad Ali, was stripped of his title and jailed.

Inspired by some of their musical icons, young people grew their hair long. Inspired by the availability, hallucinogens and other drugs replaced their parents' martinis as the youth cocktail of choice. The new lifestyle demanded a new soundtrack. For some it was soul like Otis Redding and Joe Tex, for some it was pop like Motown and Tom Jones, and for others it was rock that spanned the gamut from pop to soul, from the Who to the Grateful Dead.

The summer of 1967 has gone down in the history books as the Summer of Love. With the Vietnam conflict as a far-off backdrop, the reaction to it at home was peaceful decadence—tune in, turn on, and drop out; free love; lots of good tunes. It had a utopian feel. The boomers were so numerous, they were finally beginning to feel their power. They developed a strong alternative to the entrenched way things were done. Part of that power emanated from the music.

"In '66 and '67," remarked Grateful Dead right-hand-man Dennis McNally, "in large part due to the influence of the Diggers in San Francisco, the Dead played free in Golden Gate Park and the Panhandle any number of times, partly because it was fun, partly as a political act, to give music a way to move, to take it out of the ballroom scene and all that. Nobody paid them. At that point they were small enough that it was possible to do it where your entire expense was the twenty-five dollars it took to rent the flatbed truck. They literally powered the stage on extension cords strung from apartments. Believe it or not, that was the level of equipment they had at the time. You're playing for five hundred or a thousand people. It just doesn't have to be elaborate. Simple as that. In '66, '67, they'd literally wake up on a sunny morning and say, 'It's a good day to play in the park. It's sunny today. Let's go play.' Everybody lived together. Somebody would rustle up a truck, string the power cords and go out and play. No effort."

During the Summer of Love, the Diggers had bigger fish to fry (which was a good thing, as one of the roles they took on was passing out food). They had been approached by John Phillips of the Mamas and the Papas and producer Lou Adler, who were involved in putting together a fairly ambitious show up the Pacific Coast Highway in Monterey. They were busy getting permission from the town and the police, but they also needed to get the support of the opinion makers.

The first great rock festival, the Monterey International Pop Festival proved to be a pivotal point in the commercialization of rock and roll, and turned into a feeding frenzy for the music business. But before that could happen, they had to sure up the venue and convince both the town and the intended audience that the festival would be a good idea. "We had to convince the alternative society as well as the Establishment," publicist Derek Taylor noted.

Monterey was a radical idea in many ways. A gathering of the youth culture seemed risky to the "Establishment," who had visions of vandalism and rowdiness. What they got was three days of peace, flowers, and music. "We've had more trouble at PTA conventions," one of the sheriff's deputies said.

"There were no arrests at Monterey," Michele Phillips added. "There were no fights, no problems. It was a beautiful weekend."

It also marked one of the first times the American public came to grips with the popularity of rock. There had been decades of classical gatherings, over ten years of jazz gatherings, but that represented established culture. Rock and roll was still the outlaw sound.

"The idea for the Monterey International Pop Festival came out of the mid-'60s belief that what had been pop music was now a much more serious art form, and could take its place alongside jazz," Taylor said.

Another revolutionary aspect of the show was the sheer volume of talent presented, and the ideals that drew the talent there. Thirty artists, including Otis Redding, the Who, the Byrds, and Simon and Garfunkel appeared. They also asked Chuck Berry, but having been burned through the '60s, he had started looking out exclusively for number one: "I told him on the phone," recalled John Phillips, "'Chuck, it's for charity,' and he said to me, 'Chuck Berry has only one charity and that's Chuck Berry. $2,000.' We couldn't make an exception."

Additionally, a large number of future stars made their initial leap at Monterey. It was one of the first times Big Brother and the Holding Company had performed outside the Bay Area. Everyone from Ravi Shankar to Clive Davis was taken with their front person, a gritty, soulful blues singer named Janis Joplin. Davis started negotiating their contract with Columbia Records the day of their performance. Another performer who earned his stripes at Monterey was a young unknown guitarist from Seattle who had been tearing up Europe the previous year, Jimi Hendrix.

Joel Selvin, long-time rock critic for the *San Francisco Chronicle*, recalled seeing Hendrix and thinking the guitarist had "rewritten the rule book of the role of the guitar in rock. [Even] if he had fallen dead in the wings he would have made his mark."

Along with Joplin and Hendrix, the Jefferson Airplane and several other groups were signed to recording contracts owing to their performances at Monterey. The freak barrier was broken, and the music business was betting large amounts of money (rumors flew that some of these signings went for a quarter of a million dollars or more, huge sums for the '60s) that these new, "hippie" rock bands were the wave of the future.

This only grew when the film *Monterey Pop* hit theaters. People who weren't there could see the Who make wreckage of their instruments, could see Jimi Hendrix's incendiary guitar playing ending with a literally incinerated guitar.

The promoters set up the show as a charity event. While the cost of tickets for the show ran between three dollars and six-fifty per performance in the main arena, most chose to listen to the music from the outside "strolling area." All the artists played the show for free (though they did get flown in and put up). Artists John Phillips, Johnny Rivers, and Paul Simon, along with producers Lou Adler and Terry Melcher, put up the seed money. All profits would go to a foundation and be donated to charity. The Monterey Foundation still continues to award grants. "It showcased the fact that we were doing rock 'n' roll for the spirit of it," Art Garfunkel said.

"There was no price that could have been set for this particular group of talent at that time," Lou Adler added. Over the next two years, that would change.

The coverage of the event was remarkable and wide-ranging. *Time* and *Newsweek* reported on the event. In the *New York Post,* Pete Hamill noted how peaceful the event was: "What these kids are is the avant-garde of the Leisure Generation. . . . This country will have to come to grips with everything these kids are dealing with right now in Haight Ashbury in San Francisco, in the East Village in New York and along Fairfax and the Strip and in Venice in Los Angeles."

Stalwart jazz critic Leonard Feather remarked how, "the growing suspicion that rock 'n' roll has become important was substantiated to say the least. . . . The old beat was still there and still intoxicating, but none of the Monterey sounds resembled rock's embryonic stage."

Suddenly, rock and pop festivals sprang up all over. In 1968, a young promoter named Michael Lang put together a one-day event in Miami. "Just seeing the effect that the music and the atmosphere had on the kids there was an inspiration to do more of those kinds of events," Lang remarked from his office in the formerly bohemian East Village of New York City. "I felt that the timing was right for a big generational gathering. It had been a lot of years of protests and issues and struggles and freedom and fun. There was this kind of disjointed family out there in America that everybody, I think, sort of felt related to and attached to."

This gathering of the tribes was originally set for Woodstock, New York, an area already attracting some of the New York City arts community, a two-hour drive from the heart of Greenwich Village. When the residents changed their minds at the specter of a hundred thousand people running around their town, Lang made arrangements to move the festival grounds to a farm about seventy miles southwest, in the town of Bethel, near the border between New York and Pennsylvania. The move came so late that they couldn't change the name of the festival. All the ads, posters, and tickets said the Woodstock Music and Arts Fair. They ultimately didn't even have the chance to put up a ticket gate.

"The last thing to go up were the gates, and they just never got into place," Lang recalled. "People, in large numbers, had shown up on Monday and Tuesday. By the time the weekend rolled around there was probably, going into Friday, about 100,000 people there."

It had been an enormous summer for "pop festivals." There were the two that Jimi played in Denver and Newport at Northridge, California. The Soul Bowl played the Astrodome. Toronto, Atlanta, Dallas, Atlantic City, and New Orleans all held music festivals. Seattle hosted two, Seattle Pop and Sky River Rock.

"Some of the artists at Woodstock played Mile High," noted Lang. "Atlantic City had probably twenty or thirty percent of our bill. It's the way you book a tour. You're on a routing and agencies tend to keep you on some sort of a coherent order, rather then sending you back and forth across the country. Since Atlantic City was two weeks before Woodstock, it was sort of naturally part of the route.

"There were quite a few festivals that summer. I went to all of them to see what the problems would be. It was a summer that was fraught with incidents at rock shows: Gate-crashing, tear gassing, police confrontations. I found, as I was sort of a guinea pig at all of these shows, that there was always a reason for the problem. You put two hundred cops in tear gas masks and helmets, and give them clubs and stand them on one side of the arena, you're going to set up a confrontation."

Lang avoided this in two ways. The off-duty police he hired were not given weapons of any sort. They didn't wear uniforms. Rather than call them "security," they called the peace officers at Woodstock the "peace patrol." Crowd control was handled by the Hog Farm. "They had a very nice, natural way of dealing with things," Lang said. "Pies in the face instead of clubs over the head."

Tickets for the three-day "music and art fair" ran eighteen dollars for the three days, "if you bought it in advance," Lang smiled. "Kind of a bargain."

The reason Woodstock is so celebrated is severalfold. Perhaps the apex of what rock and roll was all about, it was gentle, loving, and musical; it was drugged out, bugged out, and dug out; it was sloppy, muddy, and ultimately so badly overrun that they had to figure out how to feed the 500,000 people who showed up, nearly three times the number they had expected.

For most of the people who didn't pay in advance, it was even more of a bargain. "It became a free show on Friday because there were no gates," Lang said. "We created quite a site. We did parks and trails and swimming holes. We tried to make it as good a facility for people to spend a weekend as we could. You go into a beautiful country setting and your first reaction is not to get uptight. Nature has a way of soothing, and we felt that if we offered people something better than what they were expecting, if the experience when they came was something more than what we were promising, not less, those sorts of things would tend to get people to open up and relax."

Tickets at the gate were supposed to cost about twenty-one dollars. The promoters had hoped to use this money to pay the second half of the guarantees for the bands. However, without the gates, they had to draw the money other ways. Afterwards, stories started to circulate that bands had to threaten the promoters to get the second half of their guarantee. One story had the Who's John Entwhistle lifting one promoter off the ground by his collar and threatening to throw him into the crowd.

"It wasn't that the bands had trouble getting paid after the show, it was getting paid *at* the show," said Lang. "Everyone got paid. I think we managed to get the bank to open up in the middle of the night to draw checks for some of the bands."

Festivals had grown up. Where Monterey, two years previous, had the utopian purity of a nonprofit event with the artists performing free for charity, Woodstock was definitely a for-profit venture, for both the bands and the promoters.

"I paid them more than they'd ever been paid before," said Lang. "We set a maximum of $15,000 per act, but most acts had topped at $10,000 at that point. Once the groundswell started, we were being deluged with acts. There was some difficulty with some of the acts we booked. The Who had to be convinced to come from England to do it. There were a few of those kinds of issues."

Some of the baby bands from Monterey were the heavyweights at Woodstock. Janis Joplin and the Jefferson Airplane had emerged as full-blown stars in the ensuing two years. The Who had made history with an elaborate rock opera called *Tommy*. They performed the entire piece at Woodstock, and that was only part of their set.

"*Tommy* had been a huge, fluid success, partly, maybe because of Woodstock," the group's Pete Townshend said. "What the Who had done on stage at Woodstock is the opera with guitar, bass, and drums, and it held together."

This double album had brought rock into the realm of "serious music" as the first true "rock opera." So serious that it got played at the Metropolitan Opera House and remains as vital a work today as the day it was released. It also triggered waves of writers who saw that rock could be used in a wider context than just a three-minute song. Yet, at Woodstock, the group was very unhappy with their performance and the fact that they didn't even get onstage until around three in the morning. Added to that, yippie leader Abbie Hoffman jumped on the stage to try and raise some consciousness, raving about imprisoned White Panther leader John Sinclair. Who guitarist Pete Townshend found this disruptive and inappropriate. He kicked Hoffman off the stage—literally—to the cheers of the crowd. Townshend later came to regret having done that, though. "What he was arguing for," he said, "was very valid." At the 1998 A Day in the Garden concert held at Yasgur's Farm, the site of the original 1969 festival, Townshend dedicated "Behind Blue Eyes" to Hoffman.

Woodstock also showcased what might just be the zenith of rock and roll. Jimi Hendrix had become an amazing live draw between

Monterey and Woodstock. He was set to close the show, debuting his new band Gypsy Suns and Rainbows, playing music from his ground-breaking *Are You Experienced*, *Axis Bold as Love*, and *Electric Ladyland* albums. With these releases, Hendrix had entirely redefined the sound of the guitar and indeed the rock band from that time until today. Beyond being a great and very instinctive musician, he was also a consummate showman. At Monterey, he had astonished the audience by setting his guitar on fire. At Woodstock, the shocks were more musical, as he launched into a version of America's national anthem that made the song into a war zone, with bombs bursting out of his guitar and ambulances running around the sonic battlefield he created.

Most of the musicians had never made so much for one show, nor had they ever played for such a large audience. It was the largest single gathering for a musical event ever, nearly half a million people. Due to the problems with the gate, most of them didn't pay. Although the movie and several albums have come out since, "it turned a profit of inches about ten years ago, " Lang concedes, "but not a huge profit."

In many ways Woodstock was the highwater mark of the rising tide of utopian spirit started at Monterey. While the music was remarkable, the human portion of the equation was equally important.

"For a city that size," said Stu Cook, bassist for Creedence Clearwater Revival, one of the Saturday night headliners, "I guess you have to call it a city, there had to be half a million there, which made it one of the largest cities in just about any state. It was certainly the biggest crowd we ever played for. The fact that they made it through the weekend without any really out-of-control aggressiveness, considering the amount of chemicals that were being passed around, I think that was the most amazing feat of all."

As large as the crowd that made it to the festival grounds was, more people were stuck on the road. The concert closed down nearly every major highway in that area of New York state. The artists had to be flown in by helicopter. Since no one had anticipated the size and scope of the crowd, there was a shortage of sleeping areas and sanitation and food. Certainly any kind of large-scale deliveries were impossible. The Hog Farm somehow generated a huge amount of granola for the crowd. During her set, Janis Joplin told the audience, "If you have any food, share it with your brother and sister—that's the person on your right, the person on your left." And people did it.

"The vibe of the place," adds Cook, "was the most amazing thing, under those kind of conditions, with limited sanitary (facilities) and no accommodations. The fact that everybody showed some respect for the people around them was probably the most amazing thing for me, outside of the musical aspect. We were just in awe of the whole thing. As advertised originally, it was supposed to be the biggest thing ever, but it turned out to be triple that."

"They were the most courteous, considerate, and well-behaved group of kids in my twenty-four years of police work," one of the officers on the scene recalled.

"The most surprising thing was how well the people behaved," Lang agreed, "how helpful they were to each other, how they just opened up and gave to each other. It was just phenomenal to see it on that scale. You see things like that happening here and there, but to see it across such a huge demographic . . ."

Like Monterey, Woodstock "made" its share of performers, especially after the film came out. "I was doing really nicely before the Woodstock film came out," Alvin Lee from Ten Years After remembered. "When it came out, suddenly we were doing these huge obelisk places, finding ourselves playing to a fifty-foot pit full of policemen and you can't see the audience and the sound is bouncing around . . . ya' know, you do twenty of those in a row and you don't see the point."

Where most everything started to become can-you-top-this in America during the '70s and '80s, nobody tried to best this temporary city of half a million anytime soon thereafter. Perhaps the task was too daunting, perhaps the upshot too great, or perhaps the financial losses of the principals too scary. In the early '70s, festivals of Woodstock's ilk became rarer and rarer.

"After Woodstock, strangely enough, festivals sort of dried up in America," Lang noticed. "But it became a tradition in Europe. Festivals sprang up and continued every year in Europe, in England and Scandinavia. A lot of festivals grew and maintained through the years. There became a tradition of festivals. Strangely enough, they've remained fairly consistent in the way that they're put together. I was always surprised that that didn't follow in America."

Perhaps America sensed that anything after Woodstock would be anticlimactic. Or, perhaps it was on account of what happened across the country, a bit over one hundred miles as the Harley flies from the Monterey fairgrounds where it had all started, some four months after that utopia of perception called Woodstock. At Altamont, everything that everyone was afraid of about rock and roll came to pass.

It started when the Rolling Stones realized they had blown big-time exposure in the U.S. by blowing off appearing at Woodstock. So they decided to throw their own show and make their own movie about it. Initially they hoped to play a free concert in Golden Gate Park with special guests the Grateful Dead, the Jefferson Airplane, and Ike and Tina Turner.

They had recently played a similar show in London's Hyde Park and it had gone extremely well. For security at that show, they had hired the Stepney chapter of the Hell's Angels, and that had worked out so well, they decided to do it again in San Francisco. Which they did, over the objections of the Dead, for a truckload of beer and ice.

They applied for permission to play the show in the park that December. The parks department said that they would issue a permit only if no public announcement of the show was made more than twenty-four hours before the actual show. Stones lead singer Mick Jagger couldn't contain himself. He mentioned the show during a radio interview and the permit went poof.

Finding an alternative venue on short notice was not easy. They finally found a place about forty miles out of the city at the Altamont Speedway. It defeated part of the vision they had for the concert. Holding it in the park would have allowed them to bring everyone together. However, you needed to be able to *drive* to get out to Altamont.

People were actually flying in from all over the country to see the Stones for free. The desert surrounding Altamont was alive with cars, camping and traffic, backed up six miles in every direction. The radio was telling people not to go there. Ultimately 300,000 people showed up.

By the time the show got under way, it was clear that the afternoon would be a disaster. Melees broke out all over the grounds, with the Hell's Angels beating on each other and the audience with pool cues. Both Jagger and Marty Balin got punched. Grace Slick of the Airplane got onstage, looked out over the sea of battling bodies, and wondered aloud into the microphone, "What the fuck is going on?" The Dead just got onto their bus and left. The Stones, who threw the party after all, had to go on.

"It felt great and sounded great," recalled Keith Richards. "Then there's a big ruckus about one of the Angels' bikes being knocked over in front of the stage. Oh dear, a bike got knocked over. I'm not used to bein' upstaged by Hell's Angels—over somebody's motorbike. Yes, I perfectly understand that your bike's got knocked over, can we carry on with the concert? But they're not like that."

While the exact cause of what happened next is open to conjecture, the upshot is this: A young black man pulled a gun and was knifed to death. He was with a pretty white woman, so some suspect that the Angels were on him about that. Some suspect he was out to pop Jagger. Some feel that he was the object of the Angels' wrath for knocking over the bike and was protecting himself. No matter how you slice it, though, he was dead. And the Maysles brothers, who were making the documentary of the concert, captured the whole thing on film. In one of the most chilling scenes in cinema, they play the footage of the knifing over and over for Jagger, who pulls deeper into himself with each repeated viewing.

Whether because of Altamont or because people felt like they'd been there and done that or because the simple economics of such an event proved much more than anyone had anticipated, festivals became less ambitious, fewer and further between. George Harrison managed to pull off a concert that was festival-like in 1971 at Madison Square Garden, a benefit concert for the beleaguered people of Bangladesh, but over the next two decades American festivals of the size and scope of Woodstock, or even Monterey, became scarce.

In Europe, however, the Castle Donnington Festival, Reading Festival, and others would draw hundreds of thousands every year. This helped to revive the festival in America.

Jane's Addiction signed on to play the 1990 Reading Festival in England. Vocalist Perry Farrell lost his voice on the way. While Farrell went from doctor to doctor to try to reclaim it, drummer Steven Perkins took in the festival with the band's booking agent, Marc Geiger.

"We had a wonderful time," Geiger recalled. "We went back another day, and at one point we looked at each other and said, 'How come we can't have something like this in the States?' We just really loved the vibe of the festival. And we went back to talk to Perry about putting on a festival like that in America, and he was very much into the idea."

The next year, Farrell, Geiger, and Jane's Addiction's manager, Ted Gardner, made it reality. They called the event Lollapalooza. Not content to do things the way their parents had done it (it had, after all, been over twenty years since Woodstock), the Lollapalooza trio figured to bring their music to the people rather than having the people come to the music. They took the bands on tour with them, reminiscent of the old 1950s tours that took half-a-dozen acts from theater to theater.

Lollapalooza was also very reminiscent of the traveling caravan Jimi Hendrix had envisioned to Ververt Turner all those years ago. Where Woodstock spoke to the beginning bulge of the baby boom, Lollapalooza addressed the tastes of Generation X, celebrating the alternative music that Jane's Addiction had heralded. Farrell and company brought favorite acts like English new wavers Siouxsie and the Banshees; Body Count, the hardcore band fronted by rapper Ice-T; and a new band beginning to make a name for themselves, Nine Inch Nails.

They also had a midway that addressed the needs and interests of their audience. It included Internet kiosks, a film tent, an art tent, places to get body piercings, vegetarian food, booths for Greenpeace and AIDS information. "I've been to Lollapalooza, which is very reminiscent of the style of Woodstock in terms of the way it's laid out," Lang noted. "It's kind of a nice idea to travel with it."

Like Woodstock, Lollapalooza caught an audience at the height of ripeness. In 1991, "alternative music" made its move to the mainstream. Nirvana topped the charts at the turn of the year. Almost symbolically, the album it replaced was Michael Jackson's *Dangerous*. Unlike Woodstock, the promoters grew the idea, expanded it, and took it back on the road the next year. It became the breaking ground for bands like the Red Hot Chili Peppers and Pearl Jam.

Unlike the fizzle effect that happened after Woodstock, Lollapalooza happened after the more, more, more era of the '80s. They could take it out every year. People wanted them to, but it had to be bigger and better every time they did it. "Every year we try and reinvent ourselves and what Lollapalooza is to keep it fresh, 'cause we assume that people that go to it go more than one year," Geiger said. "I'd like to see Lollapalooza stay on the edge as much as possible and try not to be a reflection of the times, but always pushing the times forward musically and artistically."

Eventually they decided they couldn't grow it any more and folded up their caravan tents. However, that didn't put an end to the idea. Like music criticism, the traveling festivals just became considerably more focused in their approach and execution. Skate-music fans (ska-core, hardcore, etc.) were offered the Warped Tour, sponsored by a shoe manufacturer. The initial outing featured Bad Religion, the Specials, Cherry Poppin' Daddies, and others. The Guinness Fleadh tour, sponsored by the Irish brewery, reached out to roots fans with The Chieftains, Chumbawamba, John Lee Hooker, Richard Thompson, Squeeze, and Los Lobos. Blues Traveler's HORDE (Horizons of Rock Developing Everywhere) tour took out bands like Smashing Pumpkins, Fastball, Robert Bradley's Blackwater Surprise, Barenaked Ladies, and Ben Harper. Heavy metal fans got Limp Bizkit, Megadeth, Tool, Sevendust, and others on the Ozzfest, hosted by former Black Sabbath frontman and metal icon Ozzy Osbourne. Dead heads got the Other Ones, a band composed of former Dead members Mickey Hart, Phil Lesh, and Bob Weir joined by Bruce Hornsby, Dave Ellis, Stan Franks, and John Molo who headlined the Further Festival with fellow jam bands Rusted Root and Hot Tuna.

Perhaps the most notable of Lollapalooza's children, though, was the Lilith Fair, 1998's most successful touring festival. It addressed an audience no one had even thought of seeking on its own: women. As Woodstock changed the perception of society at large regarding the financial viability of rock and youth culture, and Lollapalooza once again reenergized perceptions about the commerciality of the "underground," Lilith opened the eyes of those who thought of rock predominantly as a man's game. With a rotating lineup of ten or so women artists ranging from festival founder Sarah McLachlan to the pop stylings of former Bangle Suzanna Hoffs to the Celtic undertones of the Cardigans, Lilith demonstrated that classifying someone as a "woman rocker" made as much sense as calling someone a male rocker. The performers at Lilith might have been largely of one gender, but they made music every bit as diverse, and rocked as convincingly as the big boys.

"We wanted to show that these rules don't apply anymore," McLachlan said, "that you can play two women back-to-back on the radio, that you can have a lineup with all women as headliners. In a sense, we're talking more to the industry than the public. Because the industry thinks the public only responds to the lowest common denominator, and I think the public deserves more credit than that. We're proving it."

That they did. Lilith confounded expectations by rising to the status of the highest grossing of the summer caravan festivals in 1998. Artists that joined the fair at one time or another read like a who's who of performers who just happen to be women—Bonnie Raitt, Queen Latifah, Sheryl Crow, Erykah Badu, Emmylou Harris, and Neneh Cherry to name but a few. However, McLachlan never saw this as "the women taking over." To her, Lilith just leveled the playing field a little. "We're not trying for an upper hand," she said, "we just want to even the scales a little bit and promote equality. That's what this has been good for. You bring such talented people together and you start to hear a sense of things shifting. You realize that we do have power—as a group, certainly, but also as individuals."

Another important aspect of Lilith was the enterprise's level of social responsibility. On the one hand, it had corporate sponsors, but as much as they put into the operating expenses of the show, they also made donations in the tour's name.

This brings up two very important aspects of the modern festival gestalt—the yin and yang of the contemporary festival, the balance between the ideals of the foundation endowing Monterey and the for-profit venture that became Woodstock—corporate sponsorship and altruism. Touring festivals like the Vans' Warped tour and the Guinness Fleadh tours are sponsored by specific corporate entities. However, most have a midway that at least pays lip service to social responsibility.

This yin-and-yang relationship between art and commerce is not the sole province of the caravan festivals. Two other types of musical events go by the festival name. Anyone who went to Woodstock would recognize a festival as an event that brings a bunch of bands to one place at one time. Many radio stations throw "Weenie Roasts" and other types of sponsored shows that might bring together over a dozen artists on one bill. The converse of this event is the Tibetan Freedom Festival. The first one was held at New York's Randall's Island (a traditional site for New York City festivals from the '70s and the

New York Pop Festival—another Hendrix-headlined show—to the New York City dates for Lollapalooza). It brought together such diverse acts as the Beastie Boys, U2, and Radiohead to promote the cause of Tibetan nationals oppressed by the Chinese government.

Another kind of event that has taken on the sobriquet of "festival" is a gathering of musical events that takes place across an entire city. The Newport (now JVC) Jazz Festival evolved into this when it came to New York and spread into a week's worth of performances at venues—on the East Side, on the West Side, all around the town—such as Town Hall, the Blue Note, and Avery Fischer Hall. Such a festival "takes over" Midtown Atlanta on an annual basis as well over the course of three days in May.

Similarly, the Intel festival would take over Manhattan clubs in mid-July, the ghost of a festival that accompanied the New Music Seminar, a music-business event that brought literally thousands of bands of all shapes, sizes, and genres to New York City for over a decade. The Intel festival marked a watershed of its own, happening both in reality and in virtual reality on the Web, offering millions of music fans worldwide the ability to participate.

Whether the show springs from the navel of corporate sponsorship or the most charitable instincts of the performers, they always have had one common denominator. Festivals offer a place for thousands of people to share and enjoy a musical and cultural experience, to explore the things that make us different and the things we share. They are yet another way that music brings us together.

The Sex Pistols Tour America

Toward the middle of the '70s, the world started to come unhinged while fighting, grasping desperately, for some level of status quo. Unfortunately for the youth of the late '70s, lots of things were wrong. The economy, worldwide, had taken a dive, causing double-digit inflation. Unemployment also achieved double-digit status—though through statistical hocus pocus, the government was able to keep it down to single digits on paper lest panic ensue. At least in the U.S.

In England, some estimate 25 percent of the population under twenty-five were "on the dole." Within five years, the official overall unemployment rates in England would top double digits. Riots broke out among youth that writer Jon Savage aptly described as "doubly disenfranchised from work (no jobs) and leisure (no money to fill the gap left by no jobs) . . ."

This led to a lot of disaffection, to say the least. Beyond that, even *music* had stopped speaking to them. In the fall of 1975, the charts were topped by such behemoth rockers as David Essex in England and John Denver in the U.S. Over the course of the decade the popular rock had mutated into the letter-perfect studio confections of Queen; their "Bohemian Rhapsody" topped the English charts in November 1975. KISS offered up the grittiest rock in the Stateside pop charts with a live version of "Rock and Roll All Night."

Yet the spirit of rock was still around. You just had to look harder for it and away from the radio—a trend that continues to prevail. New York homeboys the Ramones and the New York Dolls brought a loud, fast, visceral sound back to the music, as did bands like DMZ in Boston and groups playing clubs and pick-up gigs where they could get them in most major cities. Not part of the mainstream, rock critic Lester Bangs suggested that they reminded him of his favorite '60s bands, loud, neopsychedelic rock bands like the Seeds and the Count Five. He gave them the same name he called those old beloved groups: punk rock.

Among the stalwarts of this scene in New York were Johnny Thunders and the Heartbreakers. With the limited opportunities in New York, they took their show to London, where they developed a good-sized following, though drugs would eventually destroy the band. However, hearing about the London scene, lots of New York bands made the trip over the pond, including Patti Smith, Television, Blondie, Talking Heads, and the Ramones.

"At our soundcheck at Dingwalls," Joey Ramone recalled of their trip to England, "all these kids—Johnny Lydon, Joe Strummer—were there telling us that we were responsible for turning them on. England was like a freak show, a circus, with the different-colored hair and all. It was great but kinda crazy."

Another band that made the trip were elder statesmen of the scene, the New York Dolls. The Dolls had a lot going for them. They were theatrical to the point of high camp, cross-dressing in high heels and makeup. They played loose, raunchy rock and roll. They had a great frontman in David Johansen, who continues to be possessed of one of the great voices in pop music into the twenty-first century. They had some great songs and had been one of the first New York "underground bands" to land on a major label. However, that didn't help the scene because their records, one brilliant and one just so-so, didn't sell well.

Nonetheless, this impressed fashion designer and King's Road clothing-store owner Malcolm McLaren, whose shop, Too Fast to Live, Too Young to Die, attracted the Dolls as the Dolls attracted him. He'd had some experience in rock, making a student film on English rocker Billy Fury. He offered to manage the Dolls and followed them home to New York. "The trouble with the Dolls," McLaren said, "was their hype was so much bigger than they were. They really had an opportunity to change it all around, but instead of ignoring all that bullshit about signing up with a company and a big advance, they got sucked in."

The Dolls' disappointment reflected badly on the scene. "Everybody was unique and worked hard," said Ramone, "but there was a black cloud in that nobody was signing New York bands because of the failure of the New York Dolls."

McLaren's sojourn with the Dolls lasted for a bit under a year. By 1975 McLaren was back in his shop on King's Road. By then the shop had shortened its name simply to Sex, with its clothing line leaning heavily on leather and rubber fetishwear. This brought out the punks in force. Three of them had a band built on the spiv ethic—they manifestly wanted to avoid the dead-end jobs that loomed in their future. They bought their leather at Sex and, knowing McLaren's history with the Dolls (and hoping for a discount), started asking his advice on the band and eventually goaded him into managing them.

His first move was to have vocalist/guitarist Steve Jones drop doing the vocals. He brought in John Lydon, who hung out a bit by the jukebox at Sex. McLaren then changed the band's name to the Sex Pistols, British slang for male genitalia. He changed Lydon's name to Johnny Rotten, another bit of British slang for a bad condom.

Lydon/Rotten didn't have the greatest voice, but he had the right level of intensity. "I hate shit," he said. "I hate hippies and what they stand for. I hate long hair. I hate pub bands."

Pub rock was the prevalent style of the day, bands making music for drinking. "They're all full of people," McLaren said of the pub rockers, "playing what a crowd wants rather than what they want because they can make a reasonable living from it. If you want to change things, you can't play pubs. You don't have the freedom."

In this, McLaren tipped his hand as to what the Sex Pistols were all about. The Sex Pistols reached a level of infamy that made them exciting culturally—though they were no less a fabrication than, say, the Monkees. The whole reason behind their creation—beyond shits and giggles for McLaren—was to act as agents provocateurs for rock's third generation, a generation that in England and to a lesser degree in the U.S. really felt what the Pistols would sing in their controversial debut hit—that there was "no future."

When Rotten sang "I am an anarchist" in the opening lines of that song, it might have been his voice singing, but the idea was McLaren's. As a student, McLaren fell under the sway of the teachings of an artistic movement called the Situationists, which espoused creating situations that exposed the faults of society and provoked reactions. The movement's motto was, "Nothing is true. Everything is permitted." Selling bondage ware was one way he espoused this, but the Sex Pistols probably represented the apex of his work.

"Instead of using the canvas," he said, "I have to use human beings.

"To poke fun at the world is to provoke its collapse," he added. "For me, the very destructive nature [of punk] was ultimately its most creative point. To me, that was what it was all about."

This attitude trickled down to the group. "I'm against people who just complain about *Top of the Pops* and don't do anything," said Rotten. "I want people to go out and start something, to see us and start something, or else I'm just wasting my time."

And start something they did.

By 1977 the Sex Pistols had done one of the things they were designed to do—started a storm of controversy. Their live performances caused near riots, mostly incited by Rotten, who would throw furniture at the band and the audience to goad them into action. They earned a great deal of coverage in the papers, which spurred a bidding war among several record companies. They signed with EMI and put out the single "Anarchy in the U.K." The mainstream promotion of the record got derailed when the band cursed—extensively—during a BBC interview. The resultant brouhaha caused EMI to sever their contract and withdraw the single.

McLaren then signed them with A&M Records. The Pistols lasted a week on that roster, with the company paying them $75,000 in severance. They were making more money not releasing records than most bands did putting them out.

They finally signed with Virgin, and their first single for the label, "God Save the Queen," released in time for the Queen's Silver Jubilee, went to #2. But this was almost incidental. The biggest effect they had was on other musicians or musical wannabees. In a rock atmosphere pulsating with note-perfect performances, the raw, amateurish rock of the Pistols was a cold slap in the face to the music establishment and a bracing reminder about the core of rock. "There we were," said Joe Strummer of one of the bands that saw the Pistols and realized they could do it too, the Clash, "following Emerson, Lake & Palmer to the brink of disaster, but luckily everybody snapped out of it."

The Sex Pistols showed musicians that being sonically clean and technically perfect didn't matter if you had a level of commitment and generated a level of excitement. Suddenly new bands, inspired by the do-it-yourself ethic of the Sex Pistols, started forming all over England: the Clash, the Buzzcocks, Joy Division, the Jam, the Damned all arose in the Pistols' wake.

"I just wonder what exactly was it that was influencing them," Rotten said, "because they seemed to get it quite wrong. I've been completely—all my life—thoroughly anti-drug culture, anti-gloom and doom. I think everything I've done has been constructive and there to help people, not destroy them."

Caroline Coon—who managed the Clash for a hot minute—saw it and understood immediately. "*Participation* is the operative word," she wrote. "The audiences are reveling in the idea that any one of them could get up on stage and do just as well, if not better, than the bands already up there. Which is, after all, what rock and roll is all about."

By the end of 1977, no venue in England would book the Sex Pistols, but word of this new band was spreading, and eventually reached the U.S. The circus had come to town. They booked a tour so bizarre that it was guaranteed to generate more publicity than it did music. After initial difficulty getting visas, the group opened up their American tour in front of four TV cameras and a hall full of press in Atlanta. The show introduced the group's newest member to the U.S. Bass player Glen Matlock had left to form a new band and had been replaced by one of Rotten's homeboys, John Ritchie, who was redubbed Sid Vicious. The set was sloppily magnificent, but no one on stage did anything worse than spit, which disappointed the audience mightily.

The next night, in Memphis, only seven hundred of the nine hundred paying ticket holders were allowed in the venue. A riot ensued, which pleased the band mightily. Several days later, they cursed their way through live interviews on San Francisco radio. During one interview Vicious declared that he would be dead in two years. Many, aware of his heroin usage, suspected that estimate was optimistic. As it panned out, they were right.

By the end of the tour, Rotten had had it. He reverted back to being John Lydon and broke up the band. He surfaced again in a more musically malleable unit called Public Image Ltd. that eventually turned into a solo vehicle. A little over a year after the Pistols disbanded, Sid Vicious was dead of an overdose.

All the pandemonium surrounding the Sex Pistols had several remarkable effects on rock in the late '70s. The group almost single-handedly managed to reinvigorate the form. Suddenly rock was back to a point where if the energy was there, if the feeling was there, then it could build. You didn't have to be an accomplished musician to be in a band, though it proved to be far better if you actually had something to say.

"Then the world changed," said Joey Ramone. "Everything changed. It wasn't just the music. There was a whole new philosophy and attitude. Everything changed drastically for the better—'76–'77 was like '64–'65 and the English Invasion. We put the spirit and guts back into rock 'n' roll."

The media, however, and especially the record companies, disliked the punk appellation. American spinmeisters felt that it had far too negative a connotation (which was, in part, the point). So bands that started sprouting like spring weeds, nurtured by the urine and spittle of the Sex Pistols, started being called "new wave." A lot of good music fell under this rubric: Veterans of the New York City scene like Talking Heads, Television, and Blondie became vanguard new wave artists. And, as with so many rock movements, a lot of meaningless music fell into this genre, then fell by the wayside. But new wave, more than anything else, was a marketing concept, a way of channeling and coopting this new music in a safer manner so as to sell many, many recordings. On that count, it worked about as well as any music marketing concept, perhaps better than most. By the '80s, Blondie and Talking Heads had broken pop, without selling too big a portion of their souls to accomplish it.

"Our record company felt that we should tour with Black Sabbath, to get some more exposure," Ramone recalled of a late 1978 stint on the road. "We never felt it was right, though we were big fans of Black Sabbath in their heyday. In those days there was a real barrier between punk and heavy metal and when we arrived in San Bernardino, California, the promoter, who was pretty ignorant, did this billing which was 'The Kings of Heavy Metal Versus the Kings of Punk Rock.' He made it like a battle. . . . There were all of these motorcycle, redneck farmers there, drinking pints of whiskey. We were twenty minutes into our set, doing 'Surfin' Bird,' and it started raining whiskey bottles, carburetors, spark plugs, ice picks, and food. It was getting pretty hairy, so we left the stage, and the stage manager, about eighty-five years old, said, 'Last time I saw a reaction like that was the first time the Rolling Stones played America.'"

By 1978, "new wave" bands had begun crossing over to that bastion of the arena act, the album-oriented, rock FM stations. A band made up of two former English jazz fusion players and the drumming son of a CIA agent dyed their hair blond and took their name from the drummer's dad's profession—they called themselves the Police. Another band that had been big in Boston released their debut album in 1978. The Cars never professed to be anything but a rock band, although their leader Ric Ocasek had some unusual ideas and influences, including the minimalist, New York punk duo, Suicide. "The combination of people was perfect for that particular time," he said of his group. "To have a band that has a group sound, a sound that comes from that band and elements of what they know. It had a unique sound just using those elements."

The Pistols' DIY ethic washed over on some American bands that got caught up in the tide of the "new wave." "We all hung out as sort of a group," recalled B-52s vocalist and keyboard player Kate Pierson.

"Then we started jamming one night and we started writing. Sort of spontaneous combustion. And when the smoke cleared, someone asked us to play at a party."

For many of the original punk bands, survival required growth. The chainsaw guitars of punk grew tiresome—even to them—after a while. The Clash, for example, broke out of the mode with one of the most magnificent rock albums ever made, *London Calling*. To make it, though, they had to come to grips with some realities, that punk, whatever it had been, was just a part of a larger whole. "We're just a band and we release records," said Joe Strummer, "and that's the fact of the situation, I'd say, but people think they've got to swallow all the bullshit with it."

Others tried to keep punk alive, but only managed to embrace facets of it. The punk scene that sprang up in Los Angeles had the essential energy of its predecessors, but all focused on the music's nihilism, missing an essential point in the Pistols' nihilism: when the Pistols said, "No future," they were trying to provoke. When the Circle Jerks said it, they meant it—all they saw was no way out. The scene took punk credibility to very high levels. People in the scene saw themselves as preservers of the purer faith of punk; everyone else was a sell-out.

This brought to light a very important aspect of what punk accomplished. Punk was supposed to be about anarchy, but McLaren and the Pistols' anarchy was a very different thing from the blank generation of L.A. teens that turned to violence and punk in the early '80s, what filmmaker Penelope Spheeris documented and so aptly titled in her film *The Decline (of Western Civilization)*. Where McLaren and the Pistols sought to provoke, many in the L.A. scene sought nothing short of total destruction.

This, of course, was antithetical to what was really going on, even among some of the L.A. punk bands with "cred." By 1980, X, one of the most popular bands on the L.A. punk scene, was making critically acclaimed records for Slash, an L.A. punk/new wave label that had a pressing-and-distribution deal with one of the major label behemoths, Warners.

As time fled from 1976, more and more people, both on the musical and critical front, watched as the punk vortex got sucked and subsumed into the larger vortex of both rock and the business that had surrounded it. All but the most uncommercial or stalwartly DIY bands either fell by the wayside or were drawn into the mainstream, usually then to fall by the wayside.

Additionally, the perception of punk began to mellow with age. Many began to equate it with the mod movement of a dozen years earlier, the platform from which Pete Townshend (often, along with Iggy Pop, called "Daddy Punk"), the Small Faces, and so many other bands launched. Where punk had started more as a street movement, mod had begun in the English art schools. New wave had more of that feel, even with the name, which recalled French cinema more than music. "I guess we've always appealed to college kids," conceded the B-52s' Fred Schneider, certainly more of a "new waver" than a punk.

On the other hand, the punk ethos continued to crop up, even in bands within the mainstream vortex. "They always say that Jane's Addiction is some sort of art students band," railed the group's vocalist, Perry Farrell. "When I first heard that, I got mad. And then I thought to myself, 'Hey, we're not [an] art school band, we never went to art school.' And I thought about that and fuck, I would love to be in art school, right now at this present time . . . seems like fun. Plus, you're not working."

In the '90s, Jane's Addiction was a band that seemed to get the Situationist vibe of the Pistols, whether they were aware of it or not. "We are a grungy, street band," said the group's drummer, Steve Perkins. "We could have polished our sound, change lyrics so that no one would be offended, but that's not us. Like our album cover (a Farrell sculpture of naked Siamese twins with their hair on fire), we're not going to change it . . ."

Many in musical, critical, and even academic circles tried to make some sense of the punk ethic, punk credibility, and how it translated into a postpunk world. Some saw it as an economic model, stressing the importance of a combination of political awareness and the DIY ethos. They would cite bands like Washington, D.C.'s Fugazi and groups on Southern California's SST as "Rotten's children."

Even "cred" had its downside. Although the Sex Pistols started as a manufactured band, when they staged a reunion in the '90s, the reaction was brutal (could they have *wanted* it that way?). "1996 looks to be the pretty vacant summer," wrote *Rolling Stone*'s David Wild, "when we lose our remaining punk innocence . . ."

The further irony of the situation is that the second-edition Sex Pistols have lasted at least three times as long as the first edition. Furthermore, by 2003, the reunited group were playing casinos in both Atlantic City and Las Vegas. "As I sit around and think about what I do," Lydon said, "it amuses me greatly. I can't believe the cheek I have sometimes."

Nonetheless, the Sex Pistols gave rock and roll a wake-up call when it seemed the big sleep was upon it. The rawness, simplicity, and nihilism of the Sex Pistols' music helped spawn several movements in rock and roll, many of which still exist, though they have mutated over the years. From contemporary punk to "alternative rock," all still bear the spittle of the Sex Pistols.

MTV Launches

In January of 1986, Dave Marsh received a letter addressed "from the cloud of Lester Bangs." Written in an abbreviated version of Bangs' style, the curious note, reprinted in the front of the collection of Bangs' prose, *Psychotic Reactions and Carburetor Dung*, in part, reads: "Met God when I first got here. I asked him why. You know, 33 and all. All he said was 'MTV' He didn't want me to experience it, whatever the fuck it is."

Actually, MTV launched about nine months before Bangs passed on, but had yet to find a home on New York cable (not that Lester had cable). The Music Television Network went on the air on August 1,

1981, to the tune of the Buggles' "Video Killed the Radio Star." In retrospect you have to wonder if they meant that prophetically.

MTV changed popular music from a primarily audio medium to a medium requiring a very strong visual component. It ushered in the era of the pretty boy rocker, and also the inevitable backlash. It spawned a generation of people who "listened" to rock with the sound off—a behavior to which even some younger rock critics admit.

It started, however, mostly as a way to use bandwidth cheaply in the early days of cable TV. "A friend of mine was involved in a venture being sponsored by Warner Bros. and American Express," television producer (and bumper creator extraordinaire) Tom Pompasello recalled, "something called Warner-Amex Satellite Entertainment Corporation, or WASEC. WASEC had a little project going on called Television Music, which by the time it got on the air was called MTV."

The channel was partially the brainchild of WASEC VP James Lack and one of his hirelings, Bob Pittman. Pittman had previously worked as the program director of WNBC-FM, overseeing its change to one of the first totally automated radio stations in New York in the late '70s. He had previously produced a show for WASEC's kid channel, Nickelodeon, called *Album Tracks*, which followed a paradigm laid down on a previous Nickelodeon show, *Popclips*, produced by Pacific Arts, the company owned by former Monkee Mike Nesmith.

Neither *Popclips* nor *Album Tracks* set the world on fire. The format had obviously been used before, even as far back as *Bandstand*. The rock concert programs like *Don Kirschner's Rock Concert* and *The Midnight Special* that entertained teens as they came in late from their Friday and Saturday evening adventures also aired these clips interspersed with original concert footage. Pittman was convinced he had a winner and, being a pretty persuasive guy, convinced the powers at WASEC. The new channel was announced late in 1979. Soon, youth-oriented programs on the broadcast networks featured artists like Sting and hard-rock chanteuse Pat Benatar in spots declaring "I want my MTV!" It went live at midnight, August 1, 1981, via three hundred cable systems.

It was the most earthshaking thing to happen to popular music since punk, and it couldn't have come at a more propitious time. The most exciting music on the pop scene at the time was dance music, and it was reviled by most die-hard rockers, who wore "Disco Sucks" on their clothes and rolled with it on the back of their cars. A lot of cool music was falling under that rubric, however, including the hot blast out of Plainfield, New Jersey, and Detroit called Parliament-Funkadelic, the cheeky urban chic of August Darnell, and the "precision rock" of Nile Rogers' Chic.

Punk had never become "pop" in the U.S., and the "new wave" had splintered many ways. Several rock bands took a lesson from the dance music, creating a fusion called, aptly enough, dance rock. Groups like Blondie fell into this bag, along with the B-52s, and Talking Heads.

The top singles that summer included such scintillating fare as Rick Springfield's "Jesse's Girl," Air Supply's "The One That You Love," "Stars on 45," Diana Ross and Lionel Richie's "Endless Love," and Foreigner's "Urgent." The latter was also one of that year's top tracks on album radio, along with the Moody Blues' "The Voice," and Blue Oyster Cult's "Burning for You." Rock had had better years.

In this pond, the MTV pebble caused vast ripples. Artists like Todd Rundgren, who had dabbled in video for years, suddenly found an outlet for that aspect of their creativity. "I got involved in video in about 1973 or 1974," said Rundgren, who has a deserved reputation for technological precociousness. "I got interested because of the development of video art tools, the video synthesizer that was being used on educational television a lot, particularly on the *Electric Company*. I got very interested in video from the abstract standpoint, the Nam June Paik school. About 1975 or 1976 or so, I moved out of New York City and bought a house. That gave me space to install some video equipment. I had a home video studio from about 1976."

He got to show this off in legendary fashion when he was asked to host *The Midnight Special*. One song, "Can We Still Be Friends?" featured a ballet dancer that seemed to pirouette in miniature on the grand piano Rundgren was playing. "'Can We Still Be Friends?' was done at my house," he said. "I told them I wouldn't host it unless they let me do things like that.

"I proceeded to do broadcast-quality experimental video, a lot of what turned out to be the seminal music-video works," he added. "I think we had what turned out to be the third video shown when MTV went on the air. I think it was 'Feat Don't Fail Me Now.'"

Initially, the channel played like a radio station on television, complete with a crew of half-a-dozen veejays. "I was first attracted to the art of video music," said one of these original MTV veejays, Nina Blackwood, "because it seemed so logical to blend two of our most popular pastimes—listening to music and watching TV."

Groups like Duran Duran seemed to exist solely to appear in slick videos on MTV. They hit the scene simultaneously with MTV and the pairing suited both. The music might have been bland, but it was no blander than Journey or Foreigner, and the Duran boys (and the half-naked women in their videos) were a lot easier on the eyes.

Suddenly, in addition to needing a story for print and radio, artists had to have an easily projected and communicated image for MTV in order to become a hit. The more skilled an artist (or the artist's keeper) was at manipulating this image, the more success and longevity that artist would likely have.

The music videos developed a defining style, pioneered by artists like Rundgren and former 10cc members Kevin Godley and Lol Creme, inspired by video art pioneers like Nam June Paik, Charlotte Moorman, Frank Gillette, and Eric Siegel. The videos used quick cuts to blend with and often amplify the beat of the music, and to keep the interest of the restless eyes and attention spans of the audience. The style spread. Pretty soon any commodity that was sold as attitude, from cars to skin cream, was sold via MTV-like images.

"Most music videos don't have a story," director Marcus Nispel explained, "especially if you do dance videos. There's rhythm and you need graphic breaks. They help you a lot to create that rhythm."

The videos themselves were little more than commercials for the artists and their records. Before they were known as "music videos," the term most often applied to these four-minute films was "promotional clip." They could make stars out of artists who had struggled for years. A case in point was Billy Idol, who had fronted a moderately successful quasi-punk band called Generation X. Around the time he split from the band, MTV came along. He became one of the channel's biggest stars. "I think, sometimes people get caught up in, 'Is Billy Idol an MTV cartoon character,'" he remarked. "I have people standing outside my gigs with signs saying, 'Billy Idol, Antichrist.'"

Another artist that benefited in a big way during the early years of MTV was Robert Palmer. He had recorded an eclectic array of albums that became critical favorites, working with artists ranging from Little

Feat to reggae greats Toots and the Maytals. However, when he hooked up with two of the Duran's in a side project called the Power Station, he got something that all the critical accolades couldn't buy him: the spotlight. He capitalized on this with his next project, oddly one of his most mainstream (read "prosaic") recordings, becoming a chart-topping artist in his own right. "Obviously," he said, "the MTV thing has something to do with the exposure."

"In the '60s," added John Lodge of the Moody Blues, "you couldn't get this kind of exposure. There was no MTV, there were probably five TV channels. Nowadays, the exposure that people expect you to do is enormous."

"By the time we got to the '80s," said Rundgren, "music had become secondary to a personality. We became an art of the person-ality or a personality cult as embodied by people like Madonna and Michael Jackson. This is not to demean their music, although much of it is demeanable, but the music was an adjunct to the selling of their personality."

Being videogenic, though, didn't necessarily mean being classi-cally pretty. Another act that exploded from MTV exposure was ZZ Top, a boogying blues trio from Texas. Possessed of two of the most impressive beards in rock and roll, Billy Gibbons and Dusty Hill demonstrated you don't gotta be a "Sharp Dressed Man" to make an impression on MTV.

Slightly over two years after going live, MTV had increased the number of cable companies that carried the channel by 600 percent. It was in over 16 million homes. In the early days, MTV basically fused two radio formats for TV, showing predominantly modern rock artists and album rock artists. "MTV," said the head of MTV's European operations, Brent Hanson, "had set themselves up in a format radio world, which is the reason why there was very little black music orig-inally. But it became very clear that MTV was a phenomenon and had to open up. Radio dictates certain formats, but MTV had to break out of that mold."

"In the radio world," added Tom Hunter, who served as the chan-nel's VP of programming, "there are twenty competing signals. You pretty much have no choice but to pick a narrow target and super-serve that audience. It hasn't developed in the video world yet.

"We have the ability to deal with a lot of different kinds of music," he continued, "which is very difficult in radio. In radio, formats are designed to appeal to a very narrow segment of the audience, so it would be pretty much impossible to successfully program a radio station that might play Sinead O'Connor into Faith No More into Paula Abdul. We do that on MTV. It's pretty magic."

African-American artists had started complaining that the channel should call itself white rock TV. "We were disturbed to see the Police, Pat Benatar, and David Bowie doing commercials for MTV," wrote the rock 'n' politics newsletter *Rock & Roll Confidential* (now called *Rock & Rap Confidential*), "so we called the management of the bands to ask why these performers would urge people to watch a channel that systematically excludes black music." The magazine urged artists to withhold their videos and not to go on the channel.

Epic records had already considered this option. They were incensed that the channel would not play videos from their hot-selling album *Thriller* by Michael Jackson, even though one had a cameo by Eddie Van Halen, a stalwart of the channel. Word circulated through the music grapevine that they were considering pulling permission to play their videos, which included MTV favorites at the time like Culture Club, Adam and the Ants, and the Clash. By extension, the rumor had it, all the Sony-owned companies would follow suit. MTV started to play Jackson's "Beat It," and then the fifteen-minute, John Landis directed minifilm version of Jackson's "Thriller." Jackson became the Jackie Robinson of MTV, opening the channel for artists like Lionel Richie, Diana Ross, Prince, and even Rick James.

A good video could make a hit out of even a mediocre song. This was amply illustrated by a Norwegian group called a-ha. They had a nice, polite, slightly hooky synthpop song called "Take On Me." The video, directed by Steve Baron, contained some very stylish animation—more like an animatic, actually—that gave the video a unique look. The song, propelled by this video, topped the charts.

Even already popular groups took note. Dire Straits, who had been making hit records since their debut in 1979, kicked their career up a notch by doing a-ha one better. They took a song that poked fun at MTV and added some cutting-edge (for the time) computer graphics. The song even featured Sting reprising his roll as MTV pitchman singing, "I Want My MTV." The group's lead vocalist and guitarist Mark Knopfler got the idea for the song while he was shopping with his wife for some appliances for their new space in New York City. "They had all this kitchen stuff in the front and there was a wall of TV sets in the back," Knopfler recalled. "All the sets were tuned to MTV. A couple of guys [watching the TVs] were discoursing on the acts that were appearing. They didn't seem to think musicians did much for their money." The video for the song, "Money for Nothing," inaugurated MTV's European service when it launched on August 1, 1987.

In the late '70s, a phenomenon started growing in New York City's African-American neighborhoods, particularly in the Bronx and Harlem. Growing out of "toasting," the Jamaican music where a master of ceremonies at a dance hall might create long, stream-of-consciousness poems and patter over a reggae dub-plate, people who were deejaying at house parties and in clubs started rapping over instrumental breaks. These "personality jocks" were celebrated in the Gap Band's hit "King Tim." A group called the Sugarhill Gang took this pop with a song called "Rapper's Delight." Blondie, enamored with the new sound, added a rap break to their hit, "Rapture," that name-checked such notables in the genre as Fab Five Freddy and Grandmaster Flash.

The sound's biggest crossover came when a group from suburban Queens called Run-D.M.C. hooked up with one of MTV's hard-rock heroes, Aerosmith, and cut a rap version of the rock group's patter song "Walk This Way." The video became the first rap video on MTV in 1986. It was the perfect vehicle for MTV, the perfect invitation to white suburban kids to get a taste of this "urban culture."

"I used to always use rock records for Run and D.M.C. to rap over before we even started making records," said their deejay, Jason "Jam Master Jay" Mizell. "We used to use Billy Squier and Aerosmith, a whole bunch of records I used to use, but mainly Billy Squier and Aerosmith. We had routines off them, Run and D. used to rap over that, and I used to let a little rock come in."

Within two years, the genre became so important and successful, the channel had to add a block devoted to the music. *Yo! MTV Raps* became one of the channel's most successful shows.

The channel's success did not go unnoticed or unchallenged. One genre of music that from the git-go was even more conspicuously absent from MTV than any kind of black music was country music. MTV was designed to attract an audience with a mean age of sixteen, the *Bandstand* audience, the audience sneaker companies and skin-care companies and soft-drink companies craved. Country audiences skewed much older. In the mid-'80s, TNN (the Nashville Network) was launched. It supplemented its programming of videos by the country stars of the day with morning shows on fishing and hunting.

BET (Black Entertainment Television) launched, pretty much as an answer to the early plaints about MTV being a white music ghetto. As the name insinuated, however, it was about more than music. BET programmed sports from African-American colleges like Howard and Grambling. They broadcast talk shows with African-American hosts talking to African-American guests for a predominantly African-American audience. "There is a change in the message," said the channel's founder and president, Robert Johnson. "I suppose a psychiatrist could play with it for days. . . . The tone and temper of the discussion is different."

"As far as what is considered urban or black music," added the channel's director of Music and Program Management, Lydia Cole, "we cover all formats."

Through the competition, which continues to grow, MTV has kept ahead of the curve. While music continued to be its *raison d'être,* it also started to expand into more "televisionlike" programming. The channel started programming game shows (*Remote Control* in 1987), lifestyle programming (Cindy Crawford's *House of Style* in 1989), the first reality-TV series (*The Real World* in 1992), a soap opera (*Undressed* in 1999), and entertainment programming (the animated *Liquid TV* in 1991). *Liquid TV* gave MTV one of its first major nonmusical hits, and one of the first hits it could really call its own, *Beavis and Butthead.*

Beavis and Butthead were the caricature of the core MTV viewer—a pair of teenaged males who would get into trouble, hang out, coop on the couch, and watch MTV. Once again, as with "Money for Nothing," Beavis and Butthead found MTV watching itself. And often, as one or the other would say about the videos they saw on the channel, "It sucked." It caused *Time* magazine to proclaim the program "perhaps the bravest show ever run on national TV." To which Beavis would likely reply, "Heh, heh, heh, right." They ran until 1997 and were spun off into a movie.

Another idea MTV had was to have rock bands come into a studio with an audience and play acoustic. Starting with venerable English pub rockers Squeeze, the *Unplugged* series eventually enticed artists ranging from veteran rockers Bruce Springsteen and Eric Clapton to soul upstart Babyface and rappers Arrested Development.

By 1994, MTV Europe had even more viewers than the original American service. Additionally, the brand's international presence grew to the point that they had a Brazilian version, another in Asia, one solely for Japan, three different channels for Latin America: South, North, and Central, as well as channels in New Zealand, Germany, the U.K. and Ireland, Italy, Australia, Russia, Korea, India, China, Taiwan, Hong Kong, Poland, Spain, France, Holland, the Philippines, Belgium, Austria, Switzerland, Romania, Israel, South Africa and Argentina. Each of the countries has a mandate to keep at least 30 percent of the programming indigenous to that country.

Beyond spreading internationally, the channel also has several offshoots. Video Hits One (VH-1) offered videos for a demographic that skewed higher than the teens and twenties MTV shot for. As MTV offered more and more alternative programming, they launched M2, which took the channel back to a 24/7 music presence. New shows sprang up regularly, including a reality show centering on the family life of heavy-metal icon Ozzy Osbourne. The channel recognizes the need to consistently reinvent itself and remain fresh if it is to remain viable. "The twenty-one-year-old of today," noted president of Entertainment Brian Graden, "does not like the same thing as the twenty-one-year-old of last year."

"We are very interested in what the audience likes," said Hunter, "and in that sense, if there's something really happening on the street, we'll pick up on that lead the audience gives us. There are also things we've taken a real active role in from the very beginning because we're very passionate about it. When dance music is hot, there's a lot of it on MTV, there's a lot of it on radio, and there's a lot of it selling in the stores. We're going to reflect that pattern. We say, 'MTV, Your TV.' I don't think we define trends. I think consumers do that."

As this book goes into publication, MTV International and all its ancillary channels reach over a billion people in 164 countries and eighteen different languages. Fully 80 percent of the people watching MTV do so outside of the U.S. The company nets nearly $1.5 billion a year. Its planetary reach is enormous and can only grow on a planet where fewer than half of the homes can receive the channel. Hard to imagine in the U.S., but not everyone has cable!

"I'm sort of in the nexus of the popular culture," said the channel's head, Tom Freston. "Our talent is riding that line. We're sort of on the edge."

Yet, as many cosmetic changes as that line might cross, some things don't change. Every weekday, a gaggle of teenagers gather outside of the Times Square studio that houses MTV's after-school show *Total Request Live*. You could almost imagine it as a similar scene fifty years ago, with girls in Catholic school uniforms in Philadelphia.

Live Aid

If John Fogerty has anything to be proud of in his post–
Creedence Clearwater Revival work (and there's quite a bit there, actu-
ally), one of those would be a specific cover of his minor hit "Rocking
All Over the World" from his 1975 solo album. Ten years later, Status
Quo used it to kick off Live Aid, one of the most notorious and suc-
cessful fund and consciousness raising events ever perpetrated.

It started out in a moment of outrage and depression. Bob Geldof's
band the Boomtown Rats were going nowhere fast. Despite having a

handful of minor European hits and critical acceptance, they had never had an album break the Top 100 in the U.S. The closest thing they ever had to a U.S. pop hit was "I Don't Like Mondays," the musical retelling of a shooting spree in a California school. It hit #73.

By 1984, even the English hits and good press were slowing down. In a lousy mood, Geldof turned on his television and was galvanized by Michael Buerk's BBC report on the famine in Ethiopia. "The pictures," Geldof recalled, "were chilling and Buerk's reportage was spectacularly brilliant. It was like he couldn't speak. The silence is what I remember predominantly. And when he did speak it felt like there was such a contained, venomous rage in his voice that you were left speechless.

"The picture that remains with me," he added, "was that of the twenty-three-year-old nurse who had to choose from ten thousand, three hundred of whom could be fed. The people picked to be fed stood ashamed at their good fortune . . . the ones left behind, in effect condemned to die, stood and watched with such beautiful dignity."

Only Geldof didn't see any dignity in people going hungry on such a fat planet. "It defies all human logic, all human morality, for people to be dying of starvation in a world of surplus," he said.

"I felt disgusted, enraged and outraged," he recalled, "but more than all those, I felt deep shame."

He went to his record company, saying that he had it in mind to create a record to benefit Ethiopia in some way. Most of the people he had talked to had also seen the BBC report, both at the record company and among his musical peers. Very quickly, he had collected the cream of Britrock in a recording studio—Bono from U2, Midge Ure from Ultravox, members of Duran Duran, Genesis, and George Michael, perhaps fifty in all—recording "Do They Know It's Christmas?" under the name Band Aid. Even then, he realized that anything they could do, help as it might, was likely to be spit in the ocean as far as the enormity of the problem was concerned. He expected that the recording might, if they were lucky, raise $120,000. He grossly underestimated the effect of the special and the allure of the celebrities on the recording. Released in the fall of 1984, the record became the hit of the holiday season in Britain that year, selling $11 million worth of singles.

Not to be outdone, a group of American superstars led by Michael Jackson and including Bruce Springsteen, Paul Simon, Bob Dylan,

Cyndi Lauper, Quincy Jones, Ray Charles, and Lionel Richie recorded "We Are the World" as USA for Africa. That single raised $20 million. Similar efforts from Canada to Yugoslavia were released.

While perhaps the most widespread and successful rock charity campaign, it certainly wasn't the first. Even before rock rolled, popular singers like Frank Sinatra and Tony Bennett sang to raise money and awareness for the cause of civil rights. Amid huge amounts of media coverage, John Lennon and Yoko Ono took a bed in a Montreal hotel room and spent eight days in bed for peace, recording "Give Peace a Chance" from bed. In 1971, his Beatle bandmate George Harrison, responding to a remarkably similar scene to what Geldof saw, in this case springing out of the refugee crisis in India, Pakistan, and Bangladesh, organized a concert at Madison Square Garden, tickets and album revenues to go to relief organizations. A hugely satisfying event, musically, the whole financial aspect of it turned into a logistical nightmare, with Harrison eventually writing his own check for the full amount raised by the concert. Even then, whether the relief ever got to where it was needed was questionable.

Geldof faced a similar situation. "The problem was a cartel of truck drivers operating in Port Sudan, who were charging onerous fees and holding up the distribution of grain," he recalled. "The only way to break the cartel was to buy a fleet of trucks and operate the freight for free. That's where the notion of the concert came in.

"I was brought up understanding that music was articulating my time," he said, "the sixties, which was synonymous with radical change. Music was the driving force behind that change."

"Live Aid and Band Aid were the beginning of an awareness," added singer/songwriter Jackson Browne. "In the sixties, people believed they could change things just by saying things were changed . . . there was a revolution of consciousness . . . but we never took the step of challenging the control mechanisms."

"We did Live Aid," added Darryl "D.M.C." McDaniel of the rap group Run-D.M.C. "We just want to let people know that we are conscious of what is going on in the world today. We speak up for it."

Geldof secured JFK Stadium in Philadelphia and Wembley Stadium in London for a trans-Atlantic concert event to be broadcast around the world. He worked with impresario Bill Graham and TV producers Michael Mitchell in America and former *Old Grey Whistle*

Test producer Mike Appleton in Britain. From the time the concert was confirmed until show time was a scant six weeks.

In all, over sixty acts appeared. Phil Collins flew in a donated Concorde after playing with Sting in London to play drums in lieu of John Bonham with a reconstituted Led Zeppelin in Philadelphia. Others on the bills included Paul McCartney, the Who, Bob Dylan, Tina Turner, Madonna, Crosby, Stills, and Nash, U2, Neil Young, the Cars, Eric Clapton, and Sade, a veritable who's who of pop and rock from the mid-'80s. "You pick the people that have sold a million albums," said Geldof, "so more people will watch and contribute more money."

Beyond the music, there were appearances by world leaders like Nobel Peace Prize Laureate Archbishop Desmond Tutu of South Africa and Indian leader Rajiv Gandhi, speaking about mass famine. Images from the BBC program that had inspired Geldof in the first place were broadcast.

The technology involved pushed the borders of the time. The shorter of the two shows at Wembley involved:

- Over 300 microphones
- 40 miles of cable
- 100 tons of stage equipment
- 200 people from the BBC
- 200 people from the bands' road crews

The shows were broadcast to 170 countries, simultaneously via satellite. It has been estimated that 80 percent of the 600 million TVs on the planet tuned in to some part of the show, for a potential viewing audience of 1.5 billion people. In London, 1,600 volunteers answered 200,000 phone calls for pledges. One woman donated half a million pounds herself. In the U.S., 1,126 circuits were answered by 900 volunteers, and got more traffic than they could handle. Nearly everything at the shows, from transportation to talent to catering, was donated. Geldof pledged that one hundred percent of the money raised would go to feed starving Africans. Ultimately, the shows and records raised over $150 million.

"It wasn't just a television event," said the BBC's Appleton. "It was something everybody got wound up in and wanted to be part of. It was like your best friend's party and everybody wanted to come to it."

The shows were broadcast on MTV, local channels, and radio. ABC in the U.S. devoted all its prime time to the show that Saturday. The 1.5 billion viewers around the world said more for the drawing power of rock and roll than the social conscience of the world, but it also spoke to the music's continued power to influence the masses. It even earned Irish rocker Bob Geldof a nomination for the Nobel Peace Prize for his developing what he described as a constituency of compassion. "It had to be the biggest show ever," he said. "I was aware of that. It was entertainment, but it was for an almost biblical disaster."

"Live Aid was not meant to be a career move," said Neil Young. "It was meant to be a chance to do something good for a bunch of people."

One person deeply affected by his Live Aid experience was an impressionable twenty-five-year-old singer, one of Geldof's Dublin homeboys, named Paul Hewson, who fronted the band U2 as Bono. While most of the artists playing the show did their sets and went home, Bono and his wife Alison wanted to see what it was all about firsthand. They went to Ethiopia, where they volunteered for a month and a half at an orphanage. "You'd walk out of your tent, and you'd count bodies of dead and abandoned children," he recalled. "Or worse, the father of a child would walk up to you and try to give you his living child and say, 'You take it, because if this is your child, it won't die.'"

Another artist took the idea another way. During his Live Aid set, Bob Dylan reminded people that Ethiopians weren't the only ones in trouble. Even farmers in the United States were in deep trouble, and while it hadn't reached the starvation levels that they were fighting that day, it did behoove people to look at the situation locally as well as globally. The message was caught by Neil Young, Willie Nelson, and John Mellencamp. In the spirit of Live Aid, they came up with Farm Aid, a benefit for family farmers in danger of losing their land to a year or two of bad crops and the vagaries of government subsidies (or lack thereof).

"The fact that we have to have Farm Aid is a black eye on our country," Nelson said. "We shouldn't have to have any. It's still drawing because the people know the problems. They would like to help. They're trying to help by coming and supporting it, but the people who could really help are the people in Washington, and they ain't doing it. No one there is saying 'Family Farmer.' We used to have six to eight million family farmers, and we've lost them all now. We're losing three to five hundred a week. If something is not done, we're not going to have any more. There's less than two million out there now."

In the wake of Live Aid, it seems like every musician, and indeed actors, writers, anyone with any kind of celebrity clout, took up a cause. While the level of commitment varied, some became very devoted. Live Aid also seemed to open the West's eyes to what was going on outside its bailiwick. Africa became more than just an area on the map. Jerry Dammers had already written a piece about imprisoned South African leader Nelson Mandela. Dammers and his band, the Specials, put on a concert to continue to raise awareness. Steven Van Zandt, formerly of Bruce Springsteen's E Street Band, created a record about the Sun City resort. Recorded with stars ranging from Springsteen to rappers Run-D.M.C. to jazz poet Gil Scott-Heron under the loose rubric of Artists United Against Apartheid, that also cast people's eyes toward South Africa. In a different way, Paul Simon recorded an album there, bringing the unique musical voice of the area to a far larger audience.

Van Zandt also worked with Amnesty International, touring with Springsteen, Peter Gabriel, Lou Reed, Tracy Chapman, U2, and Sting on the Conspiracy of Hope tour that helped raise awareness and membership in Amnesty. The whole face of the organization changed during the '80s. In 1981, the average age of Amnesty's 80,000 members was forty. By 1988, the membership had increased over fivefold and the average member's age was in the early twenties.

One of Amnesty's projects was helping to secure the release of an imprisoned Nigerian dissident and musician, Fela Anikulapo Kuti. "I would like to say how gratified I am for the support that all of you gave me while I was in prison, and I want to tell you all that I appreciate the support," Fela said on his release. "It has given me the complete belief that this world is for one people, and the whole different races of this world are one people, just different colors and things. I intend to enhance this concept of Human Internationalism.

"Music is supposed to have an effect," he added. "If you're playing music and people don't feel something, you're not doing shit. That's what African music is about. When you hear it, something must move. I want to move people to dance, but also to think. Music wants to dictate a better life against a bad life. When you're listening to something that depicts having a better life, and you're not having the better life, it must have an effect on you. We want to see an Africa where people can come and go as they like, and just enjoy themselves. We are not saying that pan-Africanism is going to save the world. We hope that it will open the eyes of the less progressive leaders of the world. What is stopping this from happening is the evil minds of the leaders of the world today. Once we get leaders with good minds, you will see less harassment of the citizens of the world."

An even worse scourge than famine was about to hit the planet, and hit Africa especially hard. Even Fela succumbed to it: AIDS. Cases of the sexually transmitted and blood-borne human immunodeficiency virus reached epidemic proportions during the '80s and '90s. Many rock stars, especially openly gay ones like Elton John, became heavy supporters of AIDS research. John's foundation, like the Band Aid Foundation, operated on an extremely low (4 percent) overhead, with most of the money raised by various Elton John projects, and well over 95 percent of the money raised going to help people living with the virus on six continents.

Other stars took on causes ranging from animal rights to protecting the rain forests and other such environmental issues. Singers ranging from Phil Collins to Bruce Hornsby tackled the issue of homelessness, musically and financially. In every city he played, Bruce Springsteen would donate $15,000 to food banks and veterans' organizations. When he's home, Springsteen has been known to put on a baseball cap, jeans, and a flannel shirt and load trucks at his local food bank. Whenever a new disaster happened, musicians were there to help raise funds and awareness. "I think popular music helped restore a sense of populism to U.S. foreign policy," said Amnesty International head Jack Healy.

While being a musician had allowed him to raise over $100 million dollars that helped feed the hungry and regrow the infrastructure in seven African countries, making music became increasingly difficult for Geldof. "It was a net negative—financially, professionally, and personally," he said. "With my wife, when I was there, I wasn't there. My mind was a million miles away, and the phone never stopped.

"I'd run out of money," he added, "I had no other job and yet Live Aid didn't really help the perception of me musically. The fact of my being a pop singer was incidental."

And then there was all that money to distribute. When it was all accounted for, the Band Aid Trust had an initial war chest of over $100 million that had been promised to nonpolitical, humanitarian causes, passed along without bureaucracy. They used 40 percent of it to take care of the immediate problem of feeding as many Ethiopians and Somalis as they could reach. The remaining money was to help build an infrastructure within seven countries so that events like Live Aid would become unnecessary. And money continued to come in. After seven years, the Band Aid Trust asked that no more donations be made. However, it had assets that continue to pay dividends. Every holiday season, for example, "Do They Know It's Christmas?" gets revived and the royalties continue to go right into the Trust.

"It was only meant to last seven weeks," Geldof said in 1992, "but I hadn't counted on the fact that hundreds of millions of people would respond and I hadn't reckoned on over $100 million. Seven years. You can count them now in trees and dams and fields and cows and camels and trucks and schools and health clinics, medicines, tents, blankets . . ."

For all that, however, the problems didn't go away. In 1999, the United Nations issued a challenge to make people aware of the crushing weight of poverty in so much of the world. Rock took up the gauntlet with Net Aid, fusing the information superhighway with a Live Aid–style event at three venues. The three shows were webcast, with a site that was supposed to be able to sustain a billion simultaneous viewers. Unlike Live Aid, these shows were more about raising awareness than money. "This is about getting people's attention," said Ken Kragen, who produced both Live Aid and Net Aid, of the latter event, "and getting them to start taking steps that eliminate the underlying causes of poverty—from debt relief to literacy to the empowerment of women to the environment and refugee issues."

In some ways the problems that Live Aid was formed to fight got worse. The debt that Kragen mentioned, loans from Western governments that went to the governments of many African nations, got "misappropriated" into various African leaders' Swiss bank accounts. Those leaders knew that most African governments are tenuous at best. When the inevitable coups came, the countries were still beholden to the Western governments and were still servicing these loans.

"Almost $200 million we raised for Africa there and we were jumping around the place," Bono said. "We thought we'd cracked it, you know, this was it. $200 million. Think about that, you know. That's a lot of money. You then discover that actually, that's what Africa pays every week servicing its debts to us."

In 2003, the rains failed again. A government servicing its debts couldn't feed its people. However, Geldof and Bono had been working toward a solution to that. Bono had gotten involved with Jubilee 2000, a campaign urging Western governments to forgive the debts of "developing nations."

"The task then," said Geldof of the immediate post–Live Aid period, "was to keep the people alive and wait for the political moment to pass. It passed. Now they have a pragmatic, decent government and developing indigenous businesses. . . . They're not like the chaos we remember from the 1980s. There's no kids lying in pools of diarrhea and vomit with flies everywhere."

The issues remain complex and the rock answer tends to flatten these issues into far more black-and-white pictures than they really are. However, the forum invites listeners to become more aware and join the discussion. It offers the crux of matters that rock fans might feel the urge to delve into deeper. Celebrity spokespeople put forward an entrance point for millions of people who might not ever otherwise have been exposed to issues like African debt or political prisoners of conscience or the problems of Tibetan repression under Chinese jurisdiction or the benefits of vegetarianism or the perils to the ecology of losing the rain forests. The fact that rock stars espouse these causes can open the eyes of rock fans to things which school might not have made them aware of or care about. From "rocking the vote" to annual farm benefits to buying and protecting parts of the rain forests, these attempts all help to raise funds and awareness. This may amount to putting a Band-Aid on a gaping wound, but it's better than no aid at all.

Chapter 19: 1991

Nirvana Hits #1 with "Nevermind"

During the latter half of the '80s, punk was all but invisible as new wave flavors of the month kept tumbling from both European and American shores. Groups ranging from the Knack to Culture Club became the new wave darlings of the pop charts.

But punk didn't go away. It hunkered down in the underground, hitting record stores on little labels like California's Alternative Tentacles (owned by the Dead Kennedys) and SST, home of groups like Flipper, Soundgarden, Black Flag, and Hüsker Dü. If these albums sold over ten thousand copies, everyone felt they were doing well, as contrasted to the major-label ethic where if you didn't sell a quarter of a million copies, you were losing money.

Punk tended to coagulate around various scenes and the venues that would allow them to happen. Minneapolis, for example, had a thriving punk underground even before the Brit-punk explosion. "It's always been there in Minnesota," said Hüsker Dü's Bob Mould, "even if you go back to the Litter, a real heavy guitar band from the '60s, or moving up in the '70s, the Suicide Commandos or early Suburbs. Anybody can start a band. In our case and in the case of [fellow Minneapolis bands] the Replacements and Soul Asylum, it's a matter of hard work and . . . going out and doing the grind, so to speak. It was just bands working real hard to do what they wanted to do, just become good musicians and good bands and not have to worry about appearance.

"Our intentions," he continued, "before we got technically proficient as musicians, was to go through it as fast as we could. Not too technically adept."

Similar scenes bubbled underground all around America. The L.A. punk scene with Black Flag and the Dead Kennedys was the stuff of legend. A Washington, D.C., scene featured the Bad Brains, Minor Threat and its many offspring, including Fugazi, a group that came to epitomize the egalitarian relationship of band, fan, and scene.

This relationship was key. If a band had the street credibility—if they were perceived as making their music for the "right" reasons, the bands and fans of a scene would usually embrace them. These scenes were primordial musical soups of incestuous crossbreeding. Bands would splinter into other bands featuring friends from yet other bands. Some musicians worked with two or three groups.

"Soul Asylum and the Hüskers are always real tight," Mould offered an example of this relationship. "They came on tour with us. I produced their first record, way back, the *Say What You Will* EP. Then I did the 'Tied to the Tracks' single. Then we went in and did the album stuff for *Made to Be Broken*. They're real nice guys, they're close personal friends."

In the mid-'80s, a similar scene started to evolve in Seattle, Washington. One of the key port cities on the West Coast, Seattle was the home of Boeing and the emerging computer software giant Microsoft. Already, the city had birthed two important hard-rock bands. One was Heart, fronted by the Wilson sisters, Ann and Nancy, arguably one of the most popular female-led bands to ever tread a stage. Then there was the progressive metal band Queensryche. A hint to how they fit on the scene: Although they were a multiplatinum act, by 1992 they had only been home to play twice in six years.

Groups like Soundgarden, the Melvins, Skin Yard, Malfunkshun, and Green River were chronicled on a 1986 artifact of the early days of the scene, *Deep Six*, on indie C/Z records. "You'd go check out all your friends," said Soundgarden guitarist Kim Thayil, "the guys in Green River and Skin Yard and the Melvins."

It certainly was not a wealthy scene. Most of the bands wore the Seattle version of thrift store chic—worn flannel shirts, ripped jeans, and Doc Marten boots, clothes that were cheap and would last.

As tight as the finances of most of the bands were, the record companies that catered to and spread these scenes were even more so. Mostly run by members of the scene, their money not only went back into the band, but into the pressing, packaging, and distribution of records as well: Fugazi's Discharge Records, Greg Ginn's (of Black Flag) SST, Daniel House's (of Skin Yard) C/Z. House also worked for (and distributed C/Z through) local Seattle indie Sub Pop, which put out early records by local heroes like Mudhoney and Soundgarden.

Soundgarden's Sub Pop EPs enticed many to take notice of the Seattle scene. Their 1988, SST album *Ultramega OK* cemented that, earning the group a Grammy nomination, not at all a common thing for an underground punk band on an underground punk label. It helped to nudge the Seattle underground into the light. For one thing, it brought the major labels sniffing around, especially after A&M signed Soundgarden.

Just south of the city, huge forests grew, favored by the fact that it rains there three quarters of the time. A couple of relative late-comers to the scene rolled into Seattle from one of these southern logging towns, Aberdeen.

By 1988, they had been playing together for about three years. They had worked in a Creedence Clearwater Revival cover band together, before going with their first love, hard-core punk. Guitarist Kurt Cobain had, at one time, sold all of his records to fund a trip to Seattle to see Black Flag. Inspired, he put together a band called Skid Row with fellow outsider Chris (a.k.a. Krist) Novoselic and a rotating group of drummers. When a New Jersey "hair metal" band took the name, they changed their name to Nirvana—ironic for a group with a genuinely pessimistic point of view.

Not that they didn't earn the right to be pessimistic. Cobain had been bouncing around between his divorced parents and a slew of sundry relatives since the age of eight. One started him on guitar lessons in an effort to keep him out of trouble. It didn't work. Cobain enjoyed painting, both on canvas, which freaked out the lumberjacks in Aberdeen, and on walls, which acquainted him with the local constabulary. Eventually he wore out his welcome with all his friends and relations in Aberdeen. For a while, in his late teens, he lived rough, sleeping in boxes and under bridges. Having enough of that, he and Novoselic took off for Olympia, ostensibly to attend art school. By 1988, they were part of the scene in Seattle.

"It's like the most supportive music scene in the country," said Layne Staley, late lead singer of Alice in Chains, "because every band's different and the attitude is more to get up and jam and have a good time and outdo the other band. So the bands are there to support you and they're all your friends and everyone gets up and jams together and it's an incestuous scene. It's great."

This was a revelation to Cobain, the perpetual outsider. Initially he thrived and within a year he, Novoselic, and Cobain's drumming roommate were signed to Sub Pop, where they recorded their debut album *Bleach* for the princely sum of $600 and change. It was loud, crude, and very punk, but there was something else to both the record and the band. Part of it was that under all the noise and . . . grunge, as the scene came to be called outside of Seattle, there were *hooks*. There was also the real pain and vulnerability that came through in Cobain's vocals. Nirvana was the voice of the perpetual outsider, and that touched a nerve, because in 1989 everyone felt alienated.

The band hit the road and *Bleach* sold extraordinarily well for an indie release, moving over thirty-five thousand copies. When an indie release tops twenty thousand, alarms start going off at the major record companies. A bidding war ensued over Nirvana, something that had not happened when Soundgarden had signed with A&M a year earlier. Suddenly, Seattle was on the record companies' maps.

Most indie punk bands had a love/hate relationship with even the idea of major labels. On the one hand, no one could get the music out to a broader audience. It was, after all, the concept of controlling distribution that made a major record company a major record company. However, there was always the fear factor. "Of course, we were afraid they would make us do something," Mould recalled of Hüsker Dü's similar, earlier foray with a major label, "because everyone kept telling us, 'Oh, you go with them, they're going to change you completely! Stick with us. We won't change you. We'll just mess up your artwork every time you put a record out.'

"It took a lot of soul searching just to figure out what was at stake," he added of eventually signing the deal. "We had a feeling there was a bigger audience out there that wanted to get our records. When you start getting written up in your 7-Eleven magazines, your *Spins* and *Rolling Stones*, you know, a lot of bigger publications that are around and are available to everyone, people see them and go, 'Hmmmm, this sounds interesting.' So, they go down to the hardware store, the only place they can buy records for ten miles around, and they start asking for this band Hüsker Dü on SST Records, and the guy who actually works in the seed department and just sells records part-time sort of looks at them like, 'What are you talking about? You're nuts!' So now, maybe with Warners, we have a chance of reaching some of these people in the more remote areas who might have really gotten into the band, but never could get a hold of the stuff. That was the most important thing—taking a chance at finding out if there were more people who liked us than were buying our records, and that turned out to be true."

The only major upshot to the deal Soundgarden had signed was they had more time and more money to make the album they wanted. "We were kind of the guinea pigs for what was going to happen with a lot of the other bands," Soundgarden's Matt Cameron said. "And here we are—we're still doing it."

Nirvana gave in to the inevitable, signing with the David Geffen Company. DGC had no great expectations for Nirvana's major label debut, *Nevermind*. They only pressed fifty thousand copies of it, but the record kept selling and the single, "Smells Like Teen Spirit," a caustic, sarcastic three-chord blast of alienation that the company had hoped might captivate alternative and college radio so they could "build a story," actually started to break *pop*. MTV began to play it ten times a day. The group was asked to play *Saturday Night Live*, one of broadcast TV's last great rock showcases. By the beginning of the new year (1992), *Nevermind* was the #1 record in most of the world and on its way to selling over 10 million copies, much to the amazement of everyone involved. People tried to make sense of it.

Many felt it was how well the group embodied the juxtaposition of the twenty-something slacker generation, what Simon Reynolds characterized as "a mix of faithlessness and idealism. . . . Lyrically it is confused, vacillating between the fury of the chorus 'Here we are now, entertain us/how stupid and contagious' and the fatigued fatalism of 'I found it hard, so hard to find, oh well, whatever, nevermind'. . . Perhaps the secret of their success is that their rage is unspecific enough to provide a catch-all catharsis that appeals across the political spectrum."

This echoes a much earlier piece of pop that its creator described as, "It came out of the top of my head when I was eighteen and a half. It seems to be about the frustrations of a young person who is so incoherent or uneducated that he can't state his case to the bourgeois intellectual blah blah blah." This was Pete Townshend talking about "My Generation."

Another facet of their success might just have been the timing. They were the right band to blow a sewer grate breeze of fresh air up the staid, pleated skirt of popular music in general and rock and roll in particular. Just before Nirvana charged up the charts like a bull elephant after a herd in heat during the winter of 1991–92, the charts were full of middle-of-the-road artists like Michael Bolton, Paula Abdul, Michael Jackson, and Mariah Carey. Some life was offered courtesy of REM, Prince, and Jesus Jones, but the only thing that barely presaged the coming of Nirvana was Metallica's "Enter Sandman," rising to the Top 20 that fall. It offers a glimpse of a possible side effect of going global—they might not be reaching the "right" audience. This was not news. The "grunge" sound had a lot in common with thrash metal— very similar audiences and some unexpected crossover.

"When we were touring with Danzig a few years ago," Chris Cornell of Soundgarden recalled of time on the road with the leather-and-metal, postpunk band, "and there was some big, musclebound guy causing problems in the audience, we'd always go, 'Oh, that's Danzig's fan.' But maybe it wasn't. Now that we're on our own tour, we have guys like that coming to our shows."

The punk ethos finally went pop, but there was more at stake:

Nirvana were heroes of the underground. With this level of success, suddenly the phrase *alternative rock* became an oxymoron. "I don't feel the least bit guilty for commercially exploiting a completely exhausted Rock Youth Culture because, at this point in rock history, Punk Rock . . . is, to me, dead and gone," Cobain wrote. "We just wanted to pay tribute to something that helped us feel as though we had crawled out of the dung heap of conformity. To pay tribute like an Elvis or Jimi Hendrix impersonator in the tradition of a bar band. I'll be the first to admit that we are the '90s version of Cheap Trick or the Knack."

"Sometimes," concurred Soundgarden bassist Ben Shepherd, "I feel like it's cheapened by the process of spreading it so thin over such a wide area."

Certainly the record companies were circling Seattle like flies around that proverbial dung heap. Within months of Nirvana's success, their Seattle compatriots Mudhoney, Alice In Chains, and Pearl Jam were snatched up by media giants hoping, as they always did, to capture lightning in a bottle.

"What's interesting," said Bruce Pavitt, cofounder of Sub Pop, "is that for decades the music business has been controlled by the New York–L.A. axis. What you're seeing here is a regional scene outside that axis that has developed something from scratch and is actually having worldwide impact."

Pearl Jam was one of the first signed. They were a group with deep roots in the scene. Guitarist Stone Gossard and bassist Jeff Ament had, like Soundgarden, been on the *Deep Six* EP as members of Green River. When that band broke up, the two joined the glam-grunge group Mother Love Bone; after one album, that group was left rudderless due to the overdose death of their lead singer Andy Wood. To give you an idea just how incestuous the scene was, Soundgarden's Cornell and Wood had been roommates.

Gossard and Ament had cofounded Mother Love Bone and sought a new vocalist and lyricist to work with. Word got to singer Eddie Vedder via a mutual acquaintance, Red Hot Chili Pepper's drummer Jack Irons. Vedder, at the time, was supporting his music habit pumping gas in San Diego. He exchanged tapes with Gossard and made the trip up north. "The first three songs that Eddie wrote—'Alive,' 'Once,' and 'Footsteps'—all delve into the dark side and I think we were both drawn into that at the time," Ament said. "Mother Love Bone was a really happy, fun, tongue-in-cheek rock band: on the surface, anyway. Eddie's whole trip seemed to relate to us in a good way."

Neck and neck with Nirvana, Pearl Jam's debut album *10* (after the number of basketball star Mookie Blaylock, whose name gave the band its working moniker) stormed the album charts, largely on the strength of an amazing video for the teen-suicide anthem "Jeremy." "We have a pretty big role," crowed MTV's SVP of Music and Talent John Canelli, "in spreading something from the underground to the heartland."

Suddenly, everyone was wearing flannel and Doc Martens. The style spread even further with Cameron Crowe's twentysomething film *Singles*, which featured the three principal members of Pearl Jam (Vedder giving up his vocal slot to actor Matt Dillon, playing the drums for the film). "It wasn't like somebody said, 'Let's all dress like lumberjacks and start Seattle chic,' Sub Pop cofounder Jonathan Poneman said. "The stuff is cheap, it's durable and it's kind of timeless. It also runs against the grain of the whole flashy esthetic that existed in the '80s."

Even more than punk, which after all was born out of a clothing shop, the Seattle scene was not even antifashion, but "*a*fashion." It didn't give a shit what you wore, the plainer the better. "All things grunge are treated with the utmost cynicism and amusement," said Poneman, "because the whole thing is a fabricated movement and always has been."

Differing from the fabrication of McLaren and Rhodes, "grunge" was fabricated to give the Seattle scene a handle in the press. If you listen to Nirvana, Alice in Chains, Pearl Jam, the Melvins, and Soundgarden, all they really have in common is that they're all from Seattle, loud and energetic. The latter two elements, of course, were what popular music had once again lost touch with over the post-punk years.

Beyond that, Seattle was an antistar scene. Everyone wanted to play. For some, making more money than you really needed was okay but uncomfortable. But no one wanted to be a "rock star" in the traditional smash-up-your-hotel-room and drive-your-car-into-the-pool sense. "I wish I could have taken a class on becoming a rock star," Cobain mused. "It might have prepared me for this."

"I do not want to have a long career if I have to put up with the same stuff I'm putting up with," he said at another time. "I'm not going to subject myself to being stuck in an apartment building for the next ten years and being afraid to go outside of my house. It's not worth it."

"The whole success thing," Vedder added, "I feel like everybody else in the band is a lot happier with it than me."

Yet the success didn't slack. The charismatic Vedder was asked to take Jim Morrison's place in front of the Doors when they were inducted into the Rock and Roll Hall of Fame. Pearl Jam won four MTV Video Music Awards for "Jeremy" in 1993. Nirvana won for "In Bloom." When he accepted the award, Cobain unbuttoned his pants on stage.

Shortly after the MTV win, Pearl Jam's second album, *Vs.*, came out and zoomed right to the top of the charts, selling almost a million copies in the first week, a record at the time. "It's music," Vedder sighed, "and it shouldn't be that big of a deal. But, now we can stop making videos."

They also put their celebrity to some good. Novoselic was of Slavic extraction, and had watched with horror as the "ethnic cleansing," the wholesale slaughter and rape of Bosnia, went on in 1993. He organized the band to play its only concert in months around the issue. "An epic tragedy is happening in Europe and nobody's doing anything about it," he said. "That region of the world is where my family comes from. I've been there many times, and it's a beautiful place. There's been a breakdown in society."

Part of the reason Nirvana was so quiet was Cobain had married Courtney Love, the vocalist from the band Hole. Shortly after, they had a daughter. Then the word got out about Cobain's heroin use, and Love's.

Cobain used the drug in an almost classic sense, in the way it had initially been *intended* to be used, as a painkiller. Wracked with stomach pains from childhood, he found the heroin made the physical pain go away. It also helped dull the psychic pain of dealing with his phenomenal success.

When word of their drug use got out (via an article in *Vanity Fair*), their daughter was removed from their home. Love didn't have a "problem" with the drug and tested clean. Cobain went through rehab

(not for the last time) and got treatment for a nerve disorder that doctors thought might be causing his stomach problems. The rehab didn't
take.

In the meantime, just to keep the band hot, an album of outtakes
and odds and ends called *Incesticide* came out. By the summer of 1993,
the band was ready to go into the studio. They cut *In Utero* in around
two weeks. It was even more raw than *Nevermind*. When they took it
on tour, Cobain overdosed twice, once on heroin, once on pills. When
he OD'd on the pills, he left a suicide note. The group cancelled the
rest of the tour. Cobain took time off to work with his wife on the new
Hole album, *Live Through This*. When Love went to promote the
album in April of 1994, leaving Cobain in their Seattle home, Cobain
took a shotgun to his head and ended his life.

"He joined that stupid club," was all his mother had to say to the
press—referring to Janis Joplin, Jim Morrison, and Seattle's own Jimi
Hendrix, who all died at 27, as had Robert Johnson and Brian Jones
before them.

Effectively, Cobain's passing put the breaks on grunge as a movement. Nobody had the heart to keep up the charade. Soundgarden
broke up a few years later. Love got more involved in film, displayed
some talent as an actress, and continued to get into trouble. Pearl Jam
continued to play and record and raise hell with the establishment,
especially over things like ticket prices.

But Cobain had done something that rock seems to need every
few years: He supplied it with a swift kick in the ass that got it up and
lumbering again. Once again, MTV started to rock harder, as did radio.
Groups like Green Day became pop, and "alternative music" got its
own radio format to cater to that audience, which continues to play
bands that try to capture the Cobain magic, often at the expense of
their own.

MP3, Napster, and the End of the World as We Know It

The compact disc gave the music business license to once again sell through its catalog. Historically this has been one of the things the music business does best, which is why it seems astounding that they didn't recognize the potential of digital compression.

The answer may center on a couple of things. One is control. The other is outright greed.

A compact disc, at its digital basis, is a data storage medium. This is why computer programs also come on CDs. It takes music and compiles it into the digital 1s and 0s of data. The CD is just a storage medium for that data, the CD player the means of decoding that data for use in your stereo. A good rule of thumb is that every minute of digital audio on a 16- or 24-bit CD would cost 10 megabytes of digital storage space. A song might then take up to 30 megabytes. In 1990 that was about the average size of the hard drive on the standard office desktop computer.

However, forces were converging that would change this, and the way music was enjoyed and distributed. And for the first time since Edison, they were forces outside the control of the music industry that had grown to Frankensteinish proportions in the post-Edison century.

Around the time the audio CD was peaking in penetration and popularity, in the early '90s, Karlheinz Brandenburg of the German commercial-research company Fraunhofer IIS set out to solve a problem for the movie industry. The film biz loved the idea of the compact disc and digital-quality audio in general, but they had a problem— bandwidth. The track on either side of a film that contained the soundtrack just couldn't handle the amount of information it took to encode digital music onto a CD.

Working on the problem, Brandenburg presented the idea of audio layer compression to the Motion Picture Experts Group as a possible standard for putting digital audio on this area of the soundtrack. Since the engine he presented was his third effort, he called his algorithms Motion Picture Experts Group 1 Audio Layer-3, or MPEG 3. The files compressed using these algorithms used a file extension of ".mp3."

Instead of the 10 megabytes of information per minute of music, the digital files (a.k.a. "songs") on a CD tended to use, MP3s compressed this down to about one megabyte per minute. This lost a little bit of the fidelity, some of the very high and low end of the audio spectrum, but little that all but the best playback gear would allow you to hear.

When Fraunhofer introduced these algorithms in 1991, it took very expensive, elaborate equipment to encode it, certainly nothing that could be done on the 8088 computers on most people's desks in those days, with 64 kilobytes of memory and perhaps 10 megabytes of hard-disk storage.

Around the same time, a bunch of governments and academics sought a way of sending information back and forth quickly. By the

'60s, the means of communicating with a computer over a telephone line was pretty well established—many still have memories of the acoustic couplers that held the standard phone handset, dialing up a central computer and using a teletype unit to work on programs and access information on a time-sharing basis.

As computer technology became quicker, smaller, and more powerful, acoustic couplers gave way to hard-wired modems and primitive local-area networks. People arranged electronic bulletin boards and mailboxes as central loci for data. In the late 1980s, a way was sought (and found) to interconnect these local networks. By 1991, the U.S. government, colleges, and other research facilities had linked up via this internetwork, which became known by the proper noun Internet and the nickname "the Net." In addition to making access to research that much easier to come by, it also allowed people to contact each other with electronic mail. It was further augmented by a graphic "browser" for the internet called Mosaic, which is still the foundation of the popular Internet Explorer and Netscape.

This was not a new idea. Science fiction writer Arthur C. Clarke had postulated something like it as early as the '50s. The Who's Pete Townshend wrote a never-made film concept based on the idea, as well, inspired by one of his old art school professors, Dr. Roy Ascott. "I wanted to connect everyone together," Townshend said of the concept he called Lifehouse. "I saw them all in this place where they were getting all these lifetimes of experience, so I invented this network and then thought, 'Well, why would they be on the network in the first place? They would be there because they wanted to be part of this universal experience grid.' I think actually, to some extent, this is happening to us today. You know, we can't keep up with the barrage of information that technology is serving us."

By the mid-'90s, this "grid" was robust enough to handle pretty much any information available. People started getting wind of this new means of information gathering and of just getting in contact. Personal computers came with modems built in to take advantage of it.

These personal computers also gained in speed and power, to the point that five years after the introduction of the MP3 format as something much too sophisticated for the average computer to handle, nearly every computer had the speed, memory, and power of the software engine that Fraunhofer had invented for the Motion Pictures

Expert Group. MP3s could now run on the average high-end personal computer. Fraunhofer made the code for the engine available via the Internet as shareware.

This allowed for the transfer of digital music via computer. It became a big thing among college students with access to the faster Internet connections a college offered along with large amounts of digital space at their disposal. By 1996, it had become the big thing among "computer geeks" to have bulletin boards full of pirated games and software with the copy-prevention codes removed (thus transformed, called "warez") and digital music files of favorite songs compressed or "ripped" to MP3 files from CDs.

The music industry surely became aware of it at this point. As early as 1993, *Rolling Stone* reported, "Record companies, worried that digital music broadcasts through cable and satellite systems will soon allow consumers to make CD-quality tapes, are lobbying Congress for an amendment to the copyright laws."

However, the people in power chose to ignore this innovation, since it was generally localized on college campuses where there was access to high-speed Internet. Most home PCs operated at the time at a maximum speed of 28.8 baud—it would take about 15 minutes for a three-minute MP3 file to download at that rate—whereas businesses and colleges had access to T1 lines which were roughly six to ten times faster. They figured, as things stood, who'd want to waste that much time downloading something they could buy for the money they would make in the time that it took to download—or something like that. They didn't foresee the exponential growth in computer speed and power down the road, though a look back might have provided a glimpse. In 1984, a computer with a slow operating speed, 64 kilobytes of memory and a 300 baud modem, was hot shit. A decade later, 28,800 baud was the standard and the Pentium 120 operating system with 10 megabytes of memory would run lazy circles around the old technology.

Given that, and Moore's law, which says that the speed of computers will double every eighteen to twenty-four months, it should have been evident that this technology could become a major force. But most people in the music business seemed to lack that level of imagination. Some, however, saw it. As early as 1985, Todd Rundgren had said, "I'd rather have someone just dial up my computer terminal, and punch in the questions, and the answers would all be online. Because most interviews are written for an audience where all they care about are the most surface, phenomenal aspects of what's going on, things they can relate to."

By 1992, he was predicting the downloading of music to the exclusion of physical record stores. "It will be Tower Records and Blockbuster Video, except they won't have storefronts. They'll have big, faceless buildings with giant mainframe computers in them, waiting for you to call up. Then they'll download it to your house and they'll charge you for it, just as if you walked into the record store to buy it. The difference is that prerecorded media will disappear."

If the music industry's imagination had extended beyond lobbying and legal wrangling in 1993, it might have saved itself a world of grief five years later. However, several things prevented the industry from seeing what visionaries like Rundgren saw. One was that the industry had not fully exploited the compact disc by this point. Reissues were still coming out of records by artists ranging from the most famous to the most obscure, from the Beatles to oddball, Bay Area minimalists like the Residents. The need to start selling through their catalog again was not yet imminent.

The industry also did not count on the fact that by 1997 the Internet would probe the limits of copyright laws and the concepts of fair use in ways very few could even conceive of in 1992. On the campus bulletin boards, people pooled their CD collections, ripped them, and made them available to whoever accessed the board. This made copies of near-CD-quality music available free for the asking, in clear violation of the copyright laws.

As the phenomenon tended to be localized on college campuses, none of this seemed to bother the Brahmins of the biz particularly. They felt they could control it. The managers of English rock stars Oasis sent e-mails to 140 fan-run sites that paid tribute to the group, asking them to remove "unauthorized" music and video from their sites, and threatening them with copyright infringement suits if they didn't.

An executive at Geffen Records sent letters out to many of the colleges that, wittingly or unwittingly, hosted music bulletin board sites. The letter politely explained that several of the students using space on their server were in clear violation of the copyright laws of the United States, and you might want to notify them of this and remove the offending material. "None of us had made any attempt to avoid detection," David Weekly, who ran a site that accounted for eighty percent of the traffic on Stanford University's computer network in 1997, recalled. "We had instead made our sites as visible as possible, posting their location to all the popular search engines. We had also made links to each other's pages. It was, as a result, a simple task to discover and contact all of us rapidly: indeed, in one week early in 1997, just about every popular MP3 site on the Net disappeared."

Another site out of Texas A&M proved somewhat more dicey from a legal point of view. The enormously popular site TEK didn't let you download the MP3 files, but offered to let you listen to them by means of "streaming," the digital fulcrum of college radio and a juke box. Over two million people accessed their site every month, including employees from Microsoft and Xerox who used the service for background music in their cubicles.

Since MP3 technology was not something the music business had conceived, they felt that, at its foundation, it couldn't relate to the record business per se. However, it certainly had everything to do with the music business—it was, after all, created to get better-quality sound onto film. As something that didn't fit in with the current paradigms of distribution, they didn't see it.

What's more, the business reasoned, you can't take MP3 files away from the computer. Who wants to have to boot up their computer when they want to listen to music?

The answers to these rhetorical questions came within months of each other from two separate directions with a speed that would cross the music business's eyes and generate collective and cumulative heat that would keep it putting out fires for many years to come.

Piracy is a lot like prostitution. Shut down one area to street walkers and they'll find another, and the demand will find them. With the bulletin boards shut down, the music traders started to move a little more underground. They used IRC (internet relay chat) rooms to hook up, and then exchanged the files person to person. Not satisfied with this, a Northeastern University freshman named Shawn Fanning put together a bit of code that would allow people to link to a central nexus, download his program, and access music from each other. He named the program with his IRC handle, Napster. "It was rooted out of frustration not only with MP3.com, Lycos, and Scour.net, but also to create a music community," Fanning said of his innovation. "There really was nothing like it at the time. We had good ideas for implementation, so we proceeded. I think it was an excellent solution to the reliability issues with existing search engines."

Shortly after that shot over the bow of the music business, Korean computer hardware manufacturer Saehan announced their newest innovation, the MPMan. This announcement, the liberation of the MP3 file from the computer and onto the street and into the cars of the world, made the Walkman and home taping look like a student council meeting by comparison. Suddenly, the music business saw its future, and it didn't necessarily include hard goods. Because they had not taken any steps in the years they had known about this possibility, none of the intellectual property that they made their livings on had any means of protection and they couldn't profit from this. Within the course of a year, music went from a commodity to an entitlement.

Had the music business thought ahead far enough, they might have found in MP3s the salvation to many of their most expensive problems:

- *Real estate:* Record stores occupy vast amounts of prime retail real estate, and pay for it accordingly. In a low mark-up business like sound recordings, Rundgren's faceless, massive mainframe has enormous appeal.

- *Manufacturing:* While the actual cost of making the CD became cheaper over the years, the price of the CD never went down. However, when broken down to basics, a CD, a cassette, an LP, or a wax cylinder are still, at their hearts, only containers, a storage medium for the transfer of musical ideas. With the digital transfer of music files, that medium becomes whatever bottle the end-user chooses to keep the lightning in. "The Web eliminates two-thirds of the cost factors," the Smithsonian Institution's Richard Kurin pointed out. "You don't have to produce a hard product and you don't have to pay a middleman. The prospect is for greater dissemination."

However, none of this occurred to the mainstream business. Suddenly, in 1998, it found itself with these huge fires to put out and very little to do it with. Hundreds of thousands of people, sharing millions of music files would be logged on to Napster at any given time—the software showed the number of users and the number of files available from those users on the screen. Unlike "Alice's Restaurant," you couldn't necessarily get anything you wanted, but you could find nearly any mainstream song and even a few oddballs any time you logged on. No one got royalties from any of it.

This did not greatly upset many of the artists whose files were being traded. More than anything else, they wanted *exposure*. From the '80s onward, this had become harder and harder to get. Starting with the Reagan administration, regulations that had held the media in check for five decades began to be stripped away. Where once a single company couldn't own more than two radio stations, a TV channel, and a newspaper in any given market, by the mid-'90s, any company could own all it could afford. This centralized concentration of media and money had a chilling effect on music. With the financial stakes so high, radio needed to guarantee profits. The music was flypaper, the listeners the flies, and the companies wanted to catch as many as they could. This led to disposable pop, regurgitated rock, and repetitive rap—everything began to sound the same. Anything with a modicum of personality or potential to offend had to develop somewhere outside the broadcast frequencies.

Several websites answered this call. Anyone could upload music to MP3.com, a service that invented itself as it went along. As an added value, you could put music you already owned into a "digital locker" on the site and access it from any computer anywhere. However, much of that music featured copyrights owned by the mainstream biz, and suddenly the site was entertaining a boatload of lawsuits.

Within two years, the situation had gone from dangerous to critical. A survey conducted by the Pew Internet & American Life Project reported that nearly 80 percent of the people who downloaded music didn't consider it stealing. Over 60 percent didn't care whether it was copyrighted. Nearly the same amount who didn't consider downloading piracy did not pay for their Internet music.

Still, several independent companies attempted to vault into the digital domain. Larry Rosen, one of the principles of the GRP jazz label was one of the early adapters in the business. While he didn't see giving up the CD altogether, his N2K Encoded Media company released several excellent records and made various tracks available on the Web that either became value added to the CD or stand-alone product on the company's Music Boulevard website. One of the people he brought along with him was Grammy-winning producer Phil Ramone. "It's like the beginning of LPs," Ramone said in 1997. "When we used to cut LPs, I'm telling you, they were atrocious when good vinyl was hard to come by and the way the stylus worked and repro-duction. When they first came out on the market in 1947, there was a lot to be desired. When you first started going from analog to digi-tal, there was a lot to be desired. Now we're standing on the precipice of a new generation of technology and work."

N2K partnered with a company called Liquid Audio that used a compression protocol similar to MP3, but with certain differences that required their own proprietary playback software (which they gave away). "The piracy issue is one that the industry is very concerned with," said the company's Scott Burnett. "It's one that's at the heart and soul of the system. There's an encryption device in place, as well as watermarking. In essence, you can only enable the song and play back the particular licensed records (that you purchased or are entitled to as value added)."

The late '90s were a time of incomparable chaos in music. Sales were down. The record companies found downloading a very useful scapegoat, though it bore the weight of a scape-elephant. Certainly, as Pew outlined, there were people who didn't buy music because they could get it free off the Web. But there were many other issues that the record companies never seemed to address. Primarily, the youth dollar, while still an amazingly potent economic force, had far more demands for it than just music. Video games had proliferated during the 1990s. What the music industry had always taken for granted as "their" audi-ence, the twelve-to-twenty-four-year-old consumers, had largely been coopted by Nintendo, as well as Sony, a company in both the music and video-game, hardware and software businesses.

Artist development was another problem. A 2001 report in *Bill-board* found that 0.35 percent of all records sold accounted for over half of the sales. The article claimed that of the nearly 300,000 albums tracked by the company Soundscan during the year 2000, a little over 100 of them accounted for more than 50 percent of all records sold.

This left over a quarter of a million albums fighting for the other half
of the nation's disposable income (which was also becoming less and
less due to a lousy economy). Part of the problem was getting the
music in front of potential fans.

The Internet presented the ability to do this quite nicely. "I delivered my final CD under contract," Todd Rundgren said in 1997, "and
then immediately started crafting this subscription offering. . . . The
online experience with me is twenty-five bucks, but with that you get
chat and messaging and e-mail directly to me and there will be live
Internet performance over the course of the year, as well as having a
window into the music, and also getting exposed to a lot more music
than they would get otherwise, because of the expense of putting
music onto a CD. If I'm distributing electronically, I can make music
that I might not normally put on a CD; it wouldn't fit the concept or
it's only a minute long or it's twenty minutes long. All kinds of restric-
tions to giving up real estate on a CD don't exist when you're distributing electronically."

The online world offered artists without a record company, both
new and established, access to their fans. Early on, it was seen as the
great equalizer, a means to put the creative power of music back into
the hands of musicians. For some, like Rundgren and former Bongos
leader Richard Barone, it gave a home for the oddball track that had
no other home. "This is very intriguing, to have something available
in just this format," Barone said of the Web-only release of a live version of his song "Barbarella." "I hadn't even thought about releasing
it as a record here. In this form, which someone downloads as a single,
I thought that was really appropriate."

"The Internet is definitely a friend to the music industry in so
many different ways," Pete Townshend concurred. "For new artists, it's
a direct line to the general mass of the population so they can get
some early response to their finished work."

Of course, not every artist felt this way. Although they had a long-
time, fan-friendly policy of letting tapes of their shows circulate freely,
the members of the metal band Metallica objected to having songs
from their albums being traded on Napster. They submitted a list of a
third of a million fans (or at least their e-mail addresses) who had
downloaded "illegal" Metallica songs. "It's not about interviews or
bootlegs," said the group's drummer, Lars Ulrich. "If Napster removed

'Metallica Studio Masters,' if they would just do that, thank you, we're done, bye-bye."

The record companies' lobbying and trade organization, the Record Industry Association of America or RIAA, set about the task of shutting down Napster through the courts. By the summer of 2002, the Ninth Circuit Court of Appeals had found for the RIAA that Napster was a hub for copyright violations. The company added software to remove any work whose owners didn't want it distributed through the service, effectively eviscerating Napster. However, as the service went dormant, Fanning might well have quoted *Star Wars* at the RIAA—"You can't win. You can strike me down and I shall become more powerful than you can possibly imagine."

Other file-sharing protocols were already in the wings. They all basically used the Napster model with one basic difference—there was no central hub. These protocols connected online users who wanted songs and had the program loaded with online users, also with the program loaded, who had the desired songs, eliminating the middle-man with the exception of actually getting the software. On a random morning on the East Coast, nearly 3.5 million users worldwide on the service were offering over 600 million files.

Adding to this problem was the steady increase in bandwidth available to homes. Both cable TV companies and phone companies offered consumers download speeds comparable to the T1 lines at businesses and colleges. By 2003, nearly 40 percent of all Americans had access to broadband Internet service. With this, you could down-load a song in less time than it would take to listen to it.

Of course, the peer-to-peer services were hardly perfect. Often, it took several downloads to get the actual song you wanted, despite how it was listed. People hid their own tracks under the names of popular songs to get exposure. Record companies put up tracks that started correctly and then cut out or made horrible noises. Not every-one had broadband, so sometimes a track might take hours to down-load off one of these services.

Some companies discovered that peer-to-peer downloading actually helped them promote their artists, especially as the radio noose tight-ened. Richard Egan, a principle in Vagrant Records, figures that his label would have gone out of business without peer-to-peer downloading. Peer-to-peer, after all, is like that most convincing form of marketing, word of mouth. "Our music," he said, "by and large, when kids listen to it, they share it with their friends. Then they go buy the record. They take ownership of it."

"In artist development," added Chris Blackwell, former head of Island Records and owner of Palm Pictures, "file sharing—it's not really hurting you. You want people to discover your artists. You're building for the future."

While many companies, from N2K on, tried to offer pay download services, it took them a while to get it right. Some tried to offer sub-scriptions—all you could download for $10 a month. Many people took the free month they offered and stripped all that they wanted from the service. The services couldn't feed the downloading maw fast enough with enough variety and people left. Some charged per song, but couldn't provide the variety, especially as the major labels were leery of getting involved. There was also the issue of protecting the tracks—once someone bought the download, like when someone bought the CD and ripped a song, there was no stopping that buyer from putting it up on a sharing service.

By the time this goes to press, they still won't have it right and downloading may well become the undoing of the multinational record companies. The genie escaped its bottle with no forethought and no constraints, and continues to run amok on an industry crip-pled by indecision and falling revenue. The technology grows so quickly that it has the larger organizations' heads spinning like the spectators at a NASCAR race. "Maybe in the near future it will stabi-lize," Townshend said. "It will be great if everything stabilized, the download rate stabilized for say a year or two and we just got stuck in what would feel like a rut. It would give us all time to create some standards and conventions that just sat."

Townshend said this wistfully and wishfully. He is more familiar with Moore's Law than most and must know that the only way this fire can be put out is by acting on two fronts, putting out the existing fires and figuring out how to prevent new ones from starting. To sur-vive, the music business will have to either get a grip on the new technology and what customers want or succumb to every artist owning and exploiting his own intellectual property by hiring experts to do that one thing the record companies allegedly do best—promote and create a brand name around an artist. "The record companies still have a function," Rundgren maintained. "They have to underwrite artists until they build up a core audience. That's kind of the point. That's what record companies used to be. They used to be artist development. It was not a hits machine all the time, everybody in the company oriented toward that one blockbuster that makes the bottom line."

The record companies perhaps made their biggest gaff in September of 2003, when they subpoenaed nearly three hundred music fans who allegedly downloaded illegal files from Kazaa. The suits claimed that the downloaders were liable for up to $150,000 per song. "We wish our critics would worry less about the public-relations implications of our legal strategy than the piracy problems that require it," wrote the RIAA's Cary Sherman. "They offer few solutions to the piracy epidemic other than the suggestion to throw up our hands and give in. The multiprong strategy we are pursuing is warranted and effective. Our consumer surveys suggest overwhelming support for taking legal action against those who distribute massive amounts of music online."

"We saw the advent of Napster, which was outright thievery," said veteran country artist Charlie Daniels. "I have thought for a long time that the record industry has to catch up. We're always behind in technology. As far behind as we are, the people who make the laws of the land are even further behind. It's foolish to even think about [suing fans]. I don't even know who came up with that. Probably some lawyer who wants to spend the next ten years in court."

"The music industry is estranging an entire generation of music listeners," claimed Jerry Del Colliano, who publishes the audio/video industry online magazine AudioRevolution.com. "Gen X and Y feel it is their right to download music despite copyright infringement laws. The RIAA killing off Napster was a failed experiment because peer-to-peer networks like Gnutella rage on with files being swapped by the millions."

Both sides of the conflict understand what the Beatles meant when they sang in "Revolution," "So you say you've got a real solution, we'd just love to hear the plan." Unfortunately, for all the head-banging and tub-thumping, no one has come up with something both sides can agree on.

Ironically, the lawsuits inspired the company that created the file-sharing protocol, Kazaa, to sue the record companies for . . . copyright infringement! On September 21, 2003, they filed a suit that accused the entertainment companies of using an unauthorized version of their software to ferret out the end-users they sued.

All of the confusion about online distribution might be just the kick in the ass rock needs to revive itself again. A slew of groups have created small, dedicated fan bases via the Web and live performances. This has allowed artists to make a living and maintain control of their art. Jam bands, who have long encouraged the trading of concert tapes to spread the word, see the Internet as an opportunity to increase their recognition.

Other artists, from veterans like Dean Friedman to relative newcomers like Scooter Scudieri, run their musical careers on the Web. "I'm reinventing the rock star," Scudieri—who has toured as the opening act for Jewel and been hired to talk about his remarkable self-promotions at industry events and universities—said, reflecting on the title of his website, firstrockstar.com. "It's not about excess and ridiculousness and greed. I want to put some substance behind it. . . . I came up with the name firstrockstar to get people's attention, then show them that there's more to it."

Friedman had one fair hit in the late 1970s, a song called "Ariel." Because it was set with landmarks familiar to New York suburbanites, it became a much bigger hit in the New York metro area than anywhere else, but managed to go Top 30 nationwide as well. His subsequent musical endeavors didn't go quite so well commercially, at least at home in the U.S. He remained something of a legend in England, but quickly discovered that you can't feed a family of four on legend. He moved on to interactive design, creating games for computers and working on the Nickelodeon TV show *Arcade*. When the Web came along, he put up deanfriedman.com and suddenly his fans had a nexus. "I knew they were out there," he said, "I just didn't have the means to reach them or they me. The Internet allows artists and audience to communicate directly and pass over the middlemen—the record companies, the distributors, etc. . . I am selling CDs directly to these fans. I have sort of a cottage industry."

Little wonder the conventional music business is running scared. "It's nothing new to say the recording companies are scared," said

Professor Steven E. Schoenherrr from the University of San Diego. "They've always been scared."

That brings to mind another great movie moment, this one from the Mel Brooks classic *Blazing Saddles*. The governor had learned of problems in the town of Rock Ridge and tells his inner circle, "Gentlemen! We must protect our phony baloney jobs!"

Afterword

If you want to keep learning, write a book. I learned a lot more than I expected on this one—my boxes of research (yes, I keep it all) are easily twice as extensive as the material I collected for an exhaustive bio on Creedence Clearwater Revival.

Beyond the research though, doing this book reminded me of a few things. The Seattle chapter reminded me how much I love Soundgarden, a group that I hadn't put on the stereo in some time (I was generally listening to the subjects as I wrote about them).

I was also kind of shocked at how many of the people I was writing about were dead. The day I finished this, Robert Palmer, a musician I'd interviewed a couple of times and cite in the book, died of a heart attack. He was fifty-four years old. During the course of putting this book together, Run-D.M.C. deejay Jason "Jam Master Jay" Mizel was gunned down. Other people speaking through my tape recorder and files from beyond the grave in this book include Juggy Gayles, Joey Ramone, Paul Rothchild, Layne Staley, Sam Price, Honest Tom Pompasello, and Fela Anikulapo Kuti.

An old label-mate of mine from another lifetime as a recording artist, August Darnell (a.k.a. Kid Creole of K.C. and the Coconuts) once told me he intended to live fast, die young, and leave a pretty corpse. Fortunately, he has not and as I write this—not to give him a canary—he's still around, writing and producing. He (and I) have learned one of the messages Dave Marsh once told me he took home by listening to Bruce Springsteen, which is "Hope I *don't* die before I get old," and here's why.

The key, Pete Townshend—who wrote "hope I die before I get old" at the ripe old age of twenty-one—would tell us, is not to get old. Age, after all, is largely attitude. My grandmother lived to be ninety-six, and into her nineties was traveling the world. Rock on, Goldie!

Rock and roll keeps us young. Rock and roll keeps us strong.

Quotes

Introduction

My ancestors   from Green, Jonathon, *The Book of Rock Quotes*, 1977, Quick Fox/Omnibus, New York.

I guess it's okay   Ibid.

Anyone who spent time   from author's interview.

If it doesn't   from author's interview.

Pop music   from Green, op. cit.

Dance music   from author's interview.

I was a Charleston dancer   from author's interview.

The real story   from Escott, Colin, *All Roots Lead to Rock*, Schirmer Books, 1999, New York.

Rock and Roll is   from author's interview.

Rock and roll imposes   from author's interview.

Chapter 1: Edison Invents the Phonograph

Mr. Thomas A. Edison recently   from *Scientific American*; quoted in DeGraaf, Leonard, "Thomas Edison and the Origins of the Entertainment Phonograph," *NARAS Journal*, winter–spring, 1997/98, Santa Monica, California.

You're in bed   from Chapple, Steve, and Garafalo, Reebee, *Rock 'n' Roll Is Here to Pay*, 1977, Nelson Hall, Chicago.

America was at war   from speech accepting Joel Webber Award, New Music Seminar, July 1991, New York.

The late 50s   Ibid.

Chapter 2: Robert Johnson Makes Forty-one Recordings

So he sat   from Charters, Samuel, *The Blues Makers*, 1967, 1991 Da Capo, New York.

He played ragtime   from Murray, Charles Shaar, "Taking His Own Path Back to the Crossroads, Eminent Bluesman Robert Junior Lockwood Tells Charles Shaar Murray Why He's Happy To Discuss His Stepfather, Robert Johnson," *Daily Telegraph* (London) November 25, 2000.

. . . he went over   from Charters, op. cit.

What do you mean   Ibid.

We heard a couple   Ibid.

You gotta be   Ibid.

Robert Johnson came   from Scherman, Tony, "Finding Robert Johnson," *BPI Entertainment News Wire*, December 26, 1990, New York.

I've never heard   from Richards, Keith; liner notes, *Robert Johnson, The Complete Recordings*, 1990, Columbia Records, New York.

. . . it came as   from Clapton, Eric; liner notes, *Robert Johnson, The Complete Recordings*, 1990, Columbia Records, New York.

There has not   from Murray, op. cit.

. . . I singled out   from Clapton, op. cit.

"Love in Vain"   from Richards, cit.

Although it's hip   from Scherman, Tony, "Chipping Away at the Myths That Encrust a Blues Legend," *New York Times*, September 20, 1998.

Chapter 3: Les Paul Invents the Solid-Body Electric Guitar

That probably was   from author's interview.

Friday and Saturday   from Flippo, Chet, "I Sing the Solid Body Electric," *Rolling Stone*, February 13, 1975, New York.

It just bothered   from author's interview.

All I was trying   from author's interview.

There is the guitar   from Harrington, Richard, "Electric Experience: Smithsonian Guitar Exhibit Ponders the Implications of Amplification," *Washington Post*, November 10, 1996.

Sometime in the late 30s   from Flippo, op. cit.

I built the first   from author's interview.

This is the one   from author's interview.

If Leo Fender   from author's interview.

The cutting lathe   from author's interview.

Now this was the beginning   from Flippo, op. cit.

I had a wire recorder   from author's interview.

He showed it   from Flippo, op. cit.

. . . if you can do it   Ibid.

We're about 45 minutes   from author's interview.

had a line open   from author's interview.

I was busy   from author's interview.

This did everything   from author's interview.

The first lecture   from author's interview.

This is the way   from author's interview.

Chapter 4: "American Bandstand"

The first TV   from author's interview.

To me, at the time   from Brown, Len, and Friedrich, Gary, *Encyclopedia of Rock and Roll*, 1970, Tower Publications, New York.

The white pop   from author's interview.

They segregated everything   from author's interview.

It all happened   from Sigman, Mike, ed., "Dick Clark: A Legend in His Own Time," *Dialogues: Viewpoints of the Music Industry, a Record World Magazine Special Issue*, 1974, Record World Publishing.

You have an   from author's interview.

I think it's sad   from Raddatz, Leslie, "From 'Crazy Daddy-O' to 'Right On'," *TV Guide*, June 16, 1973.

We were talking   from Burt, Rob, *Rockerama: 25 Years of Teen Screen Idols*, 1983, Delilah Books, New York.

The girls who   from Lotz, I. C., "Dick Clark over a Chinese Luncheon," *Fusion Magazine*.

That made it all right   from Bieber, David, "He'll Give It a 90—It Jingles," *Boston Phoenix*, November 13, 1973.

We would book   from Smith, Joe, *Off the Record*, 1988, Warner Books, New York.

Any time Dick   from Smith, op. cit.

It took all of 20 minutes   Ibid.

I ran a test   from Lotz, op. cit.

Payola was a modus   from author's interview.

I didn't take   from Sigman, op. cit.

We build a   from Bieber, op. cit.

At the height   from Gardner, Hy, "Dick Clark Talks About That Washington 'Thing'," *New York Times*, March 20, 1961.

What they wanted   from author's interview.

. . . sheer unadulterated greed   from Bangs, Lester, "Screwing the System with Dick Clark (Don't Laugh—He Knows a Hell of a Lot More About It Than David Crosby!)," *Creem*, November, 1973.

Chapter 5: Elvis Presley Strolls in to the Union Street Recording Studios

In later years   from author's interview.

What in the devil   from Uslan, Michael, and Solomon, Bruce, *Dick Clark's First 25 Years of Rock and Roll*, 1981, Delacorte Press, New York.

I hung up   Chapple and Garafalo, op. cit.

Sam came down   from Booth, Stanley, "A Hound Dog, to The Manor Born," from Eisen, Jonathan, ed., *The Age of Rock*, 1969, Vantage Books, New York

I'd play along   Chapple and Garafalo, op. cit.

I got hold   from Booth, op. cit.

We tried to   from author's interview.

First time   from Smith, op. cit.

Presley products sold   from Soocher, Stan, *They Fought the Law: Rock Music Goes to Court*, 1998, Schirmer Books, New York.

I didn't realize   from author's interview.

He was the hottest   from Booth, op. cit.

What happened was   from author's interview.

I just think this black   from author's interview.

I think the easiest   from author's interview.

I wanted to say   from the *Ed Sullivan Show*; January 6, 1957.

I once went   from Smith, op. cit.

I had my Midget   from Soocher, op. cit.

He's afraid   from Booth, op. cit.

When I look out   from Nixon, Mojo, "Elvis Is Everywhere" (*Bo-Day-Shus*), Muffin Stuffin Music/La Rama Music, Los Angeles, 1987.

Chapter 6: Alan Freed Changes the Name
of His Radio Show

He was always   from Chapple and Garafalo, op. cit.

I heard the tenor   Ibid.

It's hard to convey   from Hinkley, David, "Alan Freed: Rock Punk?" *New York Daily News*, March 29, 1992

Those of us   from author's interview.

Two people were   from Davidson, Neil, "A Profile: Juggy Gayles," *Music Independent*, Oakland, California, January 1991

His (WJW) show was   from Welton, Clark, "He Was King of Rock 'n' Roll," *New York Times*, n.d.

. . . swing with a   from Beaufort, John, "On and Off Broadway," *New York Herald Tribune* (1950s).

In the beginning   from author's interview.

It keeps us   from Stearn, Jess, "Rock 'n' Roll Runs into Trouble," the *New York Daily News*, April 12, 1956.

It was two   from Dannen, Fred, *Hit Men: Power Brokers and Fast Money Inside the Music Business*, 1991, Vintage Books, New York.

An agent   from Welton, op. cit.

A guy who   from author's interview.

Alan could be   from author's interview.

I am no better   from Wilson, Earl, "Alan Freed's Story," *New York Post*, November 23, 1959.

He had a self destructive   from Hinkley, op. cit.

Freed suffered   from author's interview.

Chapter 7: The Movie "Blackboard Jungle" Comes Out

There is absolutely   from Weber, Bruce, "The Rock Hall of Fame Seeks Its Groove," *New York Times*, April 21, 1999.

When the titles   from Burt, op. cit.

But do you know   from Weber, op. cit.

I got my experience   from Jones, Marty, "Rock: The Comets' Tale—the World's Oldest Rock and Roll Band Is Still Rolling," *Denver Westword*, July 10, 1997.

It was crazy   Ibid.

Lord, just what   from Wilonsky, Robert, "Stop the Music: In *The Suburbans*, One Hit Wonders Reunite for No-Laugh Movie," *Dallas Observer*, October 28, 1999.

To join   from Stern, Jane and Michael, *Encyclopedia of Pop Culture*, 1992, Harper Perennial, New York.

I'd like to see   from author's interview.

After *Easy Rider*   LaSalle, Mick, "The People Who Briefly Saved Hollywood," *San Francisco Chronicle*, May 12, 1998.

We want to   from Wilonsky, Robert, "Look Ahead: D. A. Pennebaker Doesn't Make History, But He's Captured So Much of It," *Dallas Observer*, May 24, 2001.

The original thought from Kuzmyk, Jenn, "Rockin' Docs," *Realscreen*, November 1998.

I couldn't resist from Travers, Peter, "The Best Rock Movie Ever Made," *Rolling Stone*, New York, May 9, 2002.

There's Davd Byrne from author's interview.

I didn't want from Schoemer, Karen, "A Film Pursues the Redemptive Power of Rock and Roll," *New York Times*, August 18, 1991.

Chapter 8: From the Transistor Radio to the Cassette to the Compact Disc

Without transistors from Goodale, Bob, author's correspondence.

A lot of from Solomon, Russ; author's interview.

They were referred from Smith, Joe; author's interview.

We shouldn't have been from Paul, Les; author's interview.

Right now from Weiss, George David, address to B'nai B'rith Music and Performing Arts Unit.

Our founding fathers from Rodgers, Ruth, "Report to Congress Pursuant to Section 104 of the Digital Millennium Copyright Act," Washington D.C., August 4, 2000.

Analog records from Ludwig, Bob; author's interview.

We knew that CDs from Rose, Don; author's interview.

I walked into from Rothchild, Paul; author's interview.

The first few from Clark, Rick, "Gus Dudgeon, 1942–2002" *Mix*, October 2002, California

When you tape from Weiss, op. cit.

Chapter 9: Chuck Berry Records "Maybellene"

If Chuck Berry from Smith, Joe, *Off the Record*, 1988, Warner Books, New York.

He had a style from author's interview.

Rock 'n' roll from Hilburn, Robert, "Chuck Berry Sets the Records Straight," *Los Angeles Times Syndicate*, October 17, 1987.

In East St. Louis   from author's interview.

I don't care   from author's interview

Chuck went to see   from Smith, op. cit.

I came from   from author's interview.

I took a dub   from Chapple and Garafalo, op. cit.

If I'd gotten paid   from author's interview.

I get paid   from author's interview.

They were in it   from author's interview.

The feeling of   from Wirt, John, "Berry, A Rock 'n' Roll Original," *The Advocate*, Baton Rouge, April 11, 2003.

(To me, art) was   from Hilburn, op. cit.

Everything I wrote   from Segal, David, "Kennedy Center Honors 2000; Chuck Berry's 'Goode' Deeds; The Ornery Guitarist, at His Best in Rock-and-Roll," *Washington Post*, December 3, 2000.

My mother had 12   from Himes, Geoffrey, "It's Still Rock 'n' Roll For Little Richard," *Washington Post*, May 28, 1999.

My version was banned   from author's interview.

The public   from Kamm, Herbert, "Pat Boone Takes an Old Pro's Advice on Stardom," *New York World Telegram and Sun*, January 11, 1958.

If you wanted   from Palmer, Robert, "Hail a Creator of Rock and Roll," *New York Times*, October 11, 1987.

I've lifted every lick   Cohen, Tom, "Rock Stars Gather for Chuck Berry's 60th Birthday," Associated Press, October 16, 1986.

Chuck doesn't tell   from author's interview.

Chuck opened up   from Segal, op. cit.

Chapter 10: Buddy Holly Crashes

That was a pretty naughty   from Lehmer, Larry, *The Day the Music Died: The Last Tour of Buddy Holly, the "Big Bopper," and Ritchie Valens*, 1997, Schirmer Books, New York.

Clovis is 91 miles   from Patoski, Joe Nick, "Rave On," *Texas Monthly*, September 1994.

Holly and the Crickets from Crenshaw, Marshall, "Buddy Holly," *Britannica Biography Collection*.

We had to burn from Morse, Steve, "The Day the Stars Fell," *Boston Globe*, February 3 1989.

It was crazy from Tianen, Dave, "Buddy Holly's Fame Lives 40 Years After His Death," *Milwaukee Journal Sentinel*, February 3, 1999.

Dion says from Katz, Larry, "A Survivor of the Day the Music Died," *Boston Herald*, November 9, 2000.

He held the record Ibid.

It was a real up from Morse, Steve, "VH-1 Recalls Holly Plane Crash," *Boston Globe*, February 3, 1999.

Your daddy was from Morse, op. cit.

I turned on from Jardine, Cassandra, "The Day the Music Died: It's 39 Years Since Buddy Holly Was Killed; His Widowed Bride Has Thought of Him Every Day Since, She Says in a Rare Interview," *Telegraph*, London, March 18, 1998.

At first I couldn't from Ferguson, Derek, "Holly's Band Remembers 'Day Music Died' 30 Years Ago," *Toronto Star*, February 4, 1989.

We were on the bus from Katz, op. cit.

That's one of our heroes from Purtell, Tim, "Buddy Holly's Fateful Flight," *Entertainment Weekly*, New York, February 3, 1995.

I think maybe from Hinkley, David, "The Day the Music Survived 'American Pie': Good Song, But It Doesn't Really Tell the Story," *New York Daily News*, February 4, 1999.

We had to make from Katz, op. cit.

It fills every from Scott, Anne, "The Place the Music Died," *Des Moines Business Record*, March 9, 1998.

I'm not rich Jardine, op. cit.

Chapter 11: Beatlemania

My dad was a musician from Smith, op. cit.

The Beatles, to me from Cohen, Stephanie, and Bordowitz, Hank, ed., Peter Townshend Interview, MCY.com, New York, 2000.

George's relationship   from Sheff, David, and Golson, G. Barry, ed., *The Playboy Interviews with John Lennon & Yoko Ono*, 1981, Playboy Press, New York.

George Harrison once   from author's interview.

They were doing songs   from Masley, Ed, "Remaining Beatles Risk Their Place as Rock-Solid Legends to Reunite," *Pittsburgh Post-Gazette*, November 12, 1995.

It struck me   from Harris, Kenneth, "The Beatle Backer," *Observer*, London, May 17, 1964.

. . . chains of pandiatonic   from "What Songs the Beatles Sang," *Times,* London, December 27, 1963.

Paul was one   from Shef and Golson, op. cit.

The Beatles are   from Newton, Francis, "Beatles and Before," *New Statesman*, London, November 8, 1963.

We'll have to watch   Spain, Nancy, "Blows in on the Beatles," *She*, London, November 1963.

. . . after their 14th   from Muretich, James, and McEwen, Mary-Lynn, "Now for Some Beatles Bits and Pieces," *Calgary Herald*, November 18, 1995.

. . . a British rock 'n' roll   from Whitworth, Bill, "Beatle Siege at the Plaza," *New York Herald Tribune*, February 9, 1964.

They are charming   from Whitworth, Bill, "Quiet Look at Beatles Uproar," *New York Herald Tribune*, August 30, 1964.

The early sixties   from author's interview.

I want to be   from Harris, op. cit.

In three or four   from Robards, Terry, "The Beatle Biz," *New York Herald Tribune*, March 7, 1965.

That was wholly   from author's interview.

Imagine two people   from Norman, Tony, "Lennon-McCartney: Friends or Foes," *Pittsburgh Post-Gazette*, November 11, 1995.

Gradually, things changed   from Smith, op. cit.

There were three ways   Ibid.

I remember hitting   Ibid.

Sergeant Pepper is called   from Sheff and Golson, op. cit.

. . . if I were dead   Gammage, Jeff, "Who Was the Walrus?" *Pittsburgh Post-Gazette*, December 5, 1995.

They were not happy   from Sigman, Mike, ed., "George Martin Speaks Out," *Dialogues:Viewpoints of the Music Industry, a Record World Magazine Special Issue*, 1974, Record World Publishing.

When I heard   Ibid.

George and I   from author's interview.

When you talk   from author's interview.

Lennon and McCartney   from Norman, op. cit.

The Beatles myth   from author's interview.

I was amazed   from Smith, op. cit.

John and I   Ibid.

The whole Beatles thing   from Sheff and Golson, op. cit.

It was a magical mixture   from "Harrison Sees Beatlemania as 'Pension Fund'," *Times of India*, December 30, 2000.

They all worked   from author's interview.

They all worked   Masley, op. cit.

Jeff Lynne was surprised   Ibid.

Chapter 12: Bob Dylan Goes Electric at Newport

I had about   from Shannon, Bob, and Javna, John, *Behind the Hits,* 1986, Warner Books, New York.

. . . a thousand angry plumbers   from Dylan, Bob, "Off the Top of My Head," *Newport Jazz Festival Booklet*, Newport, 1965.

I always wanted   from Crowe, Cameron; liner notes to *Biograph*, Columbia Records, New York, 1985.

I was singing   from Crowe, op. cit.

I started writing   from Harrington, Richard, "Every Revolution Needs Young Firebrands and Elder Statesmen; Bob Dylan Has Been Both," *Washington Post*, December 7, 1997.

If I didn't   from Sirak, Ron, "Bob Dylan: A Milepost in the Passing of Time," Associated Press, New York, June 12, 1991.

Before I started   from Cohen and Bordowitz, op. cit.

I don't do anything   from "Famous Songwriter Bob Dylan Mystery Man To Most Americans," *KRLA Beat*, Los Angeles, July 7, 1965.

They booed   from Kooper, Al, "Voices of the Century: Bob Dylan Goes Electric," *Newsweek*, New York, July 19, 1999.

I wasn't surprised   from Smith, op. cit.

Before the show   from Kooper, op. cit.

That tour was   from Crowe, op. cit.

They certainly booed   Ibid.

I didn't know   Ibid.

I started out   from Pareles, Jon, "A Wiser Voice Blowing in the Autumn Wind," *New York Times*, September 28, 1997.

My songs are   Ibid.

The way Elvis   from Harrington, op. cit.

The world don't   from Cooney, Michael, "Hard Reign: Bob Dylan's Song Borrowing," *Sing Out!* Fall 2001.

I don't think   from Harrington, op. cit.

To this day   Ibid.

Chapter 13: Paul Williams Launches "Crawdaddy!" Magazine

The band was putrid   from Salinger, Jerome David, *Catcher in the Rye*, 1951, Little Brown, Boston.

I just (learned . . .   from author's interview.

. . . submediant switches from   from "What Songs the Beatles Sang," *Times*, London, December 27, 1963.

. . . there is no doubt   from Pareles, Jon, "Robert Shelton, 69, Music Critic Who Chronicled the 60s Folk Boom," *New York Times*, December 15, 1995.

There are now   from Shelton, Robert, "The Beatles Will Make the Scene Here Again, but the Scene Has Changed," *New York Times*, August 11, 1965.

I read that from Williams, Paul, ed., *The Crawdaddy! Book*, 2002, Hal Leonard Books, Milwaukee.

The reason for Ibid.

The most interesting Ibid.

We were part from author's correspondence.

I was writing from Smith, op. cit.

Rolling Stone is from Chapple and Garafalo, op. cit.

It not only covers from Christgau, Robert, "Crawdaddy!" *Village Voice*, n.d.

Mr. Crumb needed from Reay, Tony, "Like Pushing a Rubber Giraffe Through a Keyhole," Rockcritics.com, January 14, 2003.

Along with Dave from Bangs, Lester, and Marcus, Greil, ed., *Psychotic Reactions and Carburetor Dung*, 1987, Alfred A. Knopf, New York.

The music became from Rizzo, Frank, "Turning 20, *Rolling Stone* Is Still Gathering No Moss," *Hartford Courant*, July 4, 1987.

In the summer from Membery, York, "Bottom of the Pops," *Times*, London, June 30, 1992.

[In] 1976 and 1977 from Bangs and Marcus, op. cit.

It's flattering saying from Scheerer, Mark, "*Rolling Stone* Founder Looks at Magazine's Past," CNN's *Showbiz Today*, New York, September 29, 1992.

There used to be forums from Ivry, Bob, "He Made Rock Criticism into an Art Form," *Bergen Record*, New Jersey, June 8, 2000.

Rock criticism is from Robertson, Lori, "Golden Oldies," *American Journalism Review*, July/August, 2000.

Do you think from Marsh, Dave; author's correspondence.

Chapter 14: Ahmet Ertegun Signs Cream— "Rock and Roll" Becomes "Rock"

The significance of from author's interview.

Albums were what from Townshend, Pete; "Meaty, Beaty, Big and Bouncy," *Rolling Stone*, New York, December 7, 1971.

It was a novelty from author's interview.

I latched on   from author's interview.

The reputation   from Houghton, Mick; "Zeus of Zeppelin: An Interview with Jimmy Page," *Circus*, New York, October 12, 1976.

The first recordings   from author's interview.

Led Zeppelin!   from author's interview.

Heavy music   from "Black Sabbath," *Beat Instrument*, London, November 1970.

A lot of music   from Sigman, op. cit.

Roger's and Nick's   from Sutcliffe, Phil, "Pink Floyd: Dark Side of the Moon," *Mojo*, March 1998.

Blues is American   from author's interview.

I always loved   from author's interview.

We were "underground"   from author's interview.

I thought I was   from author's interview.

We were sitting   from author's interview.

I remember that   from author's interview.

I'm very interested   from Houghton, op. cit.

Somebody says   from Cohen and Bordowitz, op. cit.

We both looked   from author's interview.

From the very beginning   from author's interview.

Multi-track recording   from Sigman, op. cit.

You have to realize   from author's interview.

Our genius lighting   from Cohen and Bordowitz, op. cit.

Unlike the 60s   from Robbins, Ira, "Remember Those Fabulous 70s? A Musical Stroll from Woodstock to Punk-rock," *Trouser Press*, January 1980.

Chapter 15: From Monterey Pop to Woodstock to Altamont

There was a place   from author's interview.

Jazz had become   from author's interview.

Rock saved me   from author's interview.

In '66 and '67   from author's interview.

We had to convince   from Peeples, Stephen; liner notes to *The Monterey International Pop Festival*, Rhino Records, 1992.

There were no   Ibid.

The idea for   Ibid.

I told him   from Lydon, Michael, "Montery Pops! An International Pop Festival," June 1967, Rocksbackpages.com.

. . . rewritten the book   from Dunham, Elisabeth, "Monterey Pop: Concert That Changed Rock Music 25 Years Ago," Associated Press, June 17, 1992.

We've had more trouble   from Peeples, op. cit.

It showcased the fact   Ibid.

What these kids   Ibid.

the growing suspicion   Ibid.

Just seeing the effect   from author's interview.

The last thing   from author's interview.

What he was arguing   from Marsh, Dave, "Fooled Again," *Rock and Roll Confidential*, September 1999.

Some of the artists   from author's interview.

They had a   from author's interview.

. . . if you bought   from author's interview.

It became a free   from author's interview.

It wasn't that   from author's interview.

I paid them   from author's interview.

Tommy had been   from Cohen and Bordowitz, op. cit.

. . . it turned a profit   from author's interview.

After Woodstock   from author's interview.

If you have any food   from Nadelson, Reggie, "Where Did All the Flowers Go . . . ?" *Daily Telegraph*, London, August 11, 1994.

For a city   from author's interview.

The vibe of the place   from author's interview.

They were the most from Nadelson, op. cit.

The most surpising from author's interview.

I was doing really nicely from author's interview.

It felt great from Dalton, David, "Altamont: An Eyewitness Account," *Gadfly*, November/December 1999.

We had a wonderful time from Gaar, Gillian G., "'Verse Chorus Verse': The Recording History of Nirvana," *Goldmine,* Iola, WI, February 14, 1997.

I've been to Lollapalooza from author's interview.

We wanted to show from Moon, Tom, "Lilth Fair Comes to Town," *Philadelphia Inquirer*, n.d.

We're not trying Ibid.

Chapter 16: The Sex Pistols Tour America

Doubly disenfranchised Savage, Jon, "Punk Five Years On," *Face*, London, November 1981.

At our soundcheck from Snow, Mat, "Meet the Family: Ramones, Blondie, Talking Heads," *Q*, London, October 1990.

The trouble with from Ingham, John, "The Sex Pistols Are Four Months Old . . . ," *Sounds*, London, April 24, 1976.

Everybody was unique from Snow, op. cit.

I hate shit from Ingham, op. cit.

They are full from Ingham, op. cit.

Instead of using from Turner, Steve, "The Great Rock 'n' Roll Swindle: How Malcolm McLaren Made Cash from Chaos," *The History of Rock,* London, 1983.

I'm against people from Ingham, op. cit.

There we were from Bohn, Chris, "The Clash: One Step Beyond," *Melody Maker,* London, December 29, 1979.

I just wonder from Dunn, Jancee, "John Lydon," *Rolling Stone*, New York, June 16, 1994.

Participation   Coon, Caroline, "Punk Rock: Rebels Against the System," *Melody Maker*, London, August 7, 1976.

Then the world   from Snow, op. cit.

Our record company   Ibid.

The combination of people   from author's interview.

They always say   from author's interview.

We are a grungy   from author's interview.

1996   Quoted from Sloop, John M., "The Emperor's New Makeup: Cool Cynicism and Popular Music Criticism," *Popular Music and Society*, Spring 1999

As I sit   Dunn, op. cit.

Chapter 17: MTV Launches

A friend of mine   from author's interview.

I got involved   from author's interview.

I was first attracted   from Weiss, Paulette, *The Rock Video Book*, 1985, Pocket Books, New York.

I think sometimes   from author's interview.

Most music videos   from author's interview.

Obviously   from author's interview.

By the time   from author's interview.

MTV had set themselves   from Slack, James, "Did Video Kill the Radio Star? MTV 20 Years On," *Rock's Backpages,* London, July 28, 2001.

In the radio world   from author's interview.

We were disturbed   from "Beat It, Don't Join It," *Rock & Roll Confidential*, New York, August 1983.

I used to   from author's interview.

They had all   From Shannon, Bob, and Javna, John, *Behind the Hits*, 1986, Warner Books, New York.

There is a change   from author's interview.

As far as from author's interview.

The 21-year-old from Romano, Angela, "MTV Operating Without a Net," *Broadcasting & Cable*, May 27, 2002.

I'm sort of in from Carter, Bill, "He's Cool. He Keeps MTV Sizzling. And, Oh Yes, He's 56," the *New York Times*, June 16, 2002.

Chapter 18: Live Aid

The pictures were from Wavell, Stuart, "St. Bob Said Let There Be Light . . . And There Will Be," *Sunday Times*, London, December 19, 1999.

The picture that from Devlin, Martina, "Geldof—The Man Who Wouldn't Take No for an Answer," Press Association, London, July 9, 1995

It defies from Pareles, Jon, "Hunger Telethon to Be Heard Around the Globe," *New York Times*, July 7, 1985.

I felt disgusted from Ockenfels, F. W. and Tannenbaum, Robert, "Bob Geldof," *Rolling Stone*, New York, November 11, 1990.

The problem was from Wavell, op. cit.

I was brought from Ockenfels and Tannenbaum, op. cit.

Live Aid and Band Aid from Coleman, M., "The Revival of Conscience," *Rolling Stone*, New York, November 15, 1990.

We did Live Aid from author's interview.

It wasn't just from Mackesy, Serena, "Ten Years After. . . ," *Independent*, London, July 14, 1995.

You pick people from Pareles, op. cit.

It had to be from Devlin, Martina, "Remembering the Day Pop World Showed Its Heart," Press Association, London, July 9, 1995.

Live Aid was not from Morse, Steve, "1985 Live Aid: The Last Time Rock Found Unity . . . ," *Boston Globe*, July 11, 1995.

You'd walk out from Tyrangiel, Josh, and Nugent, Benjamin, "Bono," *Time*, New York, March 4, 2002

The fact that from author's interview.

I would like from author's interview.

It was a net from Ockenfels and Tannenbaum, op. cit.

I'd run out from Sandall, Robert, "Just the Job for Bob," *Sunday Times*, London, August 30, 1992.

It was only from Clark-Meads, Jeff, "Band Aid No Longer Seeking Funds," *Billboard*, New York, January 25, 1992.

This was about from Uhelszki, Jaan, "Live Aid, '90s Style," *Rolling Stone*, New York, September 16, 1999.

Almost $200 million from Mabrey, Vicki, "Rock Singer Bono of the Band U2 Discusses His Music and His Dedication to Reducing Third World Debt," *60 Minutes*, February 20, 2002.

The task then from Vallely, Paul, "Interview: Two Worlds: Things Have Changed. . . ," *Independent*, London, May 31, 2003.

Chapter 19: Nirvana Hits #1 with "Nevermind"

Even if you from author's interview.

Soul Asylum from author's interview.

You'd go check from Neely, Kim, and Selinger, Mark, "Soundgarden," *Rolling Stone*, New York, July 9–July 23, 1992.

It's like the Cabrera, Luis, "Music Makers: 'Grunge Rock' Puts Seattle In Musical Spotlight," Associated Press, Seattle, January 24, 1992.

Of course, we from author's interview.

. . . a mix of from Reynolds, Simon, "Nirvana: Smells Like a Sensation," *Observer*, London, December 8, 1991.

It came out from Townshend, op. cit.

When we were from Strauss, Neil, "The Pop Life: Speaking for Soundgarden," *New York Times*, June 15, 1994.

What's interesting from Cabrera, op. cit.

The first three songs from Snow, Mat, "Pearl Jam: 'You, My Son, Are Weird'," *Q*, London, November 1993.

We have a from Marin, Rick, "Grunge: A Success Story," *New York Times*, November 15, 1992.

It wasn't like Ibid.

All things grunge Ibid.

I wish I from Sutcliffe, Phil, "Kurt Cobain: King of Pain," *Q*, London, October 1993

I do not want from Egan, Timothy, "Kurt Cobain, Hesitant Poet of 'Grunge Rock,' Dead at 27," *New York Times*, April 9, 1994.

The whole success thing from Snyder, Michael, "Towers of Grunge Tip Toward Mainstream," *San Francisco Chronicle*, October 24, 1993.

It's music from Vercammen, Paul, "Pearl Jam Album Breaks New Release Sales Record," CNN, Atlanta, October 28, 1993.

An epic tragedy from Snyder, Michael, "Benefit Concert: Nirvana Fights Hell in Bosnia," *San Francisco Chronicle*, April 4, 1993.

Chapter 20: MP3, Napster, and the End of the World as We Know It

I wanted to from Cohen and Bordowitz, op. cit.

Record companies from Goodman, Fred, "In the News," *Rolling Stone*, New York, November 11, 1993.

I'd rather have from author's interview.

It will be from author's interview.

None of us from Weekly, David E., *mp3 Book*, e-book published by www.weekly.org, 2003.

It was rooted Varanini, Giancarlo, "Q&A: Napster Creator Shawn Fanning," ZDnet Music, March 2, 2000.

The Web eliminates from Napoli, Lisa, "Think Debate on Music Property Rights Began with Napster? Hardly," *New York Times*, September 22, 2003.

It's like the beginning from author's interview.

The piracy issue from author's interview.

I delivered my from author's interview.

This is very from author's interview.

The Internet from Cohen and Bordowitz, op. cit.

It's not about   from *Rock & Rap Confidential,* 2000.

Our music   from Nelson, Chris, "Upstart Labels See File Sharing as Ally, Not Foe," *New York Times,* September 22, 2003.

In artist development   from Nelson, op. cit.

I wish our critics   from Sherman, Cary, "File Sharing Is Illegal. Period." *USA Today,* New York September 19, 2003.

We saw the advent   from "Music Wars," *TechTV,* September 12, 2003.

The music industry   from "Instead of Suing Over Downloadable Music—The Music Business Should Take the High Road," PR Newswire, August 27, 2002

It's nothing new   from Napoli, op. cit.

I'm reinventing the rock star   from Katz, Larry, "Reinventing the Rock Star: Do-it-yourselfer Scooter Scudieri Fights the Musical-Industrial Complex," *Boston Herald,* October 23, 2002.

I knew they   from Ames, Lynne, "Rock-and-Roll Dreams Die Hard on Internet," *New York Times,* June 20, 1999

Bibliography

Books and Articles

"2500 Years of Communications History," *Adventures in Cybersound*, www.acmi.net.au/AIC/TV_TL_COMP_2.html.

"Alan Freed, Disk Jockey, Dead; Popularized Rock 'n' Roll Music," Associated Press, January 21, 1965.

Audio Home Recording Act of 1992.

"Beat It, Don't Join It," *Rock & Roll Confidential*, August 1983.

"Black Sabbath," *Beat Instrument*, November 1970.

"'Brother Teresa' Wants to Be Taken Seriously as a Musician," *Bergen Record*, NJ, August 28, 1990.

"CD-R Levy Has No Justification," *Computing Canada*, January 22, 1999.

"Clark, Dick," *Current Biography*, May 1959.

"Dick Clark, Past and Present," *Zoo World*, August 16, 1973.

"Edison, Thomas Alva," *Encyclopedia Britannica*, 2003, Encyclopedia Britannica Online, search.eb.com/eb/article?eu=109026.

"Famous Songwriter Bob Dylan Mystery Man to Most Americans," *KRLA Beat*, July 7, 1965.

"Fatboy Tops MTV Birthday Vote," BBC News, London, August 1, 2001.

"Grunge Rock Wins Honors from MTV," Associated Press, Universal City, CA, September 4, 1993.

"Harrison Sees Beatlemania as 'Pension Fund'," *Times of India*, December 30, 2000.

"Instead of Suing Over Downloadable Music—The Music Business Should Take the High Road," PR Newswire, August 27, 2002.

"It's School Soon for Pat Boone," *Rock and Roll Songs*, date unknown.

"John Hammond, 76, Critic and Discoverer of Pop Talent, Dies," *New York Times*, July 11, 1987, p. 1.

"Music Wars," *TechTV*, September 12, 2003.

"Oh No, The Righteous Rockers Are Staging a Comeback," *Sunday Times*, London, July 7, 2002.

"Les Paul," www.rockhall.com/hof/inductee.asp?id=164.

"Music Recording," *Encyclopedia Britannica*, 2003, Encyclopedia Britannica Online, search.eb.com/eb/article?eu=118777.

"Phonograph," *Encyclopedia Britannica*, 2003, Encyclopedia Britannica Online, search.eb.com/eb/article?eu=61273.

"Rock and Roll Pied Piper Alan Freed," *New York Times*, May 20, 1960.

"Sarnoff, David," *Encyclopedia Britannica*, 2003, Encyclopedia Britannica Online, search.eb.com/eb/article?eu=67486.

"Sing When You're Winning," *New Media Age*, November 14, 2002.

"VH-1 and *Spin* Magazine Team Up to Present 'VH-1 News Special: Grunge . . . '," PR Newswire, NY, September 10, 2001.

"What Songs the Beatles Sang," *Times*, London, December 27, 1963.

"Why the Record Companies Have to Play Hardball," *MSNBC/Newsweek*, September, 24, 2003.

Alles, Brent G, "Rock Films of the 50s, 60s, and 70s," Rock and Roll Movie Site, Southern Michigan University, 2003.

Ames, Lynne, "Rock-and-Roll Dreams Die Hard on Internet," *New York Times*, June 20, 1999.

Ansen, David, Hack, Janet, Ames, Katrine, and Agrest, Susan, "Rock Tycoon," *Newsweek*, July 31, 1978, p. 40–47.

Atherley, Ruth, "Band Aid's Millions," *McLeans*, October 5, 1987.

Bangs, Lester, "Screwing the System with Dick Clark (Don't Laugh—He Knows A Hell of a Lot More About It Than David Crosby!)," *Creem*, November, 1973.

———, and Marcus, Greil (ed.), *Psychotic Reactions and Carburetor Dung*, Alfred A. Knopf, New York, 1987.

Batchelder, Robert, "Commentary: Record Labels in Denial About Peer-to-Peer," Gartner Viewpoint, February 14, 2001, www.gartner.com.

Belz, Carl, *The Story of Rock*, Oxford University Press, New York, 1972.

Berliner, Oliver, "Edison's Disc Foray," *NARAS Journal*, Winter/Spring 1997/98, NARAS Foundation, Santa Monica, CA.

Beaufort, John, "On and Off Broadway," column, *New York Herald Tribune* (1950s).

Berry, Peter E., *". . . And the Hits Just Keep Coming*; Syracuse University Press, 1977.

Bessman, Jim, "Words and Music," *Billboard*, January 18, 2003.

Bieber, David, "He'll Give It a 90—It Jingles," *Boston Phoenix*, November 13, 1973.

Boehm, Erich, "Singular Dedication to Helping Others," *Variety*, Los Angeles, December 14, 1998.

Bohn, Chris, "The Clash: One Step Beyond," *Melody Maker*, December 29, 1979.

Bowe, Brian J., "Creem Rises," Creem.com, 2003.

Brown, David D., "Live Aid, 2 Years and $110 Million Later," *Christian Science Monitor*, London, July 13, 1987.

Brown, Janelle, "The Music Revolution Will Not Be Digitized," Salon.com, June 1, 2001.

Brown, Len, and Friedrich, Gary, *Encyclopedia Of Rock and Roll*, Tower Publications, New York, 1970.

Brown, Les, *Encyclopedia of Television*, Visible Ink, Detroit, 1992.

Cabrera, Luis, "Driving Final Nail Into Grunge Rock's Coffin," Associated Press, Seattle, September 23, 1993.

———, "Music Makers: 'Grunge Rock' Puts Seattle In Musical Spotlight," Associated Press, Seattle, January 24, 1992.

———, "Seattle's Sub Pop Records Has Left Grunge Behind," Associated Press, Seattle, September 23, 1993.

Capel, Kerry, Belton, Catherine, Lowry, Tom, Kripalani, Manjeet, Bremner, Brian, and Roberts, Dexter, "MTV's World," *Business Week*, February 18, 2002.

Carson, Tom, "Rock and Television," *Encyclopedia Britannica*, 2003.

Carter, Bill, "He's Cool. He Keeps MTV Sizzling. And, Oh Yes, He's 56," *New York Times*, June 16, 2002.

Castleman, Harry, and Podrazik, Walter J., *Watching TV: Four Decades of American Television*, McGraw Hill, New York, 1982.

Chapple, Steve, and Garofalo, Reebee, *Rock'n'Roll Is Here To Pay*, Nelson Hall, Chicago, 1977.

Charters, Samuel, *The Blues Makers*, Da Capo, New York, 1967, 1991.

Christgau, Robert, "Journey Through the Past," *Village Voice*, December 17, 1979, p. 63–70.

Christman, Ed, "Soundscan Numbers Show .35% of Albums Account for More Than Half of All Units Sold," *Billboard*, April 28, 2001.

Clapton, Eric, liner notes, *Robert Johnson, The Complete Recordings*, Columbia Records, New York, 1990.

Clark, Dick, and Robinson, Richard, *Rock, Roll and Remember*, Thomas Y. Crowe, New York, 1976.

Clark, Peter, "Rock and Roll and Cinema," British Studies Web Pages, elt.britcoun.org.p/ly_rockn.htm, 2003.

Clark, Rick, "Gus Dudgeon, 1942–2002" *Mix*, October 2002.

Clark-Meads, Jeff, "Band Aid No Longer Seeking Funds," *Billboard*, January 25, 1992.

Cohen, Tom, "Rock Stars Gather for Chuck Berry's 60th Birthday," Associated Press, October 16, 1986.

Coleman, M., "The Revival of Conscience," *Rolling Stone*, November 15, 1990.

Connors, Martin, and Furtaw, Julia (eds.), *Videohound's Golden Movie Retriever*, Visible Ink, Detroit, 1994.

Coon, Caroline, "Punk Rock: Rebels Against the System," *Melody Maker*, August 7, 1976.

Cooney, Michael, "Hard Reign: Bob Dylan's Song Borrowing," *Sing Out!*, Fall 2001.

Covert, Colin, "*Gimme Shelter* Documents the End of an Era," Minneapolis, *Star Tribune*, January 19, 2001.

Crenshaw, Marshall, "Buddy Holly," *Britannica Biography Collection*.

Crosby, John, "Very Wholesome Singer," *New York Herald Tribune*, October 14, 1957.

Crowe, Cameron, liner notes to *Biograph*, Columbia Records, New York, 1985.

Dalton, David, "Altamont: An Eyewitness Account," *Gadfly*, November/December 1999.

Dannen, Fredric, *Hit Men: Power Brokers and Fast Money Inside the Music Business*, Vintage Books, New York, 1991.

Davidson, Neil, "A Profile: Juggy Gayles" *Music Independent*, Oakland, California, January 1991.

Dawson, Jim, and Propes, Steve, *What Was the First Rock 'n' Roll Record?* Faber and Faber, New York, 1992.

DeGraaf, Leonard, "Thomas Edison and the Origins of the Entertainment Phonograph," *NARAS Journal,* Winter/Spring 1997/98, NARAS Foundation, Santa Monica, California.

Devlin, Martina, "Geldof—The Man Who Wouldn't Take No for an Answer," Press Association Limited, London, July 9, 1995.

———, "Geldof Relives Live Aid Memories," Press Association Limited, London, July 13, 1995.

———, "Remembering the Day Pop World Showed Its Heart," Press Association, London, July 9, 1995.

Dunham, Elisabeth, "Monterey Pop: Concert That Changed Rock Music 25 Years Ago," Associated Press, June 17, 1992.

Dunn, Jancee, "John Lydon," *Rolling Stone*, June 16, 1994.

Dyer, Gwynne, "The Age of Innocence," *The Gleaner*, Kingston, Jamaica, December 5, 2001.

Dylan, Bob, "Off the Top of My Head," *Newport Jazz Festival Booklet*, Newport, 1965.

Egan, Timothy, "Kurt Cobain, Hesitant Poet of 'Grunge Rock,' Dead at 27," *New York Times*, April 9, 1994.

Eisen, Jonathan (ed.), *The Age of Rock*, Vantage Books, New York, 1969.

Ertegun, Ahmet, speech accepting Joel Webber Award, New Music Seminar, New York, 1991.

Escott, Colin (ed.), *All Roots Lead to Rock: Legends of Early Rock 'n' Roll*, Schirmer Books, New York, 1999.

Ewen, David (ed.), *American Popular Songs*, Random House, New York, 1996.

Farren, Mick, "LA Punk," *NME*, London, April 11, 1981.

Featherly, Kevin, "Does Online Music Distribution Drive Sales? Maybe," Newsbytes, June 20, 2000.

Fein, Esther B., "Stands and Phone Lines Jammed for Aid Concert," *New York Times*, July 14, 1985.

Ferguson, Derek, "Holly's Band Remembers 'Day Music Died' 30 Years Ago," *Toronto Star*, February 4, 1989.

Fitzpatrick, Travis, *Father of Rock & Roll: The Story of Johnnie "B. Goode" Johnson*, Thomas Cooke, Houston, 1999.

Flippo, Chet, "I Sing the Solid Body Electric," *Rolling Stone*, February 13, 1975.

Gammage, Jeff, "Who Was the Walrus?," *Pittsburgh Post-Gazette*, December 5, 1995.

Gardner, Hy, "Dick Clark Talks About That Washington 'Thing'," *New York Times*, March 20, 1961.

Gaar, Gillian G., "'Verse Chorus Verse': The Recording History of Nirvana," *Goldmine*, Iola, WI, February 14, 1997.

Gillett, Charlie, *The Sound of the City: The Rise of Rock and Roll*, Da Capo, New York, 1996.

Goldman, Albert, *Freakshow*, Atheneum, New York, 1971.

Goldstein, Stewart, and Jacobson, Alan, *Oldies But Goodies*, Mason/Charter, New York, 1977.

Goodman, Fred, "In the News," *Rolling Stone*, November 11, 1993.

Goshert, John Charles, "'Punk' after the Pistols: American Music, Economics and Politics in the 1980s and 1990s," *Popular Music and Society*, Spring 2000.

Grady, Pam, "Act Naturally: Rock 'n' Roll on Film," Reel.com, 2003.

Green, Jonathon, *The Book of Rock Quotes*, Quick Fox/Omnibus, New York, 1977.

Grossman, Lloyd, *A Social History of Rock Music*, David McKay Co., New York, 1976.

Gunderson, Edna, "Kurt Cobain's Pain/Grief and Resignation at His Suicide," *USA Today*, April 11, 1994.

Guterman, Jimmy, "Getting Creative," *Industry Standard*, January, 2001.

Hackett, George, "Banding Together for Africa," *Newsweek*, July 15, 1985.

Harrington, Richard, "Electric Experience: Smithsonian Guitar Exhibit Ponders The Implications of Amplification," *Washington Post*, November 10, 1996.

————, "Every Revolution Needs Young Firebrands and Elder Statesmen; Bob Dylan Has Been Both," *Washington Post*, December 7, 1997.

Harris, Kenneth, "The Beatle Backer," *Observer*, London, May 17, 1964.

Harry, Bill, *The Beatles Who's Who*, Delilah Books, New York, 1982.

Hector, James, *The Complete Guide to the Music of Nirvana*, Omnibus Press, New York, 1998.

Heylin, Clinton, *Classic Rock Albums: Never Mind the Bollocks Here's the Sex Pistols*, Schirmer Books, New York, 1998.

Hibbert, Tom, "The Bowery Beat," *The History of Rock*, London, 1983.

Higgins, Mike, "It Was 15 Years Ago—Live Aid Rocked London, Philadelphia and the World," *Independent*, London, July 9, 2000.

Hilburn, Robert, "Chuck Berry Sets the Records Straight," Los Angeles Times Syndicate, October 17, 1987.

Himes, Geoffrey, "It's Still Rock 'n' Roll for Little Richard," *Washington Post*, May 28, 1999.

Hinkley, David, "Alan Freed: Rock Punk?" *New York Daily News*, March 29, 1992.

————, The Day the Music Survived 'American Pie': Good Song, But It Doesn't Really Tell the Story," *New York Daily News*, February 4, 1999.

Hopkins, Jerry, *The Rock Story*, Signet, New York, 1970.

Hoskins, Barney, "Black Sabbath Prole Metal to Ozzy and Beyond," *Creem*, 1982.

Houghton, Mick, "Zeus of Zeppelin: An Interview with Jimmy Page," *Circus*, October 12,1976.

Howell, Peter, "Push to Roll Out Pearl Jam CD Has Don Mills Plant Rocking," *Toronto Star*, November 17, 1994.

Ingham, John, "The Sex Pistols Are Four Months Old. . . ," *Sounds*, London, April 24, 1976.

Ivry, Bob, "He Made Rock Criticism into an Art Form," *Bergen Record*, NJ, June 8, 2000.

Jablons, Josephine, "'Moondog,' Blues, Jazz DiskAce, Gets N.Y. Show," *New York Times,* n.d.

Jardine, Cassandra, "The Day the Music Died: It's 39 Years Since Buddy Holly Was Killed. His Widowed Bride Has Thought of Him Every

Day Since, She Says in a Rare Interview," *Telegraph*, London, March 18, 1998.

Jennings, Nicholas, "The Absolutely Fab Four," *MacLean's*, Toronto, December 4, 1995.

Jones, Marty "Rock: The Comets' Tale—The World's Oldest Rock and Roll Band Is Still Rolling," *Denver Westword*, July 10, 1997.

Kahn, Stephan, "Pied Piper of the Air," *WT&S*, May 31, 1958.

Kamm, Herbert, "Pat Boone Takes an Old Pro's Advice on Stardom," *New York World Telegram and Sun*, January 11, 1958.

Katz, Larry, "A Survivor of the Day the Music Died," *Boston Herald*, November 9, 2000.

———, "Reinventing the Rock Star; Do-It-Yourselfer Scooter Scudieri Fights The Musical-Industrial Complex," *Boston Herald*, October 23, 2002.

Keen, Linda, and Willson, Duff, "Who Was Trying to Use Cobain's Credit Card?" *Toronto Star*, May 13, 1994.

Killen, Matt, "I Still Want My MTV," *Notre Dame Observer*, South Bend, IN, October 3, 2001.

Klein, Howie, "Sex Pistols: Tour Notes," *New York Rocker*, February 1978.

Kooper, Al, "Voices of the Century: Bob Dylan Goes Electric," *Newsweek*, New York, July 19, 1999.

Kramer, Michael J., "Can't Forget the Motor City," RockCritics.com, 2002.

Kronke, David, "MTV Through the Years," *Milwaukee Journal Sentinel*, July 26, 2001.

Kuzmyk, Jenn, "Rockin' Docs," *Realscreen,* November 1998.

LaSalle, Mick, "The People Who Briefly Saved Hollywood," *San Francisco Chronicle*, May 12, 1998.

Landau, Jon, *It's Too Late to Stop Now*, Straight Arrow, San Francisco, 1972.

Lawrence, Sharon, *So You Want to Be a Rock and Roll Star*, Dell, New York, 1976.

Lea, Cub, "MP3 and the 'Death' of the Music Industry," Winter Heat Production, 1999.

Lehmer, Larry, *The Day the Music Died: The Last Tour of Buddy Holly, the "Big Bopper," and Ritchie Valens*, Schirmer Books, New York, 1997.

Lenhart, Amanda and Fox, Susannah, "Downloading Free Music: Internet Lovers Don't Think It's Stealing," Pew Internet & American Life Project, Washington, D.C., September 28, 2000.

LeVere, Stephen C., liner notes, *Robert Johnson, The Complete Recordings*, Columbia Records, New York, 1990.

Lewis, "Uncle" Dave, "Thomas Edison" All Music Guide, www.all music.com.

Lotz, I. C., "Dick Clark Over a Chinese Luncheon," *Fusion*.

Lydon, Michael, "Montery Pops! An International Pop Festival," Rocksbackpages.com, London, written June 20, 1967.

Mabrey, Vicki, "Rock Singer Bono of the Band U2 Discusses His Music and His Dedication to Reducing Third World Debt," *60 Minutes*, February 20, 2002.

Mackesy, Serena, "Ten Years After . . . ," *Independent*, London, July 14, 1995.

Maken, Neil, "Father of Invention," *NARAS Journal*, Winter/Spring 1997/98, NARAS Foundation, Santa Monica, California.

Mann, Charles C., "The MP3 Revolution," *Atlantic*, April 8, 1999.

Marin, Rick, "Grunge: A Success Story," *New York Times*, November 15, 1992.

Marsh, Dave, "Fooled Again," *Rock & Rap Confidential*, September 1999.

————, "Live Through This," *Rock & Roll Confidential*, June/July 1995.

————, "Metallica vs. Napster," *Rock & Rap Confidential*, 2000.

————, "Something's In The Air," *Rock & Rap Confidential*, July 1997.

Maslin, Janet, "Critic's Notebook: Is It Time, Already, to Put Rock in a Museum?" *New York Times*, November 29, 1991.

Masley, Ed, "Remaining Beatles Risk Their Place as Rock-Solid Legends to Reunite," *Pittsburgh Post-Gazette*, November 12, 1995.

McAleer, Dave, *The Book of Hit Singles: Top 20 Charts from 1954 to the Present Day*, Backbeat Books, New York, 2001.

McGaughey, Scott, "Rock in the Movies," depaul.edu~dweinste/rock/ mediators-students.html, 2002.

Membery, York, "Bottom of the Pops," *Times*, London, June 30, 1992.

Miles, Barry, "Pink Floyd: Games for May," *NME*, London, May 15, 1976.

Millard, Andre, *America on Record: A History of Recorded Sound*, Cambridge University Press, New York, 1995.

————, "From Acoustic Horn to Magnetic Tape," *NARAS Journal*, Winter/Spring 1997/98, NARAS Foundation, Santa Monica, California.

Miller, Jim, Abramson, Pamela, McAlevey, Peter, and Kuflik, Abigail, "Brother, Can You Spare a Song?" *Newsweek*, October 28, 1985.

Millner, Greg, "Sound Scam: Are Home Computers Killing the Music Industry?" *Village Voice*, New York, July 8, 1997.

Moon, Tom, "Lilith Fair Comes to Town," *Philadelphia Inquirer*, n.d.

Moore, Hank, "TV Timeline—Chapter 8," December, 2001, www.net worksplus.net/caseyguy/December01news.htm.

Morrow, Melinda, "'But Beavis, Everything Does Suck': Watching Beavis and Butthead Watch Videos," *Popular Music and Society*, Fall 1999.

Morse, Steve, "1985 Live Aid: The Last Time Rock Found Unity . . . ," *Boston Globe*, July 11, 1995.

———, "The Day the Stars Fell," *Boston Globe*, February 3, 1989.

———, "VH-1 Recalled Holly Plane Crash," the *Boston Globe*, February 3, 1999.

Muretich, James, and McEwen, Mary-lynn, "Now for Some Beatles Bits and Pieces," *Calgary Herald,* Alberta, November 18, 1995.

Murray, Charles Shaar, "Taking His Own Path Back to the Crossroads Eminent Bluesman Robert Junior Lockwood Tells Charles Shaar Murray Why He's Happy to Discuss His Stepfather, Robert Johnson," *Daily Telegraph*, London, November 25, 2000.

Nadelson, Reggie, "Where Did All the Flowers Go . . . ?" *Daily Telegraph*, London, August 11, 1994.

Napoli, Lisa, "Think Debate on Music Property Rights Began with Napster? Hardly," *New York Times*, September 22, 2003.

Neely, Kim, and Selinger, Mark, "Soundgarden," *Rolling Stone*, July 9–July 23, 1992.

Nelson, Chris, "Upstart Labels See File Sharing as Ally, Not Foe," *New York Times*, September 22, 2003.

Newman, Melinda, "The Beat," *Billboard*, February 19, 1994.

Newton, Francis, "Beatles and Before," *New Statesman*, London, November 8, 1963.

Norman, Phillip, *Shout! The Beatles in Their Generation*, Fireside Books, New York, 1981.

Norman, Tony, "Lennon-McCartney; Friends or Foes," the *Pittsburgh Post-Gazette*, November 11, 1995.

Ockenfels, F. W., and Tannenbaum, Robert, "Bob Geldof," *Rolling Stone*, November 11, 1990.

Orshoski, Wes, "Newsline," *Billboard*, December 16, 2000.

Palmer, Robert, "Hail a Creator of Rock and Roll," *New York Times*, October 11, 1987.

Pareles, Jon, "A Wiser Voice Blowing in the Autumn Wind," *New York Times*, September 28, 1997.

———, "Blues Present and Past," *New York Times*, September 1, 1998.

———, "Clarence Leo Fender Dies at 82; His Guitar Changed Rock Music," *New York Times*, March 23, 1991.

———, "Hunger Telethon to Be Heard Around the Globe," *New York Times*, July 7, 1985.

————, "Robert Shelton, 69, Music Critic Who Chronicled the 60s Folk Boom," *New York Times*, December 15, 1995.

Parry, Richard Lloyd, "Fab in the Far East for Ever; in Japan, Beatlemania Never Went Away . . . ," *Independent*, London, February 21, 1999.

Patoski, Joe Nick, "Rave On," *Texas Monthly*, September 1994.

Peeples, Stephen, liner notes, *The Monterey International Pop Festival*, Rhino Records, 1992.

Philo, Simon, "Getting Dumber and Dumber: MTV's Global Footprint." members.tripod.com/~warlight/Philo.html.

Pitts, Leonard, "Music Business Facing New Reality," *Miami Herald*, September 23, 2003.

Purtell, Tim, "Buddy Holly's Fateful Flight," *Entertainment Weekly*, February 3, 1995.

Raddatz, Leslie, "From 'Crazy Daddy-O' to 'Right On'," *TV Guide*, June 16, 1973.

Reay, Tony, "Like Pushing a Rubber Giraffe Through a Keyhole . . . ," Rockcritics.com, January 14, 2003.

Resner, Hillel, "2001 Technical Grammy Award Recipient Les Paul: The Music Industry's Ben Franklin," www.grammy.com, March 1, 2001.

Reynolds, Simon, "Nirvana: Smells Like a Sensation," *Observer*, London, December 8, 1991.

Richards, Keith, liner notes, *Robert Johnson, The Complete Recordings*, Columbia Records, New York, 1990.

Rizzo, Frank, "Turning 20, *Rolling Stone* Is Still Gathering No Moss," *Hartford Courant*, July 4, 1987.

Robards, Terry, "The Beatle Biz," *New York Herald Tribune*, March 7, 1965.

Robertson, Lori, "Golden Oldies," *American Journalism Review*, July/August, 2000.

Robbins, Ira, "Remember Those Fabulous 70s? A Musical Stroll from Woodstock to Punk-rock," *Trouser Press*, January 1980.

————, "The New Wave Washes Out," *Trouser Press*, New York, October 1977.

Rodman, Sarah, and Brown, Joel, "George Harrison, 1943–2001; All Things Must Pass; 'Quiet Beatle' George Harrison Loses Battle with Cancer," *Boston Herald*, December 1, 2001.

Rodgers, Ruth, "Report to Congress Pursuant to Section 104 of the No. 000522150-0150-01 Digital Millennium Copyright Act, Washington, D.C., August 4, 2000.

Rodriguez, Juan, "Fab Four Were No Mere Fad: *A Hard Day's Night*, Made More Than 35 Years Ago and Now in Re-release, Still Holds Up, Just Like the Beatles . . . ," *Gazette*, Montreal, December 21, 2000.

Romano, Angela, "MTV Operating Without a Net," *Broadcasting & Cable*, May 27, 2002.

Romanowski, Patricia, and George-Warren, Holly, *The New Rolling Stone Encyclopedia of Rock & Roll*, Rolling Stone Press, New York, 1995.

Roughly, Gregg, "It's the Vinyl Countdown . . ." *Daily Telegraph*, London, September 20, 2003.

Salinger, J. D., The *Catcher in the Rye*, Little Brown, Boston, 1951.

Sandall, Robert, "Just the Job for Bob," *Sunday Times*, London, August 30, 1992.

Sanjeck, Russell, and Sanjeck, David, *Pennies from Heaven: The American Popular Music Business in the 20th Century*, Da Capo Press, New York, 1996.

Satchell, Michael, "Star-struck Charities Seek Famous Boosters," *U.S. News & World Report*, September 22, 1997.

Savage, Jon, "Punk Five Years On," *The Face*, London, November 1981.

Scheerer, Mark, "*Rolling Stone* Founder Looks at Magazine's Past," CNN's *Showbiz Today*, New York, September 29, 1992.

Scherman, Tony, "Chipping Away at the Myths That Encrust a Blues Legend," *New York Times*, September 20, 1998.

———, "Finding Robert Johnson," BPI Entertainment News Wire, December 26, 1990.

Schoemer, Karen, "A Film Pursues the Redemptive Power of Rock and Roll," *New York Times*, August 18, 1991.

Schwarz, John, "A Timely Anniversary for Copyrights," ZDNet, June 9, 2000.

Scott, Anne, "The Place the Music Died," *Des Moines Business Record*, March 9, 1998.

Segal, David, "Kennedy Center Honors 2000; Chuck Berry's 'Goode' Deeds; The Ornery Guitarist, at His Best in Rock-and-Roll," *Washington Post*, December 3, 2000.

Selvin, Joel, "Down in Monterey," *San Francisco Chronicle*, June 14, 1992.

Shannon, Bob, and Javna, John, *Behind the Hits*, Warner Books, New York, 1986.

Shaw, Greg, "New Wave Goodbye? Some Thoughts on the Economic State of the New Wave Industry in America," *New York Rocker*, September 1978.

Sheff, David, and Golson, G. Barry (ed.), *The Playboy Interviews with John Lennon & Yoko Ono*, Playboy Press, New York, 1981.

Shelton, Robert, "The Beatles Will Make the Scene Here Again, but the Scene Has Changed," *New York Times*, August 11, 1965.

Sherman, Cary, "File Sharing Is Illegal. Period." *USA Today*, New York, September 19, 2003.

Sigman, Mike (ed.), "Dick Clark: A Legend in His Own Time," *Dialogues: Viewpoints of the Music Industry, a Record World Magazine Special Issue*, Record World Publishing, 1974.

———, "George Martin Speaks Out," *Dialogues:Viewpoints of the Music Industry, a Record World Magazine Special Issue*, Record World Publishing, 1974.

Sinclair, David, "Seattle Takes the Grunge," *Times*, London, April 25, 1992.

Sirak, Ron, "Bob Dylan: A Milepost in the Passing of Time," Associated Press, New York, June 12, 1991.

Slack, James, "Did Video Kill the Radio Star? MTV 20 Years On," *Rock's Backpages,* London, July 28, 2001.

Sloop, John M., "The Emperor's New Makeup: Cool Cynicism and Popular Music Criticism," *Popular Music and Society*, Spring 1999.

Smith, Joe, *Off the Record*, Warner Books, New York, 1988.

Snow, Mat, "Meet the Family: Ramones, Blondie, Talking Heads," *Q*, London, October 1990.

———, "Pearl Jam: 'You, My Son, Are Weird'," *Q*, London, November 1993.

Snyder, Michael, "Benefit Concert: Nirvana Fights Hell in Bosnia," *San Francisco Chronicle*, April 4, 1993.

———, "Pearl Jam Still Gem Second Time Out," *San Francisco Chronicle*, October 17, 1993.

———, "Towers of Grunge Tip Toward Mainstream," *San Francisco Chronicle*, October 24, 1993.

Soocher, Stan, *They Fought the Law: Rock Music Goes to Court*; Schirmer Books, New York, 1998.

Spain, Nancy, "Blows In on the Beatles," *She*, London, November 1963.

St. Lifer, Evan, "Les Paul: No Stopping the Guitarist," *New York Times,* December 27, 1987.

Starrett, Robert A., "Copying Music to CD: The Right, the Wrong, and the Law," *Emedia Professional*, February 1998.

Stearn, Jess, "Rock 'n' Roll Runs Into Trouble," *New York Daily News*, April 12, 1956.

Stern, Jane and Michael, *Encyclopedia of Pop Culture*, Harper Perennial, New York, 1992.

Strauss, Neil, "The Pop Life: Speaking for Soundgarden," *New York Times*, June 15, 1994.

Sutcliffe, Phil, "Kurt Cobain: King of Pain," Q, London, October 1993.

———, "Pink Floyd: Dark Side of the Moon," *Mojo,* March, 1998.

Thomas, Linda, "Millions of Lives Are at Risk as Famine Follows Drought in Ethiopia. No Wonder Sir Bob Loses Patience," *Perspectives*, November 20, 2002.

Thorson, Larry, "Band Aid Evaluates Anti-Starvation Projects in Africa," Associated Press, London, January 7, 1987.

Tianen, Dave, "Buddy Holly's Fame Lives 40 Years After His Death," *Milwaukee Journal Sentinel*, February 3, 1999.

Townshend, Pete, "Meaty, Beaty, Big and Bouncy," *Rolling Stone*, December 7, 1971.

Travers, Peter, "The Best Rock Movie Ever Made," *Rolling Stone*, May 9, 2002.

Trebbe, Ann, "Berry: Child Abuse, Drug Charges False," *USA Today*, August 30, 1990.

Tselos, George, and Tarr, Douglas, "The Napoleon of Invention," *NARAS Journal,* Winter/Spring 1997/98, NARAS Foundation, Santa Monica, California.

Turner, Steve, "The Great Rock 'n' Roll Swindle: How Malcolm McLaren Made Cash from Chaos," *The History of Rock,* London, 1983.

Twetten, Susan Veitch, "Rock 'n' Roll Movies," Cinemaspot.com, 2002.

Tyrangiel, Josh, and Nugent, Benjamin, "Bono," *Time*, March 4, 2002

Uhelszki, Jaan, "Live Aid, 90s Style," *Rolling Stone*, September 16, 1999.

Ulanoff, Lance, "The RIAA Is Full of Hot Air," *PC Magazine*, September 17, 2003.

Ulto, Melissa, "The Rebirth of Creem," Free Williamsburg.com, May 2003.

Uslan, Michael, and Solomon, Bruce, *Dick Clark's First 25 Years of Rock and Roll*, Delacorte Press, New York 1981.

Vallely, Paul, "Interview: Two Worlds: Things Have Changed . . . ," *Independent*, London, May 31, 2003.

———, "It Is 17 Years Since Live Aid and Bob Geldof Is Back, Telling the World to Listen to Africa," *Independent*, London, May 13, 2002.

Varanini, Giancarlo, "Q&A: Napster Creator Shawn Fanning," ZDnet Music, March 2, 2000.

Vercammen, Paul, "Pearl Jam Album Breaks New Release Sales Record," *CNN*, October 28, 1993.

Vincent, Michael, "Run-DMC Rap Artist Shot," *AM* (transcript), Australian Broadcasting Company, November 1, 2002.

Watrous, Peter, "Robert Johnson, Once Largely Myth, Now a Hit," *New York Times*, February 26, 1991.

Wavell, Stuart, "St. Bob Said Let There Be Light . . . And There Will Be," *Sunday Times*, London, December 19, 1999.

Weaver, Jane, "Study: Downloads to Save Music Biz," MSNBC.com, August 12, 2002.

Weber, Bruce, "The Rock Hall of Fame Seeks Its Groove," *New York Times*, April 21, 1999.

Weekly, David E., *mp3 Book*, e-book published by www.weekly.org, 2003.

Weiss, George David, address to B'nai B'rith Music and Performing Arts Unit.

Weiss, Paulette, *The Rock Video Book*, Pocket Books, New York, 1985.

Welton, Clark, "He Was King of Rock 'n' Roll" *New York Times*, n.d.

Wexler, Jerry, *Rhythm and the Blues*, Alfred A. Knopf, New York, 1993.

Whitburn, Joel, *Pop Memories 1890–1954*, Record Research, New York, 1991.

———, *Billboard Book of Top 40 Hits, 7th Edition*, Billboard Books, New York, 2000.

———, *Rock Tracks*, Billboard Books, New York, 1995.

Whitworth, Bill, "Beatle Siege at the Plaza," *New York Herald Tribune*, February 9, 1964.

———, "Quiet Look at Beatles' Uproar," *New York Herald Tribune*, August 30, 1964.

Williams, Bob, "Kosovo Crisis Should Spur Music Biz to Action," *Billboard*, May 1, 1999.

Williams, Paul (ed.), *The Crawdaddy! Book*, Hal Leonard, Milwaukee, 2002.

Williams, Bob, "Freed Loses His TV Show—But Doesn't 'Feel' Fired," *New York Post*, November 23, 1959.

Wilonsky, Robert, "'Look Ahead,' D. A. Pennebaker Doesn't Make History, but He's Captured So Much of It," *Dallas Observer*, May 24, 2001.

———, "Stop the Music: In *The Suburbans*, One Hit Wonders Reunite for No-Laugh Movie," *Dallas Observer*, October 28, 1999.

Wilson, Earl, "Alan Freed's Story," *New York Post*, November 23, 1959.

Wirt, John, "Berry A Rock 'n' Roll Original," *The Advocate*, Baton Rouge, Louisiana, April 11, 2003.

Woods, Eric, "September 2003 Bandwidth Report," *URLwire*, September 23, 2003.

Younger, Richard, "A Day in the Garden," *Midtown Resident,* Summer 1998.

Zimmerman, Kevin, "Who Fears Peer-to-Peer," *Cablevision*, February 12, 2001.

Author's Interviews and Correspondence

Jan Akkerman
Richard Barone
Bill Bruford
Scott Burnett
Lydia Cole
Bobby Colomby
Stu Cook
Jonathan Demme
Willie Dixon
Mickey Dolenz
Ahmet Ertegun
Donald Fagen
Perry Farrell (1990)
Juggy Gayles (a.k.a. George Resnick)
Roger Glover
Robert Goodale
Justin Hayward
Jack Hues
Tom Hunter
Billy Idol
Johnnie Johnson (1995)
Robert Johnson (1990)
Fela Anikulapo Kuti
Alvin Lee
Jerry Leiber
John Lodge
Bob Ludwig
Dave Marsh (1986)
John Mayall (1987)
Darryl "D.M.C."McDaniel
Elias McDaniel (a.k.a. Bo Diddley) (1996)

Dennis McNally
Klaus Meine
Jason "Jam Master Jay" Mizell
Bob Mould
Willie Nelson
Marcus Nispel
Ric Ocasek
Robert Palmer
Les Paul
Carl Perkins
Steve Perkins (1990)
Kate Pierson
Tom Pompasello
Sammy Price
Phil Ramone
Malcolm "Mac" John Rebennack, Jr. (a.k.a. Dr. John)
Don Rose
Paul Rothchild
Todd Rundgren
Jack Satter
Jerry Schilling
Fred Schneider
Joe Smith
Russ Solomon
Ringo Starr
Mike Stoller
John Swenson
Koko Taylor
Ververt Turner
Don Was
George Wein

Web research

www.riaa.com/gp/database/default.asp, The RIAA Gold and
Platinum Database

www.rockhall.com/home/default.asp, The Rock and Roll Hall of
Fame Website

www.galenet.com/servlet/BioRC, Contemporary Authors Online,
Gale, 2003

www.allmusic.com, The All Music Guide Online

www.history-of-rock.com, History of Rock

Index

About the Author

Turning Points in Rock and Roll is the book Hank Bordowitz has been working toward his whole life and is uniquely qualified to write. Over the course of the last twenty-five years, there are few facets of rock and roll he has not experienced and lived to tell the tale. At one time or another, Hank:

- Worked as a recording engineer
- Played bars and dives of all descriptions
- Was a signed recording artist
- Promoted music to radio
- Promoted concerts
- Worked at one of the major music business trade magazines
- Toiled in record companies doing
  - Marketing
  - Retail
  - Distribution
  - Publicity
- Programmed radio
- Worked as a deejay
- Licensed music from publishers
- Consulted for artists and companies
- Taught the Introduction to the Music Business course at Baruch College

This background gives him peerless insight into the task of acting as a tour guide through the history of rock and roll as more than an observer: He has been a *participant*.

He also worked as a journalist for twenty-five years, covering music and musicians. His debut book, *Bad Moon Rising: The Unauthorized History of Creedence Clearwater Revival* was the first to tackle this great American band's sad story from inception through the personal difficulties that broke the band up and the legal wrangling that followed.

- *Booklist* said: "*Bordowitz's recounting of all the acrimony is well detailed and not too hyperbolic. This is must reading for CCR-philes . . .*"

- *Publishers Weekly* said: "*Bordowitz provides evenhanded treatment of highly charged issues. . . . persuasively demonstrating that CCR has earned their reputation as one of the most important bands in rock history.*"

- *Literary Journal* agreed: "*Bordowitz brings CCR's complex story to life . . . [he] never takes sides or passes judgment yet brilliantly illuminates the tragedy of CCR's lost potential.*"

- *USA Today* said: "*If Hank Bordowitz's* Bad Moon Rising *isn't 'the saddest story in rock 'n' roll,' . . . it certainly comes within kissing distance.*"

His *U2 Reader: A Quarter Century of Commentary, Criticism and Reviews*, one of the most comprehensive books on that important rock group, received similar kudos:

- *The Celebrity Café* rated it 8 out of 10, saying: "U2 fans, along with people interested in the band's cultural impact, will want to read this book."

- *Blender* gave the book three stars, noting, "Cherry picking twenty-five years of press coverage of a band as diverse as U2 is no easy gig, and as such this anthology offers . . . big name contributions—Elizabeth Wurtzel dissecting *Achtung Baby* for the *New Yorker*; Salman Rushdie recalling a pogoing sesson with Van Morrison in Bono's living room—and profiles cribbed from everything from *Time* to *Star Hits*.

His *Bruce Springsteen Scrapbook* was published in the spring of 2004 by Citadel Press, and *Every Little Thing G'wan Be All Right: The Bob Marley Reader* is due out this spring via Da Capo.

Hank lives in the exurbs of New York City with his wife and three sons.